THE AFRICAN CONTINENTAL FREE TRADE AREA
AND THE FUTURE OF INVESTOR-STATE DISPUTE
SETTLEMENT IN AFRICA

THE AFRICAN CONTINENTAL FREE TRADE AREA AND THE FUTURE OF INVESTOR-STATE DISPUTE SETTLEMENT IN AFRICA

Mouhamed KEBE

INTERSENTIA

Cambridge – Antwerp – Chicago

Intersentia Ltd
8 Wellington Mews
Wellington Street | Cambridge
CB1 1HW | United Kingdom
Tel: +44 1223 736 170
Email: mail@intersentia.co.uk
www.intersentia.com | www.intersentia.co.uk

Distribution for the UK and
Rest of the World (incl. Eastern Europe)
NBN International
1 Deltic Avenue, Rooksley
Milton Keynes MK13 8LD
United Kingdom
Tel: +44 1752 202 301 | Fax: +44 1752 202 331
Email: orders@nbninternational.com

Distribution for Europe
Lefebvre Sarrut Belgium NV
Hoogstraat 139/6
1000 Brussels
Belgium
Tel: +32 (0)2 548 07 13
Email: mail@intersentia.be

Distribution for the USA and Canada
Independent Publishers Group
Order Department
814 North Franklin Street
Chicago, IL 60610
USA
Tel: +1 800 888 4741 (toll free) | Fax: +1 312 337 5985
Email: orders@ipgbook.com

The African Continental Free Trade Area and the Future of Investor-State
Dispute Settlement in Africa
© Mouhamed Kebe 2023

ISBN 978-1-83970-314-0
D/2023/7849/26
NUR 822

British Library Cataloguing in Publication Data. A catalogue record for this book is available from the British Library.

ACKNOWLEDGEMENTS

Over the last few years I have attended and presented in many conferences and seminars where ISDS was hotly debated. Most of the points addressed in this book were presented during these events.

The participants who attended the CIArb Conference held in Johannesburg on 18–19 July 2017,[1] the AfAA Conference held on 3–5 November 2022 in Accra,[2] the SOAS Conference held virtually on 23–24 November 2021,[3] the ICC Conference held in Paris on 12 December 2019,[4] to name a few, will see that many of the ideas I advocated during these events are developed in this book.

I am deeply thankful to all of these participants. Their insights and comments helped the book along tremendously. I am also thankful to the publishers of the papers I wrote further to these events, particularly to TDM, who published two of these.

I also want to express my sincere gratitude to all my partners and colleagues in GENI & KEBE, DLA Piper Africa, and DLA Piper for their constant support and encouragement. I owe a special debt to Meghan Waters, former Senior Associate at GENI & KEBE. Her intellectual and practical support throughout the process of writing this book was critical.

My gratitude also to Alan Tolerton, who agreed to proofread the manuscript, and who provided very useful insights. I would also like to thank Intersentia UK, particularly Ahmed Hegazi, for agreeing to publish this book and the editors, especially Rebecca Moffat, for her highly professional assistance.

Last, but by no means least, I would particularly like to thank both my parents and all my family, for their boundless love, support, and patience.

---

[1]   CIArb International Arbitration Conferences 2017 Johannesburg on "The Synergy and Divergence between Civil Law and Common Law in International Arbitration".

[2]   AfAA 3rd Annual International Arbitration Conference, panel on "AfCFTA: a window of opportunity for Africanisation of Dispute Resolution".

[3]   7th SOAS Arbitration in Africa Conference, co-hosted with the Casablanca International Mediation and Arbitration Centre, Panel on "Challenges faced by African States in regard to ISDS".

[4]   ICC Africa and ICC BRI Commissions Conference on "The Belt and Road Initiative in Africa: Promises, Challenges, and Dispute Resolution".

CONTENTS

LIST OF CASES

LIST OF LEGISLATION

Agreement Establishing the African Continental Free Trade Area, 21 March 2018 (entered into force 30 May 2019), available at: https://au.int/sites/default/files/treaties/36437-treaty-consolidated_text_on_cfta_-_en.pdf.

EAC Model Investment Code (2006), available at: http://www.eac.int/.

ECOWAS Supplementary Protocol A/SP.1/01/05 Amending the Preamble and Articles 1, 2, 9 and 30 of Protocol A/P.1/7/91 Relating to the Community Court of Justice and Article 4 Paragraph 1 of the English Version of Said Protocol, available at: http://prod.courtecowas.org/wp-content/uploads/2018/11/Supplementary_Protocol_ASP.10105_ENG.pdf.

International Law Commission (2006), "Draft Articles on Diplomatic Protection", Official Records of the General Assembly, Sixty-first Session, Supplement No. 10, UN Doc. A/6/10, Article 14(1).

Investment Agreement for the COMESA Common Investment Area, UNCTAD (23 May 2007), available at: https://investmentpolicy.unctad.org/international-investment-agreements/treaties/treaties-with-investment-provisions/3547/ecowas-supplementary-act-on-investments.

Investment Agreement for the COMESA Common Investment Area, Common Market for Eastern and Southern Africa, available at: https://www.iisd.org/toolkits/sustainability-toolkit-for-trade-negotiators/wp-content/uploads/2016/06/rei120.06tt1.pdf.

SADC Model Bilateral Investment Treaty Template, SADC (July 2012), available at: https://www.iisd.org/itn/wp-content/uploads/2012/10/sadc-model-bit-template-final.pdf.

Supplementary Act A/SA.3/12/08 Adopting Community Rules on Investment and the Modalities for their Implementation with ECOWAS, ECONOMIC COMMUNITY OF WEST AFR. STATES, Dec. 19, 2008, available at: https://investmentpolicyhub.unctad.org/Download/TreatyFile/3266.

"Text of the Trans-Pacific Partnership," New Zealand Foreign Affairs & Trade, available at: https://www.mfat.govt.nz/en/about-us/who-we-are/treaties/trans-pacific-partnership-agreement-tpp/text-of-the-trans-pacific-partnership.

"UNCITRAL Arbitration Rules", United Nations Commission on International Trade Law, available at: https://uncitral.un.org/en/texts/arbitration/contractualtexts/arbitration.

United Kingdom – Vietnam BIT (2002), available at: https://investmentpolicy.unctad.org/international-investment-agreements/treaties/treaties-with-investment-provisions/3066/united-kingdom---viet-nam-bit-2002-. See Article 2(2).

LIST OF ABBREVIATIONS

AEC	African Economic Community
AfAA	African Arbitration Association
AfCFTA	African Continental Free Trade Area
AMU	Arab Maghreb Union
ASEAN	Association of Southeast Asian Nations
AU	African Union
BITs	bilateral investment treaties
BRI	Belt and Road Initiative
CAFTA	Central America Free Trade Agreement
CAJAC	China–Africa Joint Arbitration Centre
CCJA	OHADA Common Court of Justice and Arbitration
CEMAC	Central African Economic and Monetary Community
CEN-SAD	Community of Sahel-Saharan States
CETA	Canada–EU Comprehensive Economic and Trade Agreement
CFIA	Cooperation and Investment Facilitation Agreement
CIArb	Chartered Institute of Arbitrators
CIMAC	Casablanca International Mediation and Arbitration Centre
COMESA	Common Market for Eastern and Southern Africa
CPTPP	Comprehensive and Progressive Agreement for Trans-Pacific Partnership
DSB	Dispute Settlement Body
DTAA	Double Taxation Avoidance Agreement
DTT	double taxation treaty
EAC	East African Community
ECCAS	Economic Community of Central African States
ECCJ	ECOWAS Community Court of Justice
ECJ	Court of Justice of the European Union

ECOWAS	Economic Community of West African States
ECOWIC	ECOWAS Common Investment Code
ECPF	ECOWAS Conflict Prevention Framework
ECT	Energy Charter Treaty
EDEAC	Customs and Economic Union of Central African States
EU	European Union
FCN treaties	friendship, commerce and navigation treaties
FDI	foreign direct investment
FET	fair and equitable treatment
GATS	General Agreement on the Trade in Services
GATT	General Agreement on Tariffs and Trade
GDP	gross domestic product
HKIAC	Hong Kong International Arbitration Centre
ICC	International Chamber of Commerce
ICC Court	International Chamber of Commerce Court of Arbitration
ICDR	International Centre for Dispute Resolution
ICSID	International Centre for Settlement of Investment Disputes
IGAD	Intergovernmental Authority on Development
IMF	International Monetary Fund
ISDS	investor-state dispute settlement
KIAC	Kigali International Arbitration Centre
LCIA	London Court of International Arbitration
MFN	most-favoured nation
MIGA	Multilateral Investment Guarantee Agency
MIT	multilateral investment treaties
NAFTA	North American Free Trade Agreement
NT	national treatment
OECD	Organisation for Economic Co-operation and Development
OHADA	Organization for the Harmonisation of Business Law in Africa
PAIC	Pan African Investment Code
PTA	Preferential Trade Area
RECs	Regional Economic Communities
RIA	regional investment agreement

SADC	Southern African Development Community
SADCC	Southern African Development Coordination Conference
SDGs	Sustainable Development Goals
SIAC	Singapore International Arbitration Centre
TFTA	Tripartite Free Trade Area
TIR	Transports Internationaux Routiers
TPP	Trans-Pacific Partnership Agreement
TRIMs	Agreement on Trade-Related Measures
TRIPS	Trade-Related Aspects of Intellectual Property Rights
TTIP	US–EU Transatlantic Trade and Investment Partnership
UNASUR	Union of South American Nations
UNCITRAL	United Nations Commission on International Trade Law
UNCTAD	United Nations Conference on Trade and Development
USAID	United States Agency for International Development
USMCA	United States–Mexico–Canada Agreement
WAEMU	West African Economic and Monetary Union
WCO	World Customs Organization
WTO	World Trade Organization

CHAPTER 1
INTRODUCTION

The continent of Africa is ripe with economic opportunity. The continent's extractive industries alone have the potential to be some of the most lucrative in the world, given that it is home to some of the largest natural resource reserves on the planet. Approximately 30% of the world's mineral reserves,[5] 8% of the world's natural gas reserves and 12% of the world's oil reserves[6] are found on the African continent. At the same time, Africa has one of the fastest-growing populations in the world, which has a huge potential to increase demand for goods and services on the continent.[7] In 2019, four of the world's ten fastest-growing economies were in Africa: Côte d'Ivoire, Ethiopia, Ghana and Rwanda.[8] The World Bank has also predicted that several countries on the continent, including, in addition to these four countries, Senegal, will see per income capital rates rising by more than 4% during 2022.[9] All signs seem to be pointing towards strong economic growth and, therefore, opportunity in Africa, at least in the near future.

That said, even considering the increasingly positive prospects at Africa's doorstep, an overwhelming majority of the continent's 54 countries still face tremendous obstacles to meaningful growth. Poor infrastructure, an unskilled labour force, health concerns, climate change, weak security,

---

[5] Andre Pottas, "Addressing Africa's Infrastructure Challenges", Deloitte, available at: https://www2.deloitte.com/content/dam/Deloitte/global/Documents/Energy-and-Resources/dttl-er-africasinfrastructure-08082013.pdf.

[6] "Extractive Industries", The World Bank, available at: https://www.worldbank.org/en/topic/extractiveindustries/overview. See also "Africa's Oil and Gas Potential", Standard Bank, available at: https://corporateandinvestment.standardbank.com/cib/global/sector/capabilities/oil-and-gas/Africa%27s-Oil-and-Gas-potential.

[7] Wilson Chapman, "Africa to Lead World in Population Growth", US News, 10 July 2019, available at: https://www.usnews.com/news/best-countries/articles/2019-07-10/africa-to-lead-world-in-population-growth.

[8] "Africa Report", The World Bank, available at: https://www.worldbank.org/en/region/afr/overview.

[9] Ibid.

corruption and poorly functioning judicial systems continue to drag down economies on the continent.

Africa's ability to grow its economies and meet the demands of its growing population is heavily reliant on its ability to improve infrastructure. The continent continues to have inadequate transport, communication, water and power infrastructure,[10] which is, in turn, having dire consequences in terms of the amount of investment being made in many countries.

While more and more countries in Africa have moved from authoritarian to democratically elected governments, there is a question as to whether elected democratic regimes on the continent are resulting in stronger development.[11] In some cases, there is even a question as to whether elections are in fact democratic;[12] however, the bigger issue now seems to be whether elected officials are equipped to promote long-term growth (or are even interested in doing so). Investment in social services and infrastructure seems to increase in many countries around election times, and often appears to be carried out hastily.[13] A lack of long-term vision and planning has, at times, resulted in stale growth. At the same time, corruption continues to have a stifling impact on economic growth on the continent.[14]

Guinea serves as a persuasive example of how poor governance can hinder growth. The country held its first democratic election since 1958 in 2010, following decades of despotic and military regimes.[15] Even though these elections were considered democratic, the country has since been plagued by ethnic disputes and violence. The regime led by Mr. Alpha Condé has also been heavily criticised for banning demonstrations by opposition parties and civil society groups, and for allowing security forces

---

[10] Andre Pottas, "Addressing Africa's Infrastructure Challenges", Deloitte, available at: https://www2.deloitte.com/t/dam/Deloitte/global/Documents/Energy-and-Resources/dttl-er-africasinfrastructure-08082013.pdf.

[11] Ernest Aryeetey, "Is there a tension between democracy and economic development in Africa?", Brookings Institution, 11 March 2019, available at: https://www.brookings.edu/blog/africa-in-focus/2019/03/11/is-there-a-tension-between-democracy-and-economic-development-in-africa/.

[12] By way of example, Angola, Congo and Cameroon hold elections, but are seen as continuing to have authoritarian leadership.

[13] Ernest Aryeetey, "Is there a tension between democracy and economic development in Africa?", Brookings Institution, 11 March 2019, available at: https://www.brookings.edu/blog/africa-in-focus/2019/03/11/is-there-a-tension-between-democracy-and-economic-development-in-africa/.

[14] "Most Corrupt Countries 2020", World Population Review, available at: http://worldpopulationreview.com/countries/most-corrupt-countries/.

[15] "Guinea Country Profile", BBC News, available at: https://www.bbc.com/news/world-africa-13442051.

to use excessive force when there are protests against the government.[16] Moreover, the judiciary is regularly accused of failing to investigate state-sponsored violence.[17] In 2021 a military coup obliged President Condé to resign and relinquish power to a military group. As will be discussed later in this book, in Chapter 5, the ECOWAS Court of Justice recently issued a landmark decision against the government of Guinea, finding that it had unlawfully taken assets from a private company. This case could signal a shift in the legitimacy of that Court, and Guinea finds itself at the heart of the dispute, all as a result of corrupt practice.

Poor governance has resulted in the inability of local governments to respond to the massive natural disasters and health crises that have crippled many countries on the continent in recent years. In 2019 alone, more than 1,200 people lost their lives in cyclones and mudslides that hit Mozambique, Somalia, Kenya, Sudan and Malawi.[18] As a result of climate crises, 33 million people in Eastern and Southern Africa alone are at an emergency level of food insecurity.[19] West Africa also remains one of the most vulnerable regions in the world to climate variability and climate change.[20] At the same time, the continent remains plagued by communicable diseases, including dengue, cholera, trachoma and malaria, amongst others, and certain countries have been paralysed by infectious diseases such as Ebola. While the final impacts of COVID-19 are not yet known, as of the time of writing, it is almost certain that it, too, will have dire consequences on the continent.

Guinea is only one example of how a plethora of issues continue to stall economic growth on the African continent. While there are several African countries topping the list of the world's growing economies, even more countries across the continent continue to face manifold problems of the types facing Guinea. The development of individual African nations will depend on African leaders addressing these issues head-on and devoting resources to improving infrastructure and social services. It will also depend, in large part, on the ability of African nations to attract foreign investment, both intercontinental and external.

---

[16]   "Guinea Events of 2018", Human Rights Watch, available at: https://www.hrw.org/world-report/2019/country-chapters/guinea.

[17]   Ibid.

[18]   "2019: Natural disasters claim more than 1200 lives across East and Southern Africa", ReliefWeb, available at: https://reliefweb.int/report/world/2019-natural-disasters-claim-more-1200-lives-across-east-and-southern-africa.

[19]   Ibid.

[20]   "Climate Risk Profile: West Africa", ReliefWeb, available at: https://reliefweb.int/report/world/climate-risk-profile-west-africa.

The economies of African nations, like most countries in the world, are dependent on foreign direct investment (FDI).[21] The stability and growth of African economies is intricately intertwined with the ability of African governments to attract investors from outside the continent. As stated well by the International Journal of Financial Studies,

> Foreign Direct Investment can bring in much needed capital, particularly to developing countries, help improve manufacturing and trade sectors, bring in more efficient technologies, increase local production and exports, create jobs and develop local skills, and bring about improvements in infrastructure and overall be a contributor to sustainable economic growth.[22]

With this plethora of potential benefits, it is absolutely essential that African nations create favourable environments for foreign investors. At the same time, however, they must ensure that the gains derived from FDI are in fact being used to create sustainable development.

Africa has had a long history of slow growth, and has struggled more than other regions in the world to attract foreign investment. Throughout the 1980s and 1990s, African nations went to great lengths to attract greater foreign investment. Many countries liberalised their investment regulations and offered incentives to foreign investors.[23] At that same time, however, negative images of the continent continued to dominate headlines around the world, and foreign investors were, as a result, dissuaded from entering African markets. Africa's extractive industries and raw material sector were some of the first areas to see an increase in FDI, as investors began to gain a better understanding of the opportunities that exist on the continent. In the 1990s, FDI increased fourfold,[24] and

---

[21]   FDI is defined as "an investment involving a long-term relationship and reflecting a lasting interest and control by a resident entity in one economy in an enterprise resident in an economy other than that of the foreign direct investor". See IMF, "Foreign Direct Investment Trends and Statistics: A Summary", available at: https://www.imf.org/External/np/sta/fdi/eng/2003/102803s1.pdf.

[22]   Prince Jaiblai, "International Journal of Financial Studies, Determinants of FDI in Sub-Saharan Economies: A study of DATA from 1990–2017", available at: https://ideas.repec.org/a/gam/jijfss/v7y2019i3p43-d256918.html.

[23]   "Foreign Direct Investment in Africa: Performance and Potential", United Nations Conference on Trade and Development, available at: https://unctad.org/en/Docs/poiteiitm15.pdf.

[24]   Stephen Thomsen, "Foreign Direct Investment in Africa: the Private-Sector Response to Improved Governance", Chatham House, available at: https://www.chathamhouse.org/sites/default/files/public/Research/International%20Economics/bpafrica-fdi.pdf.

Africa then saw an uptick of FDI at the turn of the century, with USD 50 billion in investments between 2000 and 2003.[25] The continent has had a slow increase in FDI since then, with some exceptions, notably in 2017 when FDI fell by 21%,[26] when weak oil prices and a commodities bust hit the continent at the same time.

Notably, the *World Investment Report 2019* found that FDI to the continent rose 11% in 2018, in a year where there was global decline in FDI around the world.[27] This growth includes a strong showing from sub-Saharan Africa, where the increase in FDI to some of the poorest economies in the world grew by 13%.[28] EY (formerly Ernst & Young)'s last *Africa Attractiveness Report*, released in September 2019, found that Africa's ratio of FDI to gross domestic product (GDP) is high, which it notes is an important indicator of the importance of FDI for economic growth in the continent.[29] While the continent has seen an uptick in the number of developing-country investors, the leading investors continue to come from France, the Netherlands, and the United States, as well as from China, which has for several years now demonstrated that it is ready to become one of the leading investors in Africa, if not *the* leading investor.[30] While the total amount of FDI flowing into Africa remains lower than the rest of the world, there are clear indications that it will continue to grow in the future.

Unlike most developed nations, Africa's reliance on foreign investment does not end with monetary contributions. African nations not only rely on financial investment, but also on the technical expertise and, at times, human capital resources of investors. As one primary example of this, the leading industries for FDI in Africa continue to be the extractive industries, which attracted 36% of the overall FDI in 2018.[31] While Africa is extremely wealthy in natural resources, most countries lack the experience and technical expertise to turn this wealth into economic gain.

[25] Ibid.
[26] "WIR-Foreign direct investment to Africa fell by 21% in 2017, says United Nations report", UNCTAD, available at: https://unctad.org/en/pages/PressRelease.aspx?OriginalVersionID=461.
[27] Ibid.
[28] Ibid.
[29] "EY Attractiveness Reports (2019)", Ernst & Young, available at: https://www.ey.com/en_us/attractiveness.
[30] Mouhamed Kebe, "Dispute Settlement under China's Belt and Road Initiative – African Perspective", December 2019.
[31] "EY Attractiveness Reports (2019)", Ernst & Young, available at: https://www.ey.com/en_us/attractiveness.

Not only do the extractive industries rely on large amounts of capital to finance projects in this industry, but they also rely on the technical assistance and human capital that more experienced foreign investors may be able to bring. To a lesser extent than in the extractive industries, this is also true in other sectors that are showing strong growth,[32] such as the manufacturing and services industries. Successful growth of these sectors will also require a certain level of expertise that does not currently exist in many African countries.

At the same time, while they rely on foreign investment and, often, technical assistance, African countries are sovereign nations that must balance a vast range of different political, social and economic objectives when seeking outside resources. Governments are responsible to their citizens, and have both domestically and internationally mandated obligations that they must fulfil. This is particularly true in terms of sustainable development objectives,[33] which are absolutely essential in assuring a prosperous future for the continent. States are balancing an array of different needs, many of which were discussed above; everything from strengthening the rule of law to food security, and from providing health services to creating jobs, must be considered if countries have any hope of reducing the current level of poverty, improving the standard of living, and cultivating economic conditions for investment.

While African governments struggle to demonstrate that they have the institutional and structural capacity to support foreign investments, foreign investors that are willing to enter the market find themselves in a commanding position. Investors often overlook or ignore the internal responsibilities of governments, and misinterpret a reliance on foreign investment as a power to manipulate local law. Many foreign investors have been quick to capitalise on their upper hand, taking advantage of weak or corrupt governance for their own benefit. While examples of this are seemingly endless, certain companies top the list of culprits. For example, Glencore, the commodity trading and mining company, dealt a huge blow to the Democratic Republic of Congo in 2015 by suddenly closing a large copper mine that accounted for 20% of the country's total copper output, simply on the basis that it was no longer profitable for them. This decision

---

[32] Ayodele Odusola, "Addressing the Foreign Direct Investment Paradox in Africa," available at: https://www.un.org/africarenewal/web-features/addressing-foreign-direct-investment-paradox-africa.

[33] "About the Sustainable Development Goals", United Nations, available at: https://www.un.org/sustainabledevelopment/sustainable-development-goals/.

put masses of people out of work, and left the country scrambling to find alternative means of extracting the valuable resource.[34] Again, this is just one example of a never-ending list of foreign companies that appear to be using Africa to their own advantage, regardless of the impact.

Manipulation of vulnerable tax systems is also an excellent example of where African nations have struggled to restrict foreign investors, resulting in huge losses for their countries, often with little or no recourse. As has been highlighted by leaders in development,

> Africa is haemorrhaging billions of dollars because multinational companies are cheating African governments out of vital revenues by not paying their fair share in taxes. If this tax revenue were invested in education and healthcare, societies and economies would further flourish across the continent.[35]

Herein lies one of the most complicated challenges to future economic growth in Africa; to show real growth and development, African nations must be able to assert themselves and the needs of their countries into their negotiations with foreign investors. Foreign investment must be strategically used to the benefit of African nations, not to their detriment.

The importance of African governments, representing their constituents, being heard in determining when, and under what circumstances, investment may be made in their countries exists not only during initial negotiations, but remains throughout the lives of investment projects. Over the course of a complex transaction, the needs of a country may shift, or things may run astray from what is in the best interests of the local population. Governments may decide that certain aspects of a project need to be modified; or that new laws having no direct connection to a project, but which may have a negative impact on it need to be passed. In these circumstances, disputes will likely arise, which creates a need for sound dispute settlement mechanisms.

The most common types of disputes arising from investments in Africa include those related to contractual breaches, environmental damage,

---

[34] Parag Khanna, "These 25 Companies Are More Powerful Than Many Countries", Foreign Policy, available at: https://foreignpolicy.com/2016/03/15/these-25-companies-are-more-powerful-than-many-countries-multinational-corporate-wealth-power/.
[35] According to Winni Byanyima, the then Executive Director of Oxfam. See "Multinational companies cheat Africa out of billions of dollars", Oxfam, available at: https://www.oxfam.org/en/press-releases/multinational-companies-cheat-africa-out-billions-dollars.

breaches of local or community law, and violations of human rights. Contractual breaches often arise when African governments have entered into agreements quickly, or have been unaware of the terms being agreed to when entering into agreements governed by foreign law. These types of disputes also arise when one of the parties, in most cases an African government, is unable to meet the contractual terms. For example, disputes may be common in cases where African governments took on debt, as part of the investment agreement, which they are later unable to pay. The imbalance of contractual parties' bargaining power often leads to disputes later on as a project develops.

The nature of many of the largest foreign investment projects in Africa, many of which are associated with the extractive industries, often results in damage to the environment. In many cases, this damage is irreversible. Such damage often causes direct harm to local populations, whose mistrust of government only exacerbates weak legal systems, leading to more difficult development challenges. Examples of environmental damage from foreign investment are plentiful in Africa. Recently, a new network of railways being built in Kenya and Uganda cut directly through national reserves, creating havoc in biosystems there.[36] The Grand Inga Dam in Congo did not take into consideration the potentially huge negative impacts on biodiversity, or the long-term impacts that such a project may have on the water supply of local populations.[37] The government of Cameroon has pushed forward road construction, mining and logging projects that have caused irreparable damage to the land, and have had a substantial negative impact on the livelihoods of local farmers.[38] In order for there to be truly sustainable growth in Africa, claims against these projects, and governmental efforts to protect against further harm, must be given a forum.

The local laws of African nations are as complex as they are unique. Many countries on the continent have complex webs of common or civil law, mixed with traditional or community laws. The constitutions of

---

[36] See "Executive Summary of the Environmental and Social Assessment – Rift Valley Railways Project", African Development Bank Group, available at: https://www.afdb. org/fileadmin/uploads/afdb/Documents/Environmental-and-Social-Assessments/ RVR%20ESIA%20Exec%20Summary_English%20final.pdf.

[37] Adam Wernick, "Congo pushes for a mega-dam project, with no environmental impact studies", 3 July 2016, available at: https://www.pri.org/stories/2016-07-03/congo-pushes-mega-dam-project-no-environmental-impact-studies.

[38] Mike Ives, "China's Belt and Road Initiative Threatens to Pave the Planet", 16 December 2019, available at: https://www.sierraclub.org/sierra/2020-1-january-february/feature/chinas-belt-and-road-initiative-threatens-pave-planet.

several African nations provide a long list of individual rights to citizens, many of which may be considered as running contrary to the desires of foreign investors.[39] Project documents, including investment agreements, are often put together without regard for local laws, specifically community laws. Foreign investors, particularly those from China, tend to use their own materials and labour for completing projects, which is, at times, in direct conflict with local labour laws. Projects may also be carried out without prior consultation with local populations, which runs contrary to what is required under local law, and leads to heightened tension and distrust in communities.[40] The basic human rights of local populations, enshrined not only in local laws but in international law, are often overlooked or ignored as complex projects progress and expand. This only increases the likelihood of potential conflict.

Existing dispute settlement mechanisms under African investment agreements are, in many cases, failing to protect the needs of African nations. Currently, the dispute settlement mechanisms built into investment agreements almost always allow for investor-state dispute settlement (ISDS). Using ISDS, investors have been quick to challenge proposed local laws or policy decisions that may run contrary to their investment expectations.[41] In most cases, little consideration is given to local needs or objectives. As a result, frustrations are boiling.

Several African leaders have begun to express concern over a perceived infringement of their sovereign rights and obligations being built directly into existing dispute settlement options.[42] At the same time, African governments have historically argued that international arbitration – investors' preferred method of dispute settlement – is extremely costly, and is perceived as biased towards investors, resulting in African nations having to pay large awards that further inhibit their economic growth.[43]

[39] See H. Kwasi Prempeh, "Africa's 'constitutionalism revival': false start or new dawn?", (2007) 5(3) International Journal of Constitutional Law, pp. 495–506, available at: https://academic.oup.com/icon/article/5/3/469/647353.

[40] Larry Hanauer and Lyle J. Morris, "China in Africa Implications of a Deepening Relationship", Rand Corporation, available at: https://www.rand.org/pubs/research_briefs/RB9760.html.

[41] Tsotang Tsietsi, "International Commercial Arbitration: Case Study of the Experiences of African States in the International Centre for Settlement of Investment Disputes", available at: https://scholar.smu.edu/cgi/viewcontent.cgi?article=1582&context=til.

[42] Theobald Naud, Ben Sanderson and Andrea Lapunzina Veronelli, "Recent Trends in Investment Arbitration in Africa", DLA Piper, 11 April 2019, available at: https://globalarbitrationreview.com/insight/the-middle-eastern-and-african-arbitration-review-2019/1190119/recent-trends-in-investment-arbitration-in-africa.

[43] Ibid.

What has become clear is that there is diminishing confidence amongst African nations in the current dispute settlement mechanisms.

The purpose of this book is to explore the conflicting relationship between the African states involved in the ISDS and the application of this mechanism within the African continent over the few last decades, and what solutions can be identified and implemented to mitigate this "conflict". The book looks, first, at the current laws governing investment in Africa, followed by the existing forums for resolving disputes over investments. The book then explores the existing dispute settlement mechanisms being used to settle international disputes: state-to-state dispute settlement and ISDS. It then zooms in on current trends around the world, in different regions, and notes how there appears to be a growing movement away from ISDS. Finally, the book presents the author's position that, taking into consideration all of these aspects of dispute settlement, Africa needs a continental court with clearly defined rules and procedures that protect the sovereignty of African nations while continuing to attract much-needed foreign investment.

CHAPTER 2

GOVERNING LAW

When foreign investors enter a new market, they become subject to that country's jurisdiction. What this would generally imply is that foreign investors would be subject to the laws and regulations of the host country, no matter how favourable or unfavourable to the investor. However, recent worldwide trends have focused on eliminating discrimination against foreign investors, by applying international standards of equity (for example, fair and equitable treatment and, to a less extent, most-favoured nation (MFN) or national treatment (NT)).[44]

Countries have accomplished this by entering into international treaties, creating a complicated web of international and domestic laws and agreements that foreign investors must navigate when entering new jurisdictions.

In Africa, foreign investments are regulated by host state laws, by Regional Economic Communities (RECs), by continental agreements, by multinational and bilateral treaties, and under investment agreements.[45] Navigating the pool of differing regulations can prove challenging, and lead to confusion or frustration for foreign investors. Before delving into the current landscape for dispute settlement, to be discussed in the following chapters, this chapter provides a general overview of the types of investment regulations and how each type of regulation interplays with the others. When looking at these governing regulations, important

---

[44] This study will not address these subjects. A comprehensive analysis can be found in: Peter Muchlinski, Federico Ortino and Christoph Schreuer (eds.), The Oxford Handbook of International Investment Law, Oxford; New York: OUP, 2008, pp. lxv, 1282. See also "International Investment Agreements: Key Issues Volume I", United Nations Conference on Trade and Development, available at: https://unctad.org/en/Docs/iteiit200410_en.pdf.

[45] Tinyiko Ngobeni, "The Relevance of the Draft Pan African Investment Code (PAIC) in Light of the formation of the African Continental Free Trade Area", 15 January 2019, available at: http://www.afronomicslaw.org/2019/01/11/the-relevance-of-the-draft-pan-african-investment-code-paic-in-light-of-the-formation-of-the-african-continental-free-trade-area/.

considerations that are particularly pertinent to the African context arise. Chief considerations include looking at the extent to which the freedom and actions of State Parties are limited under each regulation type, and at the extent to which developing countries that are State Parties to these agreements are able to continue making the key decisions necessary to promote their own development. Under the latter topic, it is important to consider how much a State Party is able to influence the amount and type of foreign investment they receive, as well as the conduct of foreign investors in their country.

1. DOMESTIC LAWS

Each country on the African continent has its own unique laws and regulations that govern investment and business-related matters within its territory. These laws may include investment laws, company laws, tax laws and/or securities laws, all of which directly govern business matters. Apart from these types of laws, it is also necessary to consider secondary laws that may have an impact on business operations in a country. For example, it is essential to consider labour laws, environmental laws and human rights-related laws that may be on the books in each country. Domestic laws in Africa vary in terms of complexity and clarity, but nonetheless, all play a key role in understanding the investment landscape on the continent.

Regarding the business-related laws, one of the first things that must be taken into consideration is whether the target country has adopted the uniform or model laws of an international or regional body. The most commonly adopted laws aiming, inter alia, to promote investment will be discussed at greater length below; these include, among others, the United Nations Commission on International Trade Law (UNCITRAL) Model Law on Arbitration and the OHADA Arbitration Uniform Act, which cover several different topics, including investment, securities and arbitration.[46] For those countries that have adopted model or uniform laws, such laws will be the governing laws in such jurisdictions, and will supersede all preceding domestic laws on the same topic.

Certain African countries have recently enacted domestic investment laws that are meant to better protect domestic interests. Tanzania, for example, in its Investment Act of 1997, established a Tanzania Investment

---

[46]   Prof. Dr Mohamed S. Abdel Wahab, "ICSID's Relevance for Africa: A Symbiotic Bond Beyond Time", (2019) 34(2) ICSID Review, pp. 519–541, available at: doi:10.1093/icsidreview/siz022.

Centre, created to be "the primary agency of the government to coordinate, encourage, promote, and facilitate investment in Tanzania".[47] This created a one-stop shop for investors entering the Tanzanian market, and the Act itself provided certain incentives to foreign-owned projects investing in the country. All of this was done in an effort to better attract foreign investors while at the same time protecting the domestic economy.

In 2018, another country, Côte d'Ivoire, adopted a new investment code which aims to increase investment attractiveness but is also focused on promoting domestic interests.[48] One of the most important features of this code is its dispute settlement mechanisms, which provide for a three-tiered resolution system. The first option for disputes is for amicable settlement between parties; the next option is conciliation following UNCITRAL rules; and the final option is to submit the case to the Common Court of Justice and Arbitration of the Organization for the Harmonisation of Business Law in Africa (to be discussed at length in a later chapter).[49] At the same time, the code adds certain local content requirements and further environmental obligations.[50] This code brings a unique, Africa-centred approach to protecting investments, which ultimately helps protect the country's own interests as well.

South Africa has also enacted legislation aimed at attracting greater FDI, while at the same time bringing control over investment back into the hands of the country. The South Africa Protection of Investment Act (2015) sets forth broad protections for investments, whether domestic or foreign. It does, however, provide NT to foreign investors, meaning they are not able to be treated less favourably than South African investors.[51] National treatment is not the only provision of bilateral investment treaties (to be discussed at length below) to be codified in this Act. The Act codifies several features of standard investment treaties but adds greater protection of state interests by specifically providing protections

---

47 http://www.tic.go.tz.
48 Mouhamed Kebe, Mahamat Atteib and Mouhamoud Sangare, "Ivory Coast's New Investment Code: Focus on issues related to sustainable development and dispute settlement", Investment Treaty News, 19 September 2019, available at: https://www.iisd.org/publications/investment-treaty-news-itn-volume-10-issue-3-september-2019.
49 Ibid.
50 Ibid.
51 Lungelo Magubane, "Investment protection legislation in South Africa", Return to Africa Connected: Issue 1, DLA Piper, November 2018, available at: https://www.dlapiper.com/en/southafrica/insights/publications/2018/11/africa-connected-doing-business-in-africa/investment-projection-legislation-in-south-africa/.

to state entities, enabling them to take certain measures. These protections may be used to justify nearly any constitutional state action taken by the government, making this Act particularly interesting and, perhaps, a model for greater domestic protection, which, as will be discussed throughout this publication, is of utmost importance to African nations as they look to the future.[52] Whether more countries adopt domestic legislation similar to that adopted in Tanzania, Côte d'Ivoire and South Africa remains to be seen, but in looking at the needs of the continent, it would appear advisable.

2. REGIONAL ECONOMIC COMMUNITIES

The continent of Africa is home to several RECs, each of which has its own regional investment agreement (RIA).[53] These include: the Common Market for Eastern and Southern Africa (COMESA), which has enacted the Investment Agreement for the COMESA Common Investment Area;[54] the Southern African Development Community (SADC), whose governing investment law is its Finance and Investment Protocol, as well as the SADC Model BIT;[55] the Economic Community of West African States (ECOWAS), which has adopted the Supplementary Act Adopting Community Rules on Investment and the Modalities for their Implementation with ECOWAS;[56] and the East African Community (EAC), with its Model Investment Code.[57] The RIAs govern investments in each of the member parties to each respective REC, and not only impact on investments, but also often have

---

[52] Ibid.

[53] Talkmore Chidede, "The Right to Regulate in Africa's International Investment Law Regime", (2019) 20(2) Oregon Review of International Law, pp. 437–468, available at: https://scholarsbank.uoregon.edu/xmlui/bitstream/handle/1794/24671/Chidede_ORIL20%282%29.pdf?sequence=1&isAllowed=y.

[54] Investment Agreement for the COMESA Common Investment Area, UNCTAD (23 May 2007), available at: https://investmentpolicy.unctad.org/international-investment-agreements/treaties/treaties-with-investment-provisions/3547/ecowas-supplementary-act-on-investments.

[55] SADC Model Bilateral Investment Treaty Template, SADC (July 2012), available at: https://www.iisd.org/itn/wp-content/uploads/2012/10/sadc-model-bit-template-final.pdf.

[56] Supplementary Act A/SA.3/12/08 Adopting Community Rules on Investment and the Modalities for their Implementation with ECOWAS, Economic Community of West Afr. States, 19 December 2008, available at: https://investmentpolicyhub.unctad.org/Download/ TreatyFile/3266.

[57] EAC Model Investment Code (2006), available at: http://www.eac.int/.

an effect on finance and taxation matters at both the national and regional levels.[58] Understanding governing regulations on investment in countries that are party to one or more of these RECs not only means understanding local law and bilateral investment treaties (BITs), as discussed previously, but also the governing RIAs.[59]

RIAs in Africa generally cover the same issues addressed in BITs (i.e. reciprocal exchange of guarantees and rights of foreign investors, as well as expropriation and MFN provisions) and, at the same time, harmonise the national investment policies of their Member States.[60] An important thing to note about RIAs is that they are only binding on and between nationals from the countries that are party to them.[61] For example, in the case of ECOWAS, only nationals of the 15 countries that are party to that REC are subject to its regulations, and it is only in a circumstance where a foreign investor is a national of one of the Member States that the investor is subject to the ECOWAS laws. In other words, ECOWAS's investment regulations only apply to ECOWAS nationals that are investing in other ECOWAS countries. That said, Member States have certain obligations derived from their participation in RECs that may limit or otherwise impact on their interactions with foreign investors of any nationality entering their jurisdictions.

At the same time, one of the key purposes of RECs is to harmonise laws and regulations,[62] so as to better attract foreign investment. One of the key target groups of RECs is investors who may be looking to streamline investment in several countries within the given region and/or to keep open the potential for entering new markets in that region in the future.[63] RIAs governing the jurisdiction where investment is to take place must be examined closely prior to investment, so as to understand the obligations that they impose on Member States, the benefits given to

---

[58]   United Nations Economic Commission for Africa, "Investment Policies and Bilateral Investment Treaties in Africa", available at: https://archive.uneca.org/publications/investment-policies-and-bilateral-investment-treaties-africa.

[59]   Note that there also exists the COMESA-EAC-SADC Tripartite Free Trade Area.

[60]   United Nations Economic Commission for Africa, "Investment Policies and Bilateral Investment Treaties in Africa", available at: https://repository.uneca.org/handle/10855/23035.

[61]   "International Investment Agreements: Key Issues", United Nations (2004), available at: https://unctad.org/en/Docs/iteiit200410_en.pdf.

[62]   "Assessing the Impacts of Investment Treaties: Overview of the Evidence", International Institute for Sustainable Development (2017), available at: https://www.iisd.org/sites/default/files/publications/assessing-impacts-investment-treaties.pdf.

[63]   "International Investment Agreements: Key Issues", United Nations (2004), available at: https://unctad.org/en/Docs/iteiit200410_en.pdf.

nationals of Member States, and the potential benefits they provide to non-Member State foreign investors. Each REC on the African continent will be discussed at length in Chapter 3.

3. BILATERAL INVESTMENT TREATIES

A bilateral investment treaty (BIT) is an agreement between two states that establishes the terms and conditions for private investment by nationals, including companies, of one state in another state, in accordance with host state laws.[64] The original bilateral investment treaties were called treaties of friendship, commerce and navigation. These treaties were entered into to facilitate commerce, and to protect individuals and businesses, allowing nationals of another state to be treated as equal to nationals of the home state.[65]

The first ever treaty of friendship, commerce and navigation was enacted in 1667 between Spain and the United Kingdom. This treaty was the first to establish the principle of MFN, which requires a country to provide any concessions, privileges or immunities granted to one nation under a trade agreement to all nationals of all other nations which are parties to that agreement and, in so doing, establishes equality between countries.[66]

Another notable treaty of friendship, commerce and navigation was the one signed in 1778 between the United States and France. This treaty also acknowledged the principle of MFN.[67] These earliest friendship,

---

[64] For a comprehensive analysis of the BITs, including their interpretations by arbitral awards, see Kenneth J. Vandevelde, Bilateral Investment Treaties: History, Policy and Interpretation, Oxford/New York: OUP, 2010, pp. xii, 562.

[65] Andreas Paulus, "Treaties of Friendship, Commerce and Navigation", in Max Planck Encyclopedia of Public International Law, Oxford Public International Law, available at: https://opil.ouplaw.com/view/10.1093/law:epil/9780199231690/law-9780199231690-e1482.
See also Kenneth J. Vandevelde, The First Bilateral Investment Treaties: U.S. Postwar Friendship, Commerce, and Navigation Treaties, Oxford: OUP, 2017.

[66] Article 38 of the treaty made English merchants equivalent to the Dutch and French by awarding them MFN status. See Jean McLachlan, "2. Documents Illustrating Anglo-Spanish Trade Between the Commercial Treaty of 1667 and the Commercial Treaty and the Asiento Contract of 1713", (1934) 4(3) Cambridge Historical Journal, pp. 299–311, doi:10.1017/S1474691300000664.

[67] Peter Van den Bossche and Werner Zdouc, The Law and Policy of the World Trade Organization, Cambridge: CUP, 2018, pp. 305–340, available at: https://doi.org/10.1017/9781316662496.005.

16

commerce and navigation treaties also set forth terms for shipping between countries and use of property in host countries.[68]

After World War II, the United States entered into 22 friendship, commerce and navigation treaties (FCN treaties).[69] These treaties followed the Bretton Woods Conference, wherein the International Monetary Fund (IMF) and a fixed rate against the US dollar were both established, in an effort to support those countries that had been most heavily impacted by World War II.[70] The resulting IMF agreement sought to promote free trade in goods, which created the need for greater regulation of foreign trade and investment. This was particularly true for the United States, which had a surplus of goods following the war, and was anxious to begin trading with other countries in an effort for other countries to acquire dollars, which would also help boost the US economy. At the same time, however, the country recognised that there would be risk involved in transborder transactions, and that it would need to establish a system of regulations that would ensure that the best interests of the country were protected, and risk in such transactions diminished.[71]

The policy that arose out of the United States' desire to have increased international trade sought to balance the desire for greater private investment with the need for public lending, which was of great importance as countries began to rebuild after the war. In their early states, these agreements were meant as a means to improve the standard of living around the world and to finance development, as much as they were aimed at promoting economic development through investment.[72] However, the international view of these agreements was repeatedly revised for several years, with the United States struggling with the balancing of various interests. Eventually, President Truman announced a four-point strategy, wherein the United States would focus on developing a stronger world through four proposed focuses, one of which would be to promote a new programme for scientific advancement and industrial progress for the improvement and growth of underdeveloped areas. Cradled in this strategy, the fourth point of the plan was enhanced investment, which

---

[68]   Ibid.
[69]   Kenneth J. Vandevelde, Bilateral Investment Treaties: History, Policy, and Interpretation, Oxford/New York: OUP, 2010.
[70]   Ibid.
[71]   Ibid.
[72]   Ibid.

Truman hoped would promote countries' self-reliance. What arose out of these agreements was a series of FCN treaties in the early 1950s, wherein the US government openly and actively promoted "the investment of private American capital in foreign countries".[73] Over the next few years, these FCN treaties, under the guidance of the US State Department, started to incorporate investment as more of a key feature of international agreements, thereby laying the framework for second-generation bilateral treaties.

From the end of the 1950s onwards, the first-generation bilateral treaties, referred to today as BITs, were signed. The first such agreement was entered into in 1959, between the Federal Republic of Germany and Pakistan.[74] These agreements grew in popularity as the developed world began trading more frequently with developing nations. The BITs were seen as providing protection for investments in developing countries, where systems were not as robust as in the developed world. These agreements are not only used between developed and developing nations, but have also flourished as globalisation has come to permit greater trade between countries with all types of economies. Today, there is a total of more than 2,800 BITs, with 2,227 in force.[75] African states have signed a total of 864 BITs, 165 of which have been intra-African.[76] As with their predecessor agreements, these agreements set forth the standards of conduct that governments to a treaty are to apply to nationals of the other State Party to the agreement. The four principal concepts established in BITs are: (i) fair and equitable treatment; (ii) protection from expropriation; (iii) free transfer of means; and (iv) full protection and security.[77]

---

[73] Memorandum by Charles H. Sullivan headed "Entry of Foreign Investors into the United States under Treaties of Friendship, Commerce and Navigation," dated 23 November 1949, NARA, Record Group 59, Department of State File No. 611.004/5-350.

[74] Rudolf Dolzer and Margrete Stevens, Bilateral Investment Treaties, The Hague/Boston: Martinus Nijhoff Publishers, 1995.

[75] See "International Investment Agreements Navigator", UNCTAD, available at: https://investmentpolicy.unctad.org/international-investment-agreements.

[76] Prof. Dr Mohamed S. Abdel Wahab, "ICSID's Relevance for Africa: A Symbiotic Bond Beyond Time", (2019) 34(2) ICSID Review, pp. 519–541, available at: doi:10.1093/icsidreview/siz022.

[77] "Bilateral investment treaty", Cornell Law School, available at: https://www.law.cornell.edu/wex/bilateral_investment_treaty.

Fair and equitable treatment is a minimum standard of treatment and protection required by international law, and is owed to foreign investors and their property by host countries. It is an "absolute" standard of treatment, as opposed to the "relative" standards embodied in "NT" and "MFN" principles, which define the required treatment by reference to the treatment accorded to other investments.[78] It is worth mentioning that studies by UNCTAD and many others emphasise that discrimination as part of fair and equitable treatment (FET) is distinct from discrimination within MFN and NT, which are treaty-based notions.

The difference between NT and MFN treatment is that NT provides that State Parties to an agreement will provide the same rights and protections to nationals of another state as they do to their own people and businesses, while the MFN principle provides that the country will provide the same rights and protections to each of its trading partners.[79] Most-favoured nation treatment is particularly important under the World Trade Organization (WTO) agreements,[80] to which most countries worldwide are parties. The WTO agreements themselves do provide certain exceptions to the MFN principle, including being able to set up free trade agreements amongst a smaller subset of countries; allowing developing countries to receive more favourable treatment; and allowing barriers to products that are considered to be unfair to trade by certain countries.

Many BITs to which African nations are party have only a FET clause, rather than specified NT or MFN treatment clauses.[81] This has led to a substantial amount of confusion among states and investors, as such FET clauses weigh treatment vis-à-vis other investors, making it difficult to determine what constitutes fair and equitable treatment of an investor. This has given rise to a number of claims being brought by way of ISDS (discussed at length in Chapter 6). These claims are centred on the scope

---

[78] Martin Domke, "Government Guarantees to Foreign Investors. By A.A. Fatouros (New York: Columbia University Press, 1962. pp. xvii, 411)" (1964) 58(2) American Journal of International Law, p. 551, doi:10.2307/2196254.

[79] Ibid.

[80] These include the General Agreement on Tariffs and Trade (GATT), the General Agreement on the Trade in Services (GATS), and the Agreement on Trade-Related Aspects of Intellectual Property Rights (TRIPS).

[81] Prof. Dr Mohamed S. Abdel Wahab, "ICSID's Relevance for Africa: A Symbiotic Bond Beyond Time", (2019) 34(2) ICSID Review, pp. 519–541, available at: doi:10.1093/icsidreview/siz022.

and meaning of FET clauses.[82] More specifically, there is a debate as to whether to apply a minimum international standard to these clauses, or to look solely at other language used in the treaty. There has been no consistent response to this question, which leaves African nations more vulnerable to challenges to their policies, and investors less sure as to the protections that may or may not be given to their investments under a BIT.

Another key concept under BITs is the protection from expropriation. This concept protects against losses that may arise from a government taking partial or total ownership or control over an investment.[83] The purpose of this type of provision is to protect foreign investors from losing everything (or almost everything) if the host country, for example, decides one day that the foreigners' investment would be profitable for the State, and takes control of that investment. BITs require that if a government does take over an investment, the investor must be compensated in a fair and timely manner.[84] An excellent example of this is the Venezuelan government's expropriation of the investments of the Mobil Corporation and ConocoPhillips oil companies. These two companies invoked the expropriation protection under the BIT between the Kingdom of the Netherlands and Venezuela.[85] In this case, ConocoPhillips sought over USD 21 billion in compensation for the alleged seizure of its property by the Venezuelan government, while Venezuela argued that the company was only entitled to USD 515 million. The original decision in this case, in 2013, held that Venezuela had failed to negotiate the terms of the agreement with the company in good faith, as was required under the BIT between the two countries. Venezuela has asked the annulment committee to reconsider its decision, arguing that domestic law should be considered in the calculation; however, the court has consistently stated that the terms of the BIT must be taken into consideration, given that it governs

---

[82] Ibid.
[83] Dr Johanne M. Cox, *Expropriation in Investment Treaty Arbitration*, Oxford: OUP, 2019.
[84] M. Sornarajah, "Compensation for nationalisation of foreign investments", in M. Sornarajah (ed.), *The International Law on Foreign Investment*, Cambridge: CUP, 2010, pp. 412–452, doi:10.1017/CBO9780511841439.014.
[85] *ConocoPhillips Petrozuata B.V., ConocoPhillips Hamaca B.V. and ConocoPhillips Gulf of Paria B.V. v. Bolivarian Republic of Venezuela*, ICSID Case No. ARB/07/30, available at: https://jusmundi.com/en/document/decision/en-conocophillips-petrozuata-b-v-conocophillips-hamaca-b-v-and-conocophillips-gulf-of-paria-b-v-v-bolivarian-republic-of-venezuela-award-friday-8th-march-2019.

investment between the host nation and the home nation of the company. This case is still awaiting a final decision.[86]

The free transfer of funds principle provides that investments should be able to be transferred freely by foreign investors without delay. This means that State Parties to a BIT should not be putting in place unduly burdensome foreign exchange restrictions that make the flow of capital between the two countries involved more complicated.

Argentina has been challenged several times under this principle of free transfer of funds. In fact, during its period of economic turmoil in the late 1990s and early 2000s, at least 50 claims were brought against Argentina under its BITs.[87] Many of these claims resulted from Argentina's executive or legislative branches issuing laws that heightened regulation of the exchange market, in an effort to curb the rapid economic downturn then facing the country.[88] The country has since changed its position on BITs, to assert stronger sovereignty and the ability to develop policies to address exceptional circumstances.[89] Other BITs, however, still contain provisions that protect against overly burdensome restrictions on transfers.

The full protection and security provision has also increasingly been questioned, in terms of its scope, in recent years. This provision generally includes something along the lines of, "[i]nvestments of nationals or companies of each Contracting Party shall at all times be accorded fair and equitable treatment and shall enjoy full protection and security in the territory of the Contracting Party".[90] The question that arises, however, is what extent of protection is required in today's increasingly volatile world. This provision has been challenged several times in the last decade,

---

[86]   The case was decided and later annulled. A new resubmission panel has been constituted. See https://jusmundi.com/en/document/decision/en-conocophillips-petrozuata-b-v-conocophillips-hamaca-b-v-and-conocophillips-gulf-of-paria-b-v-v-bolivarian-republic-of-venezuela-lord-phillips-recommendation-friday-10th-july-2020.

[87]   Facundo Perez-Aznar, "The Recent Argentina–Qatar BIT and the Challenges of Investment Negotiations", 12 June 2017, available at: https://www.iisd.org/itn/2017/06/12/recent-argentina-qatar-bit-challenges-investment-negotiations-facundo-perez-aznar/.

[88]   William W. Burke-White, "The Argentine Financial Crisis: State Liability Under BITs and the Legitimacy of the ICSID System", 24 January 2008, University of Pennsylvania Carey Law School, available at: https://scholarship.law.upenn.edu/cgi/viewcontent.cgi?article=1192&context=faculty_scholarship.

[89]   Ibid.

[90]   United Kingdom–Vietnam BIT (2002), Art. 2(2), available at: https://investmentpolicy.unctad.org/international-investment-agreements/treaties/treaties-with-investment-provisions/3066/united-kingdom---viet-nam-bit-2002-.

and the number of arbitral cases falling under this provision continues to rise at a notable rate.[91] In almost all cases, the arbitral tribunals have found that states cannot be required to uphold an absolute standard, but are expected to execute a high level of diligence in ensuring that foreign investors are protected in their states. In other words, states are expected to do everything possible to ensure that investors' property is protected, even in times of civil unrest or uprising.[92] The scope of this provision is certain to be challenged more in the future, as civil unrest continues to spread around the world.

With these principles in mind, the key clauses of almost all BITs include: (i) admission and establishment of investment, including the granting of NT and MFN treatment; (ii) general standards of treatment, including fair and equitable treatment, full protection and security, and the minimum standard of treatment; (iii) expropriation; (iv) transfer of funds; and (v) any exceptions that may have been reserved. In addition, and most pertinent to this book, the dispute resolution provision provided for in BITs is of utmost importance. The mechanism for dispute settlement contained in a BIT arguably has the greatest impact on the sovereign rights of the host countries. When ISDS (to be discussed at length in Chapter 6) is selected and the choice of forum clause provides for international arbitration, host states may find their legitimate domestic policy decisions being challenged by private investors. As was discussed above, this choice of dispute settlement mechanism can then directly impact on the other key provisions of BITs, as most often seen in the challenging of FET clauses. This will be discussed at length in the following chapters, but is important to raise it here, as the dispute resolution provisions in BITs are a key component of the laws governing foreign investment in Africa.

Many African nations entered into their first bilateral agreements immediately following independence, which for most countries was in

---

[91]   Mahnaz Malik, "The Full Protection and Security Standard Comes of Age: Yet another challenge for states in investment treaty arbitration?", International Institute for Sustainable Development, November 2011, available at: https://www.iisd.org/system/files/publications/full_protection.pdf.

[92]   *Asian Agricultural Products Ltd. v. Republic of Sri Lanka*, ICSID Case No. ARB/87/3, available at: https://www.italaw.com/cases/96.
This case involved the dramatic battle between the Sri Lankan security forces and insurgents who destroyed the investor's shrimp farm and killed more than 20 of its employees during the Tamil insurrection (*AAPL v. Sri Lanka, 1990*, para. 79). Neither the investor nor the government could prove whether insurgents or security forces had caused the damage.

the 1960s or 1970s. The first BITs involving individual African nations were entered into with European countries and/or the United States,[93] and have since been viewed as a key tool for attracting foreign investment to the continent, although this is highly debated. When entered into between two developed countries or two developing countries, BITs indicate that there is a hope for trade and investment between the two parties. When the BIT involves a developing country (as an overwhelming majority of African countries are classified) and a developed country, however, the intended benefits become a bit more uneven.

The intent of developing nations in entering into BITs appears, in most cases, to be to indicate to the developed country counterparty that they are open for foreign investment, and intend to protect investment in their countries.[94] The intent of developed countries, on the other hand, in addition to opening new markets for domestic companies, may be to better dictate the terms of investment flowing from their country to the developing country counterpart. The relationship in developing country–developed country BITs can be seen as more one-directional than in other BITs, given that there is an implied, albeit not typically expressed, understanding that the main purpose of the agreement is to increase investment into a developing nation, rather than to and from both nations. The implications of this perception have, arguably, hindered greater economic growth in Africa, by limiting the sovereignty of African nations that are party to such agreements. African states that enter into BITs with developed nations limit their own ability to freely regulate areas that may impact on investment and, as will be discussed at length in the following chapters, are more often than not submitting themselves to the will of international arbitral bodies.[95]

Regardless of the possible negative implications of BITs, bilateral investment agreements have for decades now been the leading governing laws for foreign investment in Africa. As discussed previously, African states often struggle with weak economies, poor infrastructure and a faltering rule of law. These countries have used BITs to subdue the fears

---

[93]   Talkmore Chidede, "The Right to Regulate in Africa's International Investment Law Regime", (2019) 20(2) Oregon Review of International Law, pp. 437–468, available at: https://scholarsbank.uoregon.edu/xmlui/bitstream/handle/1794/24671/Chidede_ORIL20%282%29.pdf?sequence=1&isAllowed=y.

[94]   Ibid.

[95]   Alec R. Johnson, "Rethinking Bilateral Investment Treaties in Sub-Saharan Africa", (2010) 59 Emory Law Journal, p. 919, available at: https://scholarlycommons.law.emory.edu/elj/vol59/iss4/3.

of foreign investors and, in turn, to better attract foreign investment. BITs, as foreign treaties, carry with them the status of international law and, therefore, for better or worse, carry more weight than domestic law. As mentioned above, according to the United Nations Economic Commission for Africa, as of 2019, there is a total of more than 2,800 BITs, with 2,227 in force. African states have signed a total of 864 BITs, of which 165 have been intra-African.[96] Understanding the investment landscape in individual African nations, therefore, requires a clear reading and understanding of any BITs that exist between the host nation and the domicile country of the investor.

4. DOUBLE TAXATION TREATIES

Another type of bilateral agreement that may directly impact on transborder investment is a double taxation treaty (DTT). Under DTTs, two countries agree to the amount of tax one country can collect from taxpayers of the other when doing business. There are currently around 3,000 DTTs worldwide.[97] These treaties confer certain rights and obligations on the two contracting states, and are intended to benefit taxpayers from the State Parties.[98] The fundamental principle of these treaties is reciprocity, meaning that taxpayers from one state are treated the same as those of the other state, regardless of nationality.[99] While originally established with the intent of ensuring that businesses do not have to pay tax in two jurisdictions, DTTs have somewhat quickly morphed into double non-taxation arrangements, leaving businesses free from paying taxes anywhere on cross-border transactions.[100]

---

[96] United Nations Economic Commission for Africa, "Investment Policies and Bilateral Investment Treaties in Africa", available at: https://archive.uneca.org/publications/investment-policies-and-bilateral-investment-treaties-africa.
[97] Evert-jan Quak and Hannah Timmis, "Double Taxation Agreements and Developing Countries", 1 June 2018, available at: https://assets.publishing.service.gov.uk/media/5b3b610040f0b645fd592202/Double-Taxation-Treaties_and_Developing_Countries.pdf.
[98] Brian J. Arnold, "An introduction to tax treaties", available at: https://www.un.org/esa/ffd/wp-content/uploads/2015/10/TT_Introduction_Eng.pdf.
[99] Ibid.
[100] Alexander Trepelkov, Harry Tonino and Dominika Halka, "United Nations Handbook on Selected Issues in Administration of Double Tax Treaties for Developing Countries" (2013), available at: https://www.un.org/esa/ffd/wp-content/uploads/2014/08/UN_Handbook_DTT_Admin.pdf.

The initial tax agreements arose in the 1920s, with the League of Nations drafting the first model income tax treaty in 1928. This initial model was highly favourable to the resident country, providing that only the country where a company or individual resided, and not the country where it conducted business, could tax such a company or individual.[101] Later treaties attempted to deal with double taxation in one of three ways: (i) limiting source country taxation on investment income or business income that lacked a significant and continuous presence in the source country (the "permanent establishment" requirement); (ii) requiring the residence country to provide an exemption of foreign source income or a tax credit for foreign taxes paid; or (iii) coordinating the rules of both countries.[102] Today, there are two predominant double tax treaties: the United Nations Model Tax Convention and the OECD Model Tax Convention, both of which share several common traits.[103] The United Nations Model Convention draws heavily on the OECD Model Convention, but with greater focus on providing a model for tax treaties between developing and developed countries.[104] Both model treaties cover agreements on various types of tax, including income from immovable property; business profits; operation of ships or aircraft; profits on associated enterprises and transfer pricing; dividends; interest; royalties; capital gains; income derived from professional and independent services; income from employment; directors' fees and remuneration of top-level managerial officials; income derived by artistes and athletes; pensions and social security payments; income derived by government employees; income derived by students, business trainees and apprentices; and other income.[105]

---

[101] Rebecca Kysar, "Unraveling the Tax Treaty", New York University School of Law, Spring 2019, available at: http://www.law.nyu.edu/sites/default/files/upload_documents/Unraveling%20the%20Tax%20Treaty%20-%20Kysar_0.pdf.

[102] Ibid.

[103] Brian J. Arnold, "An introduction to tax treaties", available at: https://www.un.org/esa/ffd/wp-content/uploads/2015/10/TT_Introduction_Eng.pdf. Note that the OECD has 34 members, and the first Model Convention was published in 1963 and then revised in 1977 and 1992.

[104] The United Nations Model Taxation Convention between Developed and Developing Countries was originally adopted in 1980 and then amended in 2001 and 2011.

[105] Brian J. Arnold, "An introduction to tax treaties", available at: https://www.un.org/esa/ffd/wp-content/uploads/2015/10/TT_Introduction_Eng.pdf. See also Allison D. Christians, "Tax Treaties for Investment and Aid to Sub-Saharan Africa: A Case Study", (2006) 71(2) Brooklyn Law Review, pp. 639–713, available at: https://brooklynworks.brooklaw.edu/cgi/viewcontent.cgi?referer=&httpsredir=1&article=1385&context=blr.

In recent years, the early DTTs have matured, and the number of international tax treaties has continued to rise. At the same time, however, the rise of multinational corporations has given rise to a manipulation of the initially well-intentioned international tax system. Multinational corporations have the fluidity and resources to establish themselves in nearly any jurisdiction in the world. This has allowed them to establish themselves in tax haven countries, where their "residency" allows them to avoid taxes altogether.[106] Moreover, wealthier countries have been able to use the OECD Model Convention to their benefit, as it largely favours the jurisdiction where the investor is resident, and most large multinational corporations are from wealthier countries.[107] While the UN Model used by many developing nations is somewhat more favourable to them as host nations, it has also been amended to more closely resemble the OECD model, resulting in even greater difficulties for developing countries in collecting tax from foreign investors.

Developing countries, who arguably have the most to gain from collecting tax revenues from foreign investors, have consistently lost the most under DTTs.[108] In fact, DTTs have demonstrated profound power politics and gaps in negotiating outcomes between wealthier, developed countries and poorer, developing countries.[109] Moreover, studies have shown that "[d]eveloping countries that depend more on corporate income tax are more likely to sign tax treaties with wealthier countries and more likely to negotiate higher withholding tax rates in those treaties, but no more likely to obtain better results overall".[110] Developing countries have

---

[106] Evert-jan Quak and Hannah Timmis, "Double Taxation Agreements and Developing Countries", 1 June 2018, available at: https://assets.publishing.service.gov.uk/media/5b3b610040f0b645fd592202/Double-Taxation-Treaties_and_Developing_Countries.pdf.
[107] Nick Shaxson, "More unfair tax treaties may be renegotiated", Tax Justice Network, 22 June 2016, available at: https://www.taxjustice.net/topics/corporate-tax/tax-treaties/.
[108] See Martin Hearson, "Tax treaties in sub-Saharan Africa: a critical review", London School of Economics (2015), available at: http://eprints.lse.ac.uk/67903/1/Hearson_Tax_treaties_in_sub-Saharan_Africa.pdf.
[109] See Martin Hearson, "When do Developing Countries Negotiate Away their Corporate Tax Base?" (2018) 30 Journal of International Development, pp. 233–255, available at: https://onlinelibrary.wiley.com/doi/pdf/10.1002/jid.3351. See also Evert-jan Quak and Hannah Timmis, "Double Taxation Agreements and Developing Countries", 1 June 2018, available at: https://assets.publishing.service.gov.uk/media/5b3b610040f0b645fd592202/Double-Taxation-Treaties_and_Developing_Countries.pdf.
[110] Evert-jan Quak and Hannah Timmis, "Double Taxation Agreements and Developing Countries", 1 June 2018, available at: https://assets.publishing.service.gov.uk/media/5b3b610040f0b645fd592202/Double-Taxation-Treaties_and_Developing_Countries.pdf.

negotiated tax treaties in an effort to attract foreign investment, but have, in the long run, lost more in potential tax revenues, which could be used for development, than they have gained in investment.[111] At the same time, wealthy corporations are able to legally use tax systems to avoid paying taxes, by channelling investments through intermediary companies formed in convenient jurisdictions, in what is known as treaty shopping.[112] As a result, these companies are not contributing to development in countries where they conduct business. While tax treaties may initially attract foreign investment (the primary concern of most developing nations), such attraction is transitory, and often crowds out domestic investment.[113]

The African continent presents the perfect example of the negative impacts that DTTs have had on developing nations. African nations have most often used DTTs to set standards for repatriation of capital (i.e. capital gained from investments carried out under BITs) without double taxation. As mentioned in Chapter 1 of this book, however, manipulation of tax systems has been a huge drain on African systems. Over time, the DTTs to which African nations are party have, not unlike DTTs in the rest of the world, evolved from treaties that prevent double taxation to treaties that seem to allow avoidance of taxes altogether.

By way of example, investors in Africa have worked out ways to establish companies in Mauritius, which has been deemed the "lynchpin of many tax avoidance structures in Africa".[114] That country has used tax treaties as a way of competing for business in the financial services sector, which is one of its strongest industries. At the same time, the country has entered into a plethora of treaties with other African nations, which then makes those nations susceptible to tax avoidance, given the special protections for companies from Mauritius.[115] Foreign companies from outside Africa

---

[111] Bruce A. Blonigen and Ronald B. Davies, "Do Bilateral Tax Treaties Promote Foreign Direct Investment?", in Karl P. Sauvant and Lisa E. Sachs (eds.), The Effect of Treaties on Foreign Direct Investment: Bilateral Investment Treaties, Double Taxation Treaties, and Investment Flows, New York: Oxford Academic, 2009, pp. 461–484, available at: https://doi.org/10.1093/acprof:oso/9780195388534.003.0017.

[112] "Tax Treaties", Tax Justice Network, available at: https://www.taxjustice.net/topics/corporate-tax/tax-treaties/.

[113] Martin Hearson, "Tax treaties in sub-Saharan Africa: a critical review", London School of Economics (2015), available at: http://eprints.lse.ac.uk/67903/1/Hearson_Tax_treaties_in_sub-Saharan_Africa.pdf.

[114] Will Fitzgibbon, "What's a Tax Treaty and Why Should I care?" (2019), available at: https://www.icij.org/investigations/mauritius-leaks/whats-a-tax-treaty-and-why-should-i-care/.

[115] Ibid.

have taken advantage of this set-up by establishing themselves in Mauritius before engaging in other investments on the continent. While Mauritius has been able to attract substantial business by establishing itself as a tax haven, it has done so to the detriment of other countries on the continent, and to the tremendous benefit of large multinational corporations.

A growing number of countries, both on and off the African continent, have begun to express concern about the "crippling" impacts their tax treaties are having on their own economies. Tax officials from Egypt, Senegal, Uganda, Lesotho, South Africa, Zimbabwe, Tunisia and Zambia have all expressed this sentiment.[116] Several African nations have announced their intent to cancel their treaties with Mauritius altogether. Senegal has led the way, terminating its taxation treaty with Mauritius on 1 January 2020.[117] In stating his reasons for terminating this agreement, Macky Sall, President of Senegal, said that the country has lost more than USD 250 million in tax revenue to Mauritius.[118] What impacts cancelling this treaty will have on foreign investment, and which other countries may follow Senegal's lead, have yet to be seen. What is clear, however, is that corporations have flocked to use Mauritius as a tax haven when investing on the African continent, demonstrating the important role of DTTs in foreign investment.

While, in Senegal, the challenge to the DTT with Mauritius was an initiative of the executive authority, in Kenya it came from civil society – the first such challenge to a tax treaty in Africa – and was endorsed by the judiciary. The High Court, in a judgment rendered on 15 March 2019, declared void the Kenya–Mauritius Double Taxation Avoidance Agreement (DTAA) signed on 11 May 2012, on the grounds that the government failed to subject the tax agreement to the due ratification process in line with the Treaty Making and Ratification Act 2012.[119] At first glance, it appears that the invalidity of the DTT is due only to a procedural defect, but according to lots of views, the ruling, in reality, validates the call for African countries to review all their tax treaties, particularly those signed with tax havens.

---

[116] Ibid.
[117] "Tax Treaty between Mauritius and Senegal Terminated", Orbitax (2019), available at: https://www.orbitax.com/news/archive.php/Tax-Treaty-between-Mauritius-a-40865.
[118] "Taxation, Senegal denounces double taxation agreement with Mauritius and threatens to abandon the deal", AfricaNews (2019), available at: https://www.africanews.com/2019/07/11/senegal-mauritius-tax-row/.
[119] High Court of Kenya, 15 March 2019, *The Tax Justice Network v. Cabinet Secretary for National Treasury, The Kenya Review Authority and Attorney General*. The judgment is available at: http://kenyalaw.org/caselaw/cases/view/169664.

Following the judgment, the Kenyan and Mauritian governments signed a new tax treaty on 10 April 2019.[120]

5. MULTINATIONAL TREATIES

Most African nations have signed on to some of the world's largest, most notable, multilateral agreements involving international investment. These agreements include, among others, the WTO[121] Agreement on Trade-Related Measures (TRIMs); the WTO General Agreement on Trade in Services (GATS); the Convention Establishing the Multilateral Investment Guarantee Agency (MIGA Convention);[122] the Convention on the Settlement of Investment Disputes Between States and Nationals of Other States (ICSID Convention, to be further discussed in Chapter 5); and the New York Convention on the Recognition and Enforcement of Foreign Arbitral Awards (New York Convention, which is also further discussed in Chapter 5).[123]

The impact of these agreements on foreign investment in Africa is highly debatable.[124] However, they do lay a foundation of certain rights and obligations from which many BITs and RIAs have been built. The ideas of MFN and NT, for example, arise out of the WTO agreements. So, too, do the idea that FDI is a mode of supply (known as "commercial presence"), and the need for what is known as temporary movement of natural persons, both of which have a direct bearing on foreign investment.[125] Understanding the investment context, therefore, requires

---

[120] Julie Martin, "Kenya and Mauritius sign new tax treaty following court nullification of earlier agreement", MNE Tax, 15 April 2019, https://mnetax.com/kenya-and-mauritius-sign-new-tax-treaty-following-court-nullification-of-earlier-agreement-33414.

[121] Currently, 39 of Africa's 55 countries are party to the WTO, and are, therefore, bound by GATS and TRIMS. See Talkmore Chidede, "The Right to Regulate in Africa's International Investment Law Regime", (2019) 20(2) Oregon Review of International Law, pp. 437–468, available at: https://scholarsbank.uoregon.edu/xmlui/bitstream/handle/1794/24671/Chidede_ORIL20%282%29.pdf?sequence=1&isAllowed=y.

[122] 53 African nations are currently party to the MIGA Convention, which "provides risk insurance to foreign investors against political risks such as expropriation, transfer restriction, breach of contract, non-honouring of financial obligations, as well as war, terrorism and civil disturbance". See Ibid.

[123] Ibid.

[124] Peter Nunnenkamp and Manoj Pant, "Why the case for a multilateral agreement on investment is weak" (2003), available at: https://www.econstor.eu/bitstream/10419/2931/1/kd400.pdf.

[125] Ibid.

an understanding of what multilateral agreements the host government is party to, as well which it is not party to, so as to determine what sort of protections may be afforded to an investor.

6. UNDERSTANDING THE WEB OF LAWS IN AFRICA

Each type of governing agreement discussed in this chapter has a bearing on investment in Africa. The local, bilateral, regional and multilateral agreements governing a host government's actions and responses to foreign investors should be examined on a jurisdictional basis when entering a new market. As stated in the 2018 World Investment Report, "[w]orking towards maximizing synergies from policy interactions in a regime consisting of thousands of investment treaties, national laws regulating domestic and foreign investment, and other bodies of international law affecting investment is a significant challenge for all countries."[126] The web of different laws can both complicate and ease the ability of foreign investors to do business on the continent, depending on the host country. Bilateral and regional agreements can ease entrance into a country and investment in multiple countries, respectively. At the same time, however, when bilateral and regional agreements conflict with one another, foreign investors can find themselves caught between regulations, unsure of legal requirements. This confusion is only compounded when local laws conflict with bilateral or multilateral agreements, which is also often the case.

In a January 2020 report compiled in collaboration between UK Aid, the Africa Trade Policy Center and the United Nations Economic Commission for Africa, which looked closely at the challenges and opportunities facing expanded UK investment in Africa, confusion as to policies and policymaking processes were among the top hurdles to investment that were identified.[127] The report points out that local laws often run counter to other bilateral laws intended to promote foreign investment. For example, local labour laws are often viewed as confusing

---

[126]   "World Investment Report", United Nations Conference on Trade and Development (2018), available at: https://unctad.org/en/PublicationsLibrary/wir2018_en.pdf.

[127]   Max Mendez-Parra, Sherillyn Raga and Lily Sommer, "Africa and the United Kingdom" (2020), available at: https://cdn.odi.org/media/documents/africa_uk_investment.pdf.

and contrary to the intentions of foreign investors.[128] Tax laws were also highlighted as some of the most complicated to understand and operate.[129]

The need to improve the interconnection between different legal regimes within a country is of utmost importance on the African continent, as countries seek to create an environment for sustainable, development-oriented investment.[130] A complex web of policies leaves African countries vulnerable to manipulation by foreign corporations. The example referenced above of Senegal losing significant tax revenue because of its tax treaty with Mauritius is an example of this. Although Senegal has worked hard at developing strong regional policies and harmonising its regional laws to promote foreign investment, the bilateral agreement with Mauritius was undercutting its efforts. By creating better synergy between legal regimes and remedying conflicts between legal systems, African nations will also be better protecting themselves and, in turn, putting African governments in the driver's seat when it comes to sustainable development.

While this world of conflicting and/or confusing legal regulation may change to some extent with the enactment of the African Continental Free Trade Area, to be discussed in the next chapter, and at length in the remainder of this book, investment on the continent will likely continue to be governed by a complex web of regulations for the near future. It is, therefore, essential that investors understand that each individual African nation has its own unique laws, which may or may not correspond to neighbouring or other countries on the continent. At the same time, African governments must work to recognise the complexities of their regulations and seek to harmonise investment-related laws. The continent as a whole should embrace the African Continental Free Trade Area (AfCFTA) and embrace harmonisation of laws across borders.

---

[128]   Ibid.
[129]   Ibid.
[130]   "World Investment Report", United Nations Conference on Trade and Development (2018), available at: https://unctad.org/en/PublicationsLibrary/wir2018_en.pdf.

CHAPTER 3

TAKING A CLOSER LOOK AT REGIONAL INTEGRATION IN AFRICA

The AfCFTA, to be discussed at length in the following chapters, is built on the foundation of Africa's current RECs, and with the idea that the successes of those RECs can be scaled up to promote economic growth in Africa. At the same time, the AfCFTA looks to harmonise the complicated web of current, often overlapping, regulations. This chapter, therefore, will pause to look more closely at certain regional organisations currently existing in Africa, and what they can provide to the ongoing conversation regarding continental integration. The chapter will look not only at the RECs, but also at one of Africa's most singular organisations, the Organization for the Harmonisation of Business Law in Africa (OHADA).

After first providing a detailed overview of OHADA and the RECs on the continent, this chapter then looks at the strengths of these regional entities, followed by the challenges facing these bodies. The chapter will conclude with suggestions on what AfCFTA should learn from these regional bodies.

1. LAYING THE FOUNDATION FOR SUSTAINABLE DEVELOPMENT: THE OHADA MODEL

Two of the biggest hurdles to improving investment in Africa, both foreign and intra-African, are: (i) a lack of respect for the rule of law; and (ii) weak legal protections provided to businesses. For decades, investors have expressed little confidence in the ability of African governments to adhere to well-defined and established laws, which is an absolute requirement for reducing investment risk. Investors want to be able to familiarise themselves with the legal framework within which they are working. When this framework continues to shift or is not respected by a host state government, the unpredictability increases investors' risks. At the same time, investors are quick to express their distrust of African courts and legal systems. In the view of investors, these institutions do not have the necessary experience in dealing with complex business issues to have the capacity to protect their investments truly.

These blanket concerns are perhaps unfair to the continent as a whole, and hide the successes of politically strong countries such as Botswana or Mauritius, among others. However, in order to ensure that foreign investment will continue to flow to the continent in the long term, African nations need to collectively come up with ways to address the real concerns of investors, and to demonstrate that the continent is stable enough to put money into. Investors want to be able to invest in several countries, sometimes all at once, and they want to be able to have a certain level of predictability in doing so. Relearning systems and laws is time-consuming and frustrating. Investors want to reduce the burden of this process, and to avoid having to take on the inherent risks in completing this relearning phase every time they enter a new country.

One of Africa's most successful attempts to attract additional investment and move away from the negative perspectives of the continent has been the establishment of OHADA. This intergovernmental organisation aims to harmonise business laws in Member States. OHADA was originally established under a treaty, entered into on 17 October 1993 in Mauritius. This treaty has since been modified once, on 17 October 2008.[131] OHADA was formed almost out of necessity, as a response to a drop in foreign investment being made on the African continent.[132] Foreign investors all but demanded that African nations, with horrific rule of law records and crumbling legal systems, reformed to create a favourable environment for investment.[133] Colonisation left the continent with a range of different legal systems, none of which appeared to adequately respond to the economic crises that hit the globe in the 1980s. Even in countries that had been colonised by the same European power, for example francophone countries, the laws that developed following independence were fragmented and different in each individual country. The one thing that did seem to be

---

[131] Organization for the Harmonisation of Business Law in Africa, "Organization", available at: https://www.ohada.org/index.php/en/ohada-in-a-nutshell/history.
[132] Ibid.
[133] Alhousseini Mouloul, "Understanding the Organization for the Harmonization of Business Laws in Africa (OHADA)", 2nd ed., June 2009, available at: http://www.ohada.com/content/newsletters/1403/Comprendre-l-Ohada-en.pdf.

consistent, however, was that none of the post-colonisation countries appeared to have created sound legal systems.[134]

To address the issues in front of them, the finance ministers of several countries appointed a group of experts, led by Senegalese Justice Keba Mbaye, to conduct a study to determine the best path forward for economic integration between African nations. The idea was that Africa needed to find a way to better harmonise its laws, to strengthen its economies. The recommendation of this group was that the francophone countries, whose legal systems were based on the system in France, should create a supranational organisation.[135] In a move to do just that, 14 African heads of state signed on 17 October 1993 in Port-Louis, Mauritius, the Organisation pour l'Harmonisation en Afrique du Droit des Affaires (Organization for the Harmonisation of Business Law in Africa) treaty. By the time the treaty entered into force on 18 September 1995, it had 16 Member States.[136] Thereafter, the Democratic Republic of Congo also became a member, bringing the total number of Member States to 17, where it stands today.[137] These Member States have committed to improving the predictability of their systems, with the purpose of better attracting foreign investment and increasing both intra-African and foreign trade.[138]

---

[134] See Summary of the Work on the Seminar on Harmonization of African Business Law in Franc Zone African states, pp. 14 and 15, Abidjan from 19 April 1993 to 20 April 1993. Regarding the necessity of harmonisation, see also Joseph Issa Sayegh, "Legal integration of franc zone African countries", Revue Penant n° 823 Janvier ñ Avril 1997, p. 5 et seq.

[135] Renaud Beauchard and Mahutodji Jimmy Vital Kodo, "Can OHADA Increase Legal Certainty in Africa?", The World Bank (2011), available at: http://documents. worldbank.org/curated/en/266761467990085419/pdf/659890WP00PUBL010Can0O HADA0Increase.pdf.

[136] In the order of ratification, the OHADA Member States are: Guinea–Bissau (0115/1501/1994), Senegal (0614/1406/1994), Central African Republic (0113/1301/1995), Mali (02/07/02/1995), Comoros (02/20/02/1995), Burkina Faso (03/06/03/1995), Benin (03/08/03/1995), Niger (0605/0506/1995), Côte d'Ivoire (0929/2909/1995), Cameroon (1020/2010/1995), Togo (1027/27210/1995), Chad (0413/1304/1996), Congo (0528/2805/1997), Gabon (02/02/1998), Equatorial Guinea (0416/1604/1999), and Guinea (05/05/2000), See Joseph Issa-Sayegh, Paul-Gerard Pourgoue, and J. Michel Sawadogo, "OHADA: Traité et Actes Uniformes, Commentés et Annotés", Poitiers, France: Juriscope, 2002.

[137] Organisation pour l'Harmonisation en Afrique du Droit des Affaires (Organization for the Harmonisation of Business Law in Africa) signed in Port-Louis, Mauritius on 17 October 1993 (OHADA Treaty). The Democratic Republic of Congo joined in July 2012.

[138] Redaud Beauchard and Mahutodji Jimmy Vital Kodo, "Can OHADA Increase Legal Certainty in Africa?", The World Bank (2011), available at: http://documents. worldbank.org/curated/en/266761467990085419/pdf/659890WP00PUBL010Can0O HADA0Increase.pdf.

To fulfil this objective, the OHADA Member States put in place an institutional framework consisting of: (i) a Council of Ministers;[139] (ii) a Permanent Secretariat;[140] (iii) a Regional Training Centre for Legal Officers;[141] (iv) a Conference of Heads of State and Government;[142] and (v) a Common Court of Justice and Arbitration. The ministers of justice and finance from each Member State sit on the Council of Ministers, and are responsible for carrying out several administrative and regulatory functions.[143] The Permanent Secretariat is an independent body that sits in Cameroon and provides technical direction and overall coordination. The Training Centre is in Benin, and provides training to judges, lawyers, notaries and court experts, in an effort to strengthen legal systems.[144] The heads of state of each of the OHADA Member States sit on the Conference of Heads of State and Government. This body meets to determine questions pertaining to the OHADA Treaty, as they are presented by individual Member States.[145] The Common Court of Justice and Arbitration (CCJA) is arguably the most important and successful organ of OHADA. This body, the judicial arm of OHADA, will be discussed at length in Chapter 5.

In addition to forming the above-mentioned bodies, Member States developed a uniform set of laws, referred to as the Uniform Acts, which superseded all conflicting domestic provisions. There are currently ten Uniform Acts, which govern: general commercial law; commercial companies and economic interest groups law; organising securities; insolvency law; arbitration law; organising simplified recovery procedures and measures of execution; accounting and financial information; contracts for the carriage of goods by road; cooperative companies law; and mediation law.[146] As confirmed by the CCJA on 30 April 2001,[147] and later confirmed by a Paris court when upholding OHADA law over

---

[139] OHADA Treaty, Art. 27(2)–(30).
[140] OHADA Treaty, Arts. 33, 40.
[141] OHADA Treaty, Arts. 41–42.
[142] OHADA Treaty, Art. 27(1).
[143] Alhousseini Mouloul, "Understanding the Organization for the Harmonization of Business Laws in Africa (OHADA)", 2nd ed., June 2009, available at: http://www. ohada.com/content/newsletters/1403/Comprendre-l-Ohada-en.pdf.
[144] Ibid.
[145] Ibid.
[146] Organization for the Harmonisation of Business Law in Africa, "Organization", available at: https://www.ohada.org/index.php/en/ohada-in-a-nutshell/history.
[147] CCJA, Avis N° 1/2001/EP, 30 April 2001, available at: https://www.ohada.com/ documentation/jurisprudence/ohadata/J-02-04.html.

Cameroonian law,[148] these Acts are supranational, rendering domestic laws that are contrary to the Uniform Acts inapplicable.[149] The intent of each of these Acts is to create modern, simple legal rules that create a favourable economic environment within Member States. At the same time, in adopting these laws, OHADA Member States are looking to promote an independent and efficient judicial system. The Acts are updated as necessary to reflect international trends on each subject matter. For example, the General Commercial Act, the Commercial Companies and Economic Interest Group Act, the Securities Act, the Bankruptcy Act and the Arbitration Act have all been updated. Additionally, OHADA most recently adopted the Meditation Act.[150]

As will be detailed further in Chapter 5, the CCJA is the court of last resort for judgments rendered and arbitral awards pertaining to the Uniform Acts. This means that it is the court of last resort for all matters of business law that are governed by the Acts.[151] Thus, business-related disputes must first be heard in domestic courts, unless it is determined that the competent jurisdiction has not acted on a case within 30 days.[152] This includes any appeals that may be made against a domestic court judgment. The CCJA then acts in the place of domestic supreme courts, serving as the final decision-maker in cases falling under the OHADA Uniform Acts.[153] This Court does not hear matters that do not come under those acts; for example, the court does not hear criminal cases.

---

[148] CA Paris 16/25484, 20 December 2018. See Thomas Kendra, Thibaud Roujou de Boubee and Ledea Sawadogo-Lewis, "The Paris Court upholds the supranational nature of OHADA law in dismissing annulment application", 14 February 2019, available at https://www.jdsupra.com/legalnews/the-paris-court-upholds-the-76318/.

[149] It is worth mentioning that the supranationality of the Uniform Acts over domestic laws will apply only to the laws covered by these Acts. Consequently excluded are sectors like tax, employment, and other domestic laws not covered by Uniform Acts.

[150] Gaston Kenfack Douajni, "Recent Developments in OHADA Arbitration", Global Arbitration Review, 11 April 2019, available at: https://globalarbitrationreview.com/chapter/1190118/recent-developments-in-ohada-arbitration.

[151] Alhousseini Mouloul, "Understanding the Organization for the Harmonization of Business Laws in Africa (OHADA")", 2nd ed., June 2009, available at: http://www.ohada.com/content/newsletters/1403/Comprendre-l-Ohada-en.pdf.

[152] Mouhamed Kebe, "The Attractiveness of the New OHADA Arbitration Act", Geni & Kebe SCP, 13 December 2018, available at: https://www.lexology.com/library/detail.aspx?g=680f77e3-1b8c-4327-87c1-183a7abc45f4.

[153] Alhousseini Mouloul, "Understanding the Organization for the Harmonization of Business Laws in Africa (OHADA)", 2nd ed., June 2009, available at: http://www.ohada.com/content/newsletters/1403/Comprendre-l-Ohada-en.pdf.

The Uniform Acts have helped to attract investors by creating consistency and predictability, allowing investors to move from one jurisdiction to another with some confidence.[154] Since they are subject to the same set of laws in each country in which they invest within the OHADA region, investors are able to decrease the legal risks associated with investment. Moreover, the OHADA regime strengthens the rule of law by holding its Member States responsible to a supranational law. This, in turn, means that the protection of an investment is not tied to the stability of an individual country, but, rather, to well-established laws that stand regardless of the internal conflicts or political issues that may be impacting on one specific country. At the same time, investors are provided with the option to have disputes arising from their investments settled by a competent body that is well-versed not only in the laws of OHADA, but also in strong international business practices. All in all, the OHADA system has had a "significant beneficial impact on access to finance, business registration and business cost savings", according to the World Bank.[155] OHADA's success in creating a supranational organisation with harmonised laws should be applauded, particularly – as will be further explained below – in light of the number of similar attempts on the continent that have fallen short of achieving the same or similar objectives.

At the same time, however, the OHADA system has faced a number of challenges. Harmonisation of laws has been a slow process, with several domestic courts taking a significant amount of time adjusting the Uniform Acts into their systems. Moreover, local private sector actors have been slow to accept the Acts as governing law, often viewing the laws as unclear and overcomplicated.[156] The Permanent Secretariat has, at the same time, been criticised for failing to provide adequate coordination between Member States. Poor adoption of technology and failure to adequately digitalise the OHADA system have put in question its ability to meet the needs of modern businesses, and the ability of the Member States to monitor happenings.[157] Critics of the system argue that, instead of creating a modern, simplified system, OHADA has created a difficult-to-use system that is failing to keep up with a fast-moving global economy.

---

[154] Mouhamed Kebe, "How Can OHADA Boost Integration and Investment in Africa?" Geni & Kebe SCP, available at: https://www.hg.org/legal-articles/how-can-ohada-boost-integration-and-investment-in-africa-19603.

[155] "An Impact Assessment of OHADA Reforms", International Finance Corporation's OHAD Investment Climate Program (2018), available at: http://www.ohada.com/content/newsletters/4643/rapport-ohada-ifc.pdf.

[156] Ibid.

[157] Ibid.

At the same time, individual Member States continue to face many of the same issues that gave rise to OHADA in the first place, putting into question the actual successes of the system. Corruption, weak court systems and struggling economies continue to exist within most Member States. While OHADA has been able to harmonise business laws, such laws are only one part of much more extensive legal systems and economies. In addition, the fact that OHADA was established amongst francophone countries has seemingly limited its ability to further expand across the continent. This issue has come to the forefront recently in Cameroon, where demands from the anglophone minority escalated into a national crisis. During the crisis, lawyers from Cameroon's anglophone population argued that the non-existence of English versions of the OHADA Uniform Acts has put anglophone businesses and attorneys at an unfair disadvantage.[158] This is just one example of how challenges within individual Member States also pose challenges to the OHADA system. As will be discussed further in Chapter 5, the CCJA has also faced its own hurdles, which have threatened its own legitimacy. The following chapters of this book will demonstrate how the AfCFTA coming into force has the potential to address many of the challenges facing OHADA, while at the same time building on its successes. Regardless of its setbacks, OHADA is arguably the most successful model for African harmonisation and future development of the law.

2. AFRICA'S REGIONAL ECONOMIC INTEGRATION

Strength in numbers is considered to be one of Africa's most direct paths towards progress. For decades now, several regional economic blocs have been making steady progress towards growth and development.[159] Today, Africa has an array of both trade blocs and monetary blocs. These include, among others, eight economic communities recognised as the building

---

158 Stuart P. Seidel, "International Trade Compliance Update", Baker McKenzie, May 2019, available at: https://www.lexology.com/library/detail.aspx?g=fd2a8cf3-03a6-426f-89c1-7ab8dbf24ac5.

159 Faizel Ismael, "The African Continental Free Trade Area (AfCFTA) and Developmental Regionalism: A Handbook", TIPS (2021), ch. 2, "History of Regional Integration In Africa", available at: https://www.tips.org.za/research-archive/books/item/4121-the-african-continental-free-trade-area-afcfta-and-developmental-regionalism-a-handbook.

blocks of the African Union: the Arab Maghreb Union; the Community of Sahel-Saharan States; the Common Market for Eastern and Southern Africa; the East African Community; the Economic Community of Central African States; the Economic Community of West African States; the Intergovernmental Authority on Development; and the Southern African Development Community.[160]

These economic communities have the principal purposes of integrating economic policy and facilitating the movement of goods and people between countries. Many African nations are either too small or lacking in resources (both natural, and in terms of capacity) to be economically viable on their own. By combining their collective knowledge and other strengths, these communities have demonstrated success in improving economic conditions in their Member Countries. In addition to working towards improved economic landscapes, these countries are also promoting peace and stability by holding individual governments accountable to a larger community, with the governments that are party to a community acting as a sort of check and balance on the actions of each individual member.

The following subsections provide a brief overview of each of the eight economic communities in Africa.

2.1. ARAB MAGHREB UNION (AMU)

The Arab Maghreb Union (AMU) was formed in June 1988 under the Treaty of Marrakesh. The Member States of this REC are Algeria, Libya, Mauritania, Morocco and Tunisia.[161] The stated objectives of this organisation were to:

- Strengthen the ties of brotherhood which link the Member States and their peoples to one another.
- Achieve progress and prosperity of Member States' societies and defend their rights.

---

[160] These regional blocs work in parallel with the African Union in meeting its economic objectives. As stated by the African Union, "The RECs are closely integrated with the AU's work and serve as its building blocks. The relationship between the AU and the RECs is mandated by the Abuja Treaty and the AU Constitutive Act, and guided by the: 2008 Protocol on Relations between the RECs and the AU; and the Memorandum of Understanding (MoU) on Cooperation in the Area of Peace and Security between the AU, RECs and the Coordinating Mechanisms of the Regional Standby Brigades of Eastern and Northern Africa". See "Regional Economic Communities", available at: https://au.int/en/organs/recs.
[161] "Regional Economic Communities", available at: https://au.int/en/organs/recs.

- Contribute to the preservation of peace based on justice and equity.
- Pursue a common policy in different domains.
- Work gradually towards achieving free movement of persons and transfer of services, goods and capital among them.

Unfortunately, due to a conflict between Algeria and Morocco over the Western Sahara, this REC has not convened collectively since 1994. Deep economic and political disagreements, even outside of this dispute, have rendered this organisation almost completely ineffective. Several of the Member States have also opted to seek membership of other regional communities, on the continent and elsewhere.[162] However, Tunisia, following its issues with the Arab Spring, has more recently sought to reconvene the AMU in an effort to try to strengthen the North African regional economy. While there has not been any substantial movement as a result, it is notable that none of the Member States has cut ties completely with the AMU and, at least in name and under the Treaty, the AMU continues to exist. As economic transactions between these countries start picking up, as they have in recent years, it will be important to see whether the AMU is given a second life.

2.2. COMMUNITY OF SAHEL-SAHARAN STATES (CEN-SAD)

The Member States of the Community of Sahel-Saharan States (CEN-SAD) cover a substantial portion of the African continent, and include Benin, Burkina Faso, Central African Republic, Chad, the Comoros, Côte D'Ivoire, Djibouti, Egypt, Eritrea, the Gambia, Ghana, Guinea–Bissau, Libya, Mali, Mauritania, Morocco, Niger, Nigeria, Senegal, Sierra Leone, Somalia, Sudan, Togo and Tunisia.[163] This REC was established on 4 February 1998. The CEN-SAD Treaty was revised once, in February 2013, in an effort to reinvigorate the community. However, this new Treaty has not been ratified by the requisite 15 Member States needed for it to enter into force.[164]

---

[162]   For example, Morocco has created a strategic relationship with Nigeria, in an effort to become a member of ECOWAS; and Algeria and Mauritania have been focusing on work in the Sahel region and seeking to join communities focused on Sahel security.

[163]   "CEN-SAD – The Community of Sahel-Saharan States", United Nations Economic Commission for Africa, available at: https://archive.uneca.org/oria/pages/cen-sad-community-sahel-saharan-states.

[164]   Ibid.

Since its inception, this REC has worked closely with overlapping regional bodies and other organisations on the continent to consolidate its political, economic and social work.[165] The primary purposes of this REC include:

- Establishment of a comprehensive economic union based on a strategy implemented in accordance with a development plan that is to be integrated in the national development plans of the Member States. This strategy includes investment in the agricultural, industrial, social, cultural and energy fields.
- Elimination of all obstacles impeding the unity of its Member States through adopting measures that would guarantee the following: facilitating the free movement of individuals, capital, and meeting the interest of Member States' citizens; freedom of residence, work, ownership and economic activity; freedom of movement of national goods, merchandise and services; encouragement of foreign trade by drawing up and implementing an investment policy for Member States; enhancement and improvement of land, air and sea transportation and telecommunications among Member States, through the implementation of joint projects; and, the consent of the community Member States to give the citizens of Member States the same rights and privileges provided for in the constitution of each Member State.
- Coordination of pedagogical and educational systems at the various educational levels, as well as in the cultural, scientific and technical fields.

The two primary overarching objectives of CEN-SAD are to improve regional security and promote sustainable development. This region has been one of the world's biggest hotbeds for terrorism, and many of the Member States are among the poorest economically in the world.

While this organisation has had some success in addressing security concerns in the Sahel region, economic integration has been complicated because of the vastly varying capacities of Member States, as well as overlapping economic communities, including ECOWAS, ECCAS and COMESA, which are more advanced in their economic integration.[166]

---

[165] Ibid.

[166] "Egypt and Community of Sahel-Saharan States", available at: https://www.sis.gov.eg/section/2614/101?lang=en-us.

2.3. COMMON MARKET FOR EASTERN AND SOUTHERN AFRICA (COMESA)

The Common Market for Eastern and Southern Africa (COMESA) is Africa's largest REC.[167] The Member States of COMESA are Burundi, Comoros, Democratic Republic of Congo, Djibouti, Egypt, Eritrea, Ethiopia, Kenya, Libya, Madagascar, Malawi, Mauritius, Rwanda, Seychelles, Sudan, Swaziland, Uganda, Zambia and Zimbabwe. COMESA was formed to replace the Preferential Trade Area (PTA), which had existed since 1981. COMESA itself was formulated in December 1994, as an "organization of free independent sovereign states which have agreed to cooperate in developing their natural and human resources for the good of all their people".[168] While this REC has committed to the promotion of peace and security in the region, its primary focus is on economic integration.

The primary objectives of COMESA aim to promote sustainable development, and include:

- Attaining sustainable growth and development of the Member States by promoting a more balanced and harmonious development of production and marketing structures.
- Promoting joint development in all fields of economic activity and the joint adoption of macroeconomic policies and programmes to raise the standard of living of its peoples, and to foster closer relations among its Member States.
- Cooperating in the creation of an enabling environment for foreign, cross-border and domestic investment, including the joint promotion of research and adaptation of science and technology for development.
- Cooperating in the promotion of peace, security and stability among Member States, in order to enhance economic development in the region.
- Cooperating in strengthening the relations between the common market and the rest of the world, and the adoption of common positions in international forums.
- Contributing to the establishment, progress and realisation of the objectives of the African Economic Community.

---

[167] "Common Market for Eastern and Southern Africa", Office of the United States Trade Representative, available at: https://ustr.gov/countries-regions/africa/regional-economic-communities-rec/common-market-eastern-and-southern-africa-comesa.

[168] "Overview of COMESA", available at: https://www.comesa.int/overview-of-comesa/.

COMESA first implemented a free-trade area on 31 October 2000, which resulted in a majority of Member States eliminating tariffs on COMESA-originating products.[169] According to COMESA, this has resulted in an average 7% annual growth.[170] In 2018, COMESA reported that 98% of non-tariff barriers had been eliminated, which includes, among other things, the liberalisation of import licensing, removal of foreign exchange restrictions, taxes on foreign exchange, import and export quotas, roadblocks, easing of customs formalities, extending the times that border posts are open, and the creation of one-stop border posts. In addition, the REC has made substantial progress in digitising its activities, allowing for virtual trade and increased monitoring of economic activity in the region. Moreover, COMESA has been working towards establishing a monetary union, by developing a common monetary area to facilitate economic integration.[171]

While COMESA has had a number of successes, it has also faced a number of challenges, many of which are common to the other regional entities discussed in this chapter. One of the greatest challenges that COMESA has faced is the self-interest of individual states and the unwillingness, at times, of governments to put the needs of COMESA above the perceived needs of their individual countries.[172] Without full buy-in to the Community, true integration becomes quite challenging. One example of this is COMESA's inability to get all its members to join the increasingly important electronic money transfer system.[173] These sorts of setbacks have delayed the transition of this Community from a common market to a fully fledged economic community. In addition to a lack of political will, the number of conflicts in COMESA countries, both large- and small-scale, have slowed progress, and at times halted the ability of the Community to actually work together.[174] This has been a decades-long issue that must subside for COMESA to be truly successful in its efforts to create an economic community.

---

[169] Ibid.
[170] Ibid.
[171] Ibid.
[172] Torque Mude, "Challenges and Prospects for the Transformation of the Common Market for Eastern and Southern Africa by 2025", (2018) 12(6) Africology: The Journal of Pan African Studies, pp. 122–130, available at: http://www.jpanafrican.org/docs/vol12no6/12.6-9-Mude.pdf.
[173] Ibid.
[174] Ibid.

2.4. EAST AFRICAN COMMUNITY (EAC)

The East African Community (EAC) was originally established in 1967, and then dissolved in 1977. However, in 1999, Kenya, Uganda and Tanzania revived this entity, signing the Treaty establishing the East African Community. Eight years later, Rwanda and Burundi joined the EAC, and then, in 2016, South Sudan joined, following its independence from Sudan.[175] Heads of state of the EAC Member States have commonly expressed the importance of speaking with one unified voice on the world stage, particularly given these countries' long-time economic relations.[176]

The EAC has stated the Member States' desire to form a customs union, a common market, a monetary union, and a political federation. These have become the four "pillars" of the EAC.

The specific objectives of the REC, as they move towards establishing these pillars, include:

- The attainment of sustainable growth and development of the partner states by promotion of a more balanced and harmonious development of the partner states.
- The strengthening and consolidation of cooperation in agreed fields that would lead to equitable economic development within the partner states, and which would, in turn, raise the standard of living and improve the quality of life of their populations.
- The promotion of sustainable utilisation of the natural resources, and taking of measures that would effectively protect the natural environment of the partner states.
- The strengthening and consolidation of the long-standing political, economic, social, cultural and traditional ties and associations between the peoples of the partner states, so as to promote a people-centred mutual development of these ties and associations.
- The mainstreaming of gender in all its endeavours, and the enhancement of the role of women in cultural, social, political, economic and technological development.
- The promotion of peace, security and stability within, and good neighbourliness among, the partner states.

---

[175] "EAC – East African Community", available at: https://www.eac.int/.
[176] See "Ministry of East African Community and Regional Development", Republic of Kenya, available at: https://meac.go.ke/eac-achievements/.

– The enhancement and strengthening of partnerships with the private sector and civil society, in order to achieve sustainable socio-economic and political development.
– The undertaking of such other activities calculated to further the objectives of the community as the partner states may, from time to time, decide to undertake in common.

The EAC's Customs Union was established in 2005, under the Customs Union Protocol, which stipulates the following objectives for the Union:

1. To promote efficiency in production within the EAC.
2. To enhance domestic, cross-border and foreign investment in the EAC.
3. To promote economic development and diversification in industrialisation in the EAC.

To meet these objectives, the EAC Customs Union calls for the elimination of internal tariffs, and a common external tariff structure of 0% for raw materials, 10% for intermediate goods, and 25% for finished goods.[177]

Thus far, the EAC has put in place mechanisms to work towards removing non-tariff barriers, establishing a EAC single customs territory, creating tax harmonisation, harmonising standards, establishing one-stop border posts, and allowing the free movement of persons and labour.[178] Moreover, the region works towards promoting sustainable development, improving food security, and enhancing regional infrastructure.[179] This Community has had quite a bit of success in raising economic conditions and increasing trade and investment. As a result, it has been able to steadily expand its membership over time.[180] Not only has this Community been able to increase intra-regional trade and foreign investment among members, but its integrated success has also had the benefit of attracting external trade and FDI to the individual member countries.

---

[177] Ibid.
[178] Ibid.
[179] Ibid.
[180] Patricia Mukiri Mwithiga, "The Challenges of Regional Integration in the East African Community", in Adam B. Elhiraika, Allan C.K. Mukungu and Wanjiku Nyoike (eds.), Regional Integration and Policy Challenges in Africa, London: Palgrave Macmillan, 2015, pp. 89–108, available at: https://doi.org/10.1057/9781137462084_5.

Even in light of the relative successes of the EAC, the Community, as with any regional body, has also had its share of challenges. The Community has struggled to create a unified system for taxation valuation, with each country failing to relinquish its own system.[181] The economic bloc has also failed to create a single customs territory, even though it has the framework protocols in place for doing so. As with other regional communities, the EAC has struggled to get full buy-in to all of its plans, which means it has fallen short of meeting certain objectives.[182]

2.5. ECONOMIC COMMUNITY OF CENTRAL AFRICAN STATES (ECCAS)

The Economic Community of Central African States (ECCAS) was born out of its predecessor, the Customs and Economic Union of Central African States (EDEAC). The new REC, formed with the purpose of creating a wider economic community in Central Africa, was established in October 1983 between Angola, Cameroon, Central African Republic, Congo, São Tomé and Principe, Zaire (now the Democratic Republic of Congo), Equatorial Guinea, Gabon, Burundi and Rwanda.[183] This REC comprises Member States from the Central African Economic and Monetary Community (CEMAC), from the Great Lakes Countries, and two countries (Rwanda and Burundi) from the East African Community.[184] Following its inception,

---

[181]   Abdullah Makame, "The East African Integration: Achievements and Challenges", (2012) 1(6) GREAT Insights, available at: https://ecdpm.org/great-insights/trade-and-development-making-the-link/east-african-integration-achievements-challenges/.

[182]   Jaime de Melo and Yvonne Tsikata, "Regional Integration in Africa: Challenges and Prospects", Foundation Pour Les Etudes et Recherches sur le Developpement International, February 2014, available at: https://ferdi.fr/dl/df-6Lm5LieRw5yaW5shkAeNSSBj/ferdi-p93-regional-integration-in-africa-challenges-and-prospects.pdf.

[183]   Note that Rwanda pulled out of the ECCAS in order to pursue membership of the EAC, but then rejoined in 2016. See "ECCAS – Economic Community of Central African States", United Nations Economic Commission for Africa, available at: https://archive.uneca.org/oria/pages/eccas-economic-community-central-african-states.

[184]   "Central Africa Regional Integration Strategy Paper 2019–2025", African Development Bank Group, June 2019, available at: https://www.afdb.org/sites/default/files/documents/strategy-documents/central_africa_risp_2019-_english_version_020619_final_version.pdf. ECCAS is an organisation that aims to achieve collective autonomy, raise the standard of living of its populations, and maintain economic stability through harmonious cooperation. The main objective of CEMAC is to promote the harmonious development of the Member States, in the context of the establishment of a CEMAC common market, by establishing an economic and monetary union.

the ECCAS was largely inactive for over a decade, due to economic and political constraints, including several ongoing conflicts in the region. In 1999, it was designated as one of the eight principal economic communities in the African Union.

The primary focus of the ECCAS is to promote self-reliance of its Member States. The Community aims to "achieve collective autonomy, raise the standard of living of its populations and maintain economic stability through harmonious cooperation".[185] This REC has identified certain sectors in which it intends to focus in order to reach this objective: transport, communications, energy, agricultural, natural resources, trade, financial matters, human resources, tourism, education, culture, and science and technology.[186]

ECCAS's specific objectives include:

- The elimination of customs duties and any other charges having an equivalent effect on imports and exports between Member States.
- The abolition of quantitative restrictions and other trade barriers.
- The establishment and maintenance of an external common customs tariff.
- The establishment of a trade policy vis-à-vis third-party states.
- The progressive removal of barriers to the free movement of persons, goods, services and capital, and to the right of establishment.
- The harmonisation of national policies in order to promote Community activities, particularly in industry, transport and communications, energy, agriculture, natural resources, trade, currency and finance, human resources, tourism, education, culture, and science and technology.
- The establishment of a cooperation and development fund.
- The rapid development of states which are landlocked, semi-landlocked, island or part-island, and/or belong to the category of the least advanced countries.
- Any other joint activities which can be undertaken by Member States for achieving Community aims.

Under the revamped version of this REC, introduced in 1999, ECCAS Member States committed to moving towards a single market, in support

---

185   Ibid.
186   "ECCAS – Economic Community of Central African States", available at: https://ceeac-eccas.org/en/.

of the greater African continent's ambitions to do the same.[187] At the same time, ECCAS put a new focus on security and defence, in response to the widespread conflicts in the region that had slowed the start-up of the Community to begin with.

2.6. ECONOMIC COMMUNITY OF WEST AFRICAN STATES (ECOWAS)

The Economic Community of West African States (ECOWAS) was established quite early, on 28 May 1975, by way of the Treaty of Lagos, which focused primarily on economic integration in the West Africa region.[188] ECOWAS's focus was then expanded, in 1993, to include greater political and social integration. The stated vision of ECOWAS is to promote cooperation and integration, in order to raise the living standards of its peoples, to maintain and enhance economic stability and foster relations among Member States.

The current Member States of ECOWAS include Benin, Burkina Faso, Cabo Verde, Côte d'Ivoire, the Gambia, Ghana, Guinea, Guinea–Bissau, Liberia, Mali, Niger, Nigeria, Senegal, Sierra Leone and Togo.

ECOWAS's specific objectives include:

- The harmonisation and coordination of national policies and the promotion of integration programmes, projects and activities, particularly in food, agriculture and natural resources, industry, transport and communications, energy, trade, money and finance, taxation, economic reform policies, human resources, education, information, culture, science, technology, services, health, tourism, and legal matters.
- The harmonisation and coordination of policies for the protection of the environment.
- The promotion of the establishment of joint production enterprises.
- The establishment of a common market.

---

[187] "Economic Community of Central African States", International Democracy Watch, available at: http://www.internationaldemocracywatch.org/index.php/economic-community-of-central-african-states-.
[188] "ECOWAS – Economic Community of West African States", available at: https://ecowas.int/.

- The establishment of an economic union through the adoption of common policies in the economic, financial, social and cultural sectors, and the creation of a monetary union.
- The promotion of joint ventures by private sector enterprises and other economic operators, in particular through the adoption of a regional agreement on cross-border investments.
- The adoption of measures for the integration of the private sectors, particularly the creation of an enabling environment to promote small- and medium-scale enterprises;
- The establishment of an enabling legal environment.
- The harmonisation of national investment codes, leading to the adoption of a single Community investment code.
- The harmonisation of standards and measures.
- The promotion of balanced development of the region, paying attention to the special problems of each Member State, particularly those of landlocked and small island Member States.
- The encouragement and strengthening of relations, and the promotion of the flow of information, particularly among rural populations, women and youth organisations, and socio-professional organisations such as associations of the media, businessmen and businesswomen, workers, and trade unions.
- The adoption of a Community population policy which considers the need for a balance between demographic factors and socio-economic development.
- Any other activity that Member States may decide to undertake jointly with a view to attaining Community objectives.

ECOWAS has established a single large trading bloc in the West African region, through economic cooperation. In pursuing greater economic integration, the REC places primary focus on specific fields, including industry, transport, telecommunications, energy, agriculture, natural resources, commerce and financial issues, and social and cultural matters.[189] The vision of ECOWAS includes creating a borderless region, where the regional population is able to seek opportunities regardless of home country, including to seek out education and health services, where needed.

---

[189] "Basic Information", Economic Community of West African States (ECOWAS), available at: https://ecoslate.github.io/about-ecowas/basic-information/index.htm.

This REC has also committed to strengthening the rule of law, democracy and good governance.[190] In a region where there have been several substantial political disputes, including the 1990s wars in Sierra Leone, Liberia and Côte d'Ivoire, as well as consistent authoritarian regimes, the role of the regional body has proven extremely important. One of the hallmarks of this REC is its conflict prevention framework. The ECOWAS Conflict Prevention Framework (ECPF), which came to be in 2008, serves as a comprehensive guide for enhancing cohesion between different departments, to prevent conflict before it arises.[191] As will be discussed later in this chapter, this framework has paved the way for ECOWAS intervention in several political disputes, leading to diffusion of tensions and, in certain cases, the transition of power.

Another growing success of this REC is the ECOWAS Community Court of Justice (ECCJ), which has become a strong adjudicator of human rights abuses in the region. Among some of the greatest successes of this court are its judgments against the torture of journalists in the Gambia, against modern slavery in Niger, and against Nigeria for failing to regulate the environmental damages caused by oil companies.[192] One of the most important cases to come out of this court also demonstrates the strength of this REC: in *Njemanze and 3 others v. The Federal Republic of Nigeria*, the court used what is known as universal jurisdiction to apply the Universal Declaration of Human Rights in a case involving the abduction and sexual assault of women by the Nigerian police and military.[193] This landmark case paves the way for the ECCJ to exercise more expansive jurisdiction over human rights abuses in the region, which could prove of utmost importance in promoting development and human rights in a region where human rights abuses have been widespread. Further details of this court will be provided in Chapter 5.

---

190   Ibid.
191   "ECOWAS at 40 – An assessment of progress towards regional integration in West Africa", available at: https://www.uneca.org/ecowas-40-assessment-progress-towards-regional-integration-west-africa.
192   Karen J. Alter, Laurence Helfer and Jacqueline R. McAllister, "A New International Human Rights Court for West Africa: The ECOWAS Community Court of Justice" (2013) 107(4) American Journal of International Law, pp. 737–779, doi:10.5305/amerjintelaw.107.4.0737.
193   Segnonna Horace Abjolohoun, "The Njemanze ECOWAS Court Ruling and 'Universal' Jurisdiction: Implications for the 'Grand African Human Rights System'", I.CONnect, available at: http://www.iconnectblog.com/2017/11/the-njemanze-ecowas-court-ruling-and-universal-jurisdiction-implications-for-the-grand-african-human-rights-system/.

In terms of economic integration, ECOWAS is working on developing a single currency programme, which it believes will integrate Member States even further. This effort has, however, faced significant challenges in its implementation, laying bare one of ECOWAS's greatest challenges: differences between the English-speaking and French-speaking countries. One of the primary issues standing in the way of a united ECOWAS currency is the reluctance of West African Economic and Monetary Union (WAEMU) countries to relinquish their existing common currency, the CFA franc, which has had relative success in recent years.[194] At the same time, disputes between smaller and larger economies have come to the forefront in this discussion, with Nigeria, ECOWAS's largest economy, stalling negotiations. These differences have demonstrated that ECOWAS still has significant growing pains in its efforts to create economic harmony.[195] This challenge also demonstrates the political tensions that exist in the region, which may continue to stand in the way of long-lasting success for this REC.[196] Whether ECOWAS is able to overcome these challenges has yet to be seen.

2.7. INTERGOVERNMENTAL AUTHORITY ON DEVELOPMENT (IGAD)

The Intergovernmental Authority on Development (IGAD) was created in 1996 as a successor of the Intergovernmental Authority on Drought and Development (originally founded in 1986).[197] The focus of this REC is slightly different from others on the continent, with the primary focus being development. The original organisation was formed in response to extreme drought in the Horn of Africa. Today, the mission of IGAD is to assist and complement the efforts of its Member States in areas of peace,

---

[194] Aloysius Uche Ordu, "An Evaluation of the single currency agenda in the ECOWAS region", Brookings Institution, September 2019, available at: https://www.brookings.edu/blog/africa-in-focus/2019/09/24/an-evaluation-of-the-single-currency-agenda-in-the-ecowas-region/.

[195] Yomi Kazeem, "West Africa's 'Eco' single currency ambition has a slim chance of success", Quartz Africa, 3 July 2019, available at: https://qz.com/africa/1657000/will-west-africas-eco-currency-succeed/.

[196] See Adeoye O. Akinola, The Politics and Challenges of ECOWAS' Common Currency, VDM Verlag Dr. Müller, 2 September 2011.

[197] "IGAD – Intergovernmental Authority on Development", United Nations Economic Commission for Africa, available at: https://archive.uneca.org/oria/pages/igad-intergovernmental-authority-development.

security, agriculture, environment, economic cooperation and social development.[198] The current Member States are Djibouti, Ethiopia, Eritrea, Kenya, Somalia, Sudan, South Sudan and Uganda.

The stated objectives of IGAD include:

- Promoting joint development strategies and gradually harmonising macroeconomic policies and programmes in the social, technological and scientific fields.
- Harmonising policies with regard to trade, customs, transport, communications, agriculture and natural resources, and promoting free movement of goods, services and people within the region.
- Creating an enabling environment for foreign, cross-border and domestic trade and investments.
- Achieving regional food security and encouraging and assisting efforts of Member States to collectively combat drought and other natural and man-made disasters and their natural consequences.
- Initiating and promoting programmes and projects for sustainable development of natural resources and environment protection.
- Developing and improving a coordinated and complementary infrastructure in the region, in the areas of transport, telecommunications and energy.
- Promoting peace and stability in the region, and creating mechanisms within the region for the prevention, management and resolution of inter-state and intra-state conflicts through dialogue.
- Mobilising resources for the implementation of emergency, short-term, medium-term and long-term programmes within the framework of regional cooperation.
- Promoting and realising the objectives of COMESA and the African Economic Community (AEC).
- Facilitating, promoting and strengthening cooperation in research development and application in science and technology.

Several international donor agencies from North America and Europe work to support IGAD in their development objectives, given the long-term development delinquencies facing many of the Member States, as well as recurring negative environmental impacts, such as drought and flooding. The United States, for example, has affirmed its support of IGAD

---

[198] "Intergovernmental Authority on Development", available at: https://archive.uneca.org/oria/pages/igad-intergovernmental-authority-development.

through agreements with its donor agency, the United States Agency for International Development (USAID), and has stated that the leading principles of IGAD are "consistent with the principles of both the United Nations and the Organisation of African Unity", and that the entity's "aims and objectives include promoting peace and stability in the subregion and creating mechanisms within the subregion for the prevention management and resolution of inter-State and intra-State conflicts through dialogue",[199] which the United States strongly supports.

2.8. SOUTHERN AFRICAN DEVELOPMENT COMMUNITY (SADC)

The Southern African Development Community (SADC) was created in 1980 to promote economic and political integration in Southern Africa, during a time when the region was witnessing apartheid South Africa.[200] At this time, only a Memorandum of Understanding (MOU) was entered into between the members of what was then known as the Southern African Development Coordination Conference (SADCC), including Angola, Botswana, Mozambique, Tanzania, Zambia, Swaziland, Lesotho, Malawi and Zimbabwe. The key objectives under this MOU were: (i) to reduce the Member States' dependence on the then apartheid South Africa; (ii) to implement projects and programmes with national and regional impact; (iii) to mobilise Member States' resources in the quest for collective self-reliance; and (iv) to secure international understanding and support.[201]

This REC was later formalised in 1992 by way of the SADC Treaty, which detailed what is referred to as the SADC Common Agenda.[202] The Agenda significantly expanded the scope of the REC, turning it into a proper economic community. The current Member States of the SADC are Angola, Botswana, Comoros, Democratic Republic of Congo, Eswatini, Lesotho, Madagascar, Malawi, Mauritius, Mozambique, Namibia, Seychelles, South Africa, Tanzania, Zambia and Zimbabwe.[203]

---

[199] "Intergovernmental Authority on Development (IGAD)", US Department of State, 12 November 2002, available at: https://2001-2009.state.gov/p/af/rls/fs/4455.htm.
[200] "SADC – Southern African Development Community, History and Treaty", available at: https://www.sadc.int/pages/history-and-treaty.
[201] Ibid.
[202] Ibid.
[203] "Member States", Southern African Development Community, available at: https://www.sadc.int/member-states/.

The key objectives of SADC under the Common Agenda include:

- Achieving development and economic growth, alleviating poverty, enhancing the standard and quality of life of the people of Southern Africa, and supporting the socially disadvantaged through regional integration.
- Evolving common political values, systems and institutions.
- Promoting and defending peace and security.
- Promoting self-sustaining development on the basis of collective self-reliance, and the interdependence of Member States.
- Achieving complementarity between national and regional strategies and programmes.
- Promoting and maximising productive employment and utilisation of resources from the region.
- Achieving sustainable utilisation of natural resources and effective protection of the environment.
- Strengthening and consolidating the long-standing historical, social and cultural affinities and links among the people of the region.

The SADC has undergone a number of substantial reforms since its inception. These reforms have been focused on improving development, putting in place a strategic political plan, and strengthening SADC's institutional structures, among others.[204] Additionally, SADC has put in tremendous work, in recent years, to strengthen its institutional structures, aimed at strengthening the REC's governance and decision-making, and supporting oversight. Moreover, in support of greater economic integration, the SADC agreed, in 2008, to establish a free-trade zone with the EAC and COMESA, which, as discussed below, they have done successfully.

One of SADC's greatest achievements has been the region's Protocol on Finance and Investment, which promotes harmonisation of Member States' policies and laws. This same Protocol has also developed a BIT sample for SADC State Parties, which will allow a more uniform approach to external relations as well.[205] This region has also been quite successful in its harmonisation of economic policies, with almost all SADC members

---

[204] "Southern African Development Community", International Democracy Watch, available at: http://www.internationaldemocracywatch.org/index.php/southern-africa-development-community.
[205] See SADC Model Bilateral Investment Treaty Template with Commentary, July 2012, available at: https://www.iisd.org/itn/wp-content/uploads/2012/10/sadc-model-bit-template-final.pdf.

having liberalised their economies. As a result, the region has seen strong economic growth, particularly in relation to other regions on the continent.[206] SADC has also seen tremendous political peace and stability in comparison with its African counterparts, and has been able to push a more aggressive development policy.[207] The challenges facing SADC are similar to some of those discussed at the end of this chapter as plaguing most regions on the continent.

As mentioned, SADC has mostly been successful in its implementation, but faces high-level, overarching challenges that will continue to keep it from reaching its full potential. These challenges include continuing high levels of poverty in the region, which leads to income instability, and is the result of high levels of unemployment and lack of opportunity.[208] The region must also do better at addressing climate change, which has created consistent natural disasters that have also held the region back. At the same time, the region must come up with a more comprehensive way of addressing frequent inward migration, including finding ways to create more labour opportunities, and to capitalise on the human talent arriving. Moreover, there have been differing levels of development amongst Member States, which further weakens the overall system of the region.[209] The lack of trust between countries becomes evident when the region attempts to address these challenges. Again, these challenges are not wholly unique to the SADC regional bloc. Further challenges facing various regions will be addressed at greater length at the end of this chapter.

3. SUCCESSES OF REGIONAL ECONOMIC INTEGRATION

Regional Economic Communities have served as the implementing arms of the African Union.[210] Each of the RECs described above has, in some

---

[206]   Paul Baker and Victor Deleplancque, "Achievements, Challenges, and Constraints of Trade Integration in SADC", available at: https://www.tradeeconomics.com/wp-content/uploads/2019/07/Achievements-challenges-and-constrainst-of-trade-integration-in-SADC1-min.pdf.

[207]   Ibid.

[208]   Ibid.

[209]   Jephias Mapuva and Loveness Muyengwa-Mapuva, "The SADC regional bloc: what challenges and prospects for regional integration?" (2014) 18 Law, Democracy and Development, pp. 22–36, available at: http://www.scielo.org.za/scielo.php?script=sci_arttext&pid=S2077-49072014000100002.

[210]   "The Regional Economic Communities (RECs) of the African Union", available at: https://au.int/en/recs.

way, created greater peace and stability within its respective region, by bringing together countries for a common objective. RECs have proven that combining the efforts of individual developing nations can lead to stronger sustainable development than any one country alone. It is with this understanding that the African Union has moved towards continental integration with the AfCFTA, which will be discussed at length in the following chapters. This section is a description of the successes that individual RECs have had thus far, as a demonstration of the potential of the AfCFTA.

Looking at RECs collectively, regional integration in Africa has, in many cases, led to increased trade, expanded markets and more substantial FDI. It is estimated that approximately 80% of all intra-African trade flows through RECs, demonstrating that regional integration has supported greater trade within the continent.[211] There is also evidence that trade liberalisation is being made across all of the RECs.[212] RECs appear to be at least somewhat successful in bringing together small, fragmented economies, allowing them to scale up what would otherwise be minimal trade.[213] At the same time, the free movement of people, introduced under African RECs, has led to higher levels of education and more skilled labour,[214] by giving individuals the ability to pursue higher education that meets their needs, rather than relying solely on the options in their home countries. This has also allowed employers to select from a wider range of employees, as necessary.[215] In addition, RECs have, increasingly, been digitising their resources, which has provided for greater oversight of these Communities by civil society. Finally, these economic communities also strengthen bargaining power when individual members or the collective whole approach outside actors. All of these forces taken together have the potential to produce tremendous economic growth.

---

[211] "From Regional Economic Communities to a Continental Free Trade Area", United Nations Conference on Trade and Development, 12 February 2018, available at: https://unctad.org/en/PublicationsLibrary/webditc2017d1_en.pdf.

[212] "Economic Development in Africa – Report 2019", United Nations Conference on Trade and Development, available at: https://unctad.org/webflyer/economic-development-africa-report-2019.

[213] Ibid.

[214] Landry Signé, "How Africa is Bucking the Isolationist Trend", Foreign Affairs, 23 May 2018, available at: https://www.foreignaffairs.com/articles/africa/2018-05-23/how-africa-bucking-isolationist-trend.

[215] Dominic Nsikan, "Top 6 Achievements of the ECOWAS", West African Countries, 2 October 2017, available at: https://www.westafricancountries.com/top-6-achievements-of-the-ecowas/.

Individual RECs have also had their own successes. ECOWAS, for example, has largely been successful in developing a strong relationship between Member States, and has, in many ways, served as a model for integrating overlapping RECs.[216] For example, all but one of ECOWAS's members (Cape Verde) are parties to both ECOWAS and CEN-SAD, yet the region has been mostly successful in distinguishing between the objectives of each REC, allowing both RECs to move forward in reaching their stated objectives. ECOWAS has also been successful in overcoming what is one of the biggest challenges to African integration: the differences between anglophone and francophone countries. In certain matters, such as strengthening the rule of law and promoting peace, ECOWAS has been able to build a bridge between French- and English-speaking countries, which has created more profound collaboration within the region.[217] That said, in other circumstances, most particularly in its efforts to develop a common currency, ECOWAS has struggled to bring anglophone and francophone countries together.

ECOWAS is the only REC that has not reduced tariffs to zero, but, rather, has set a 0.5% levy on all goods imported into the region, which has given the region certain liquidity that it has used to fund critical activities.[218] ECOWAS's focus on improved infrastructure has also led to substantial improvements in road construction, which has resulted in greater interconnection of major cities by highway.[219]

One of the most important ECOWAS infrastructure projects is the construction of the 1,081-kilometre Abidjan–Lagos highway. Valued at USD 15.6 billion, and led by ECOWAS, this transformative public–private partnership will have a significant impact on the economies of five West African countries: Côte d'Ivoire, Ghana, Togo, Benin and Nigeria. The new highway will start at Bingerville, in the eastern suburbs of Abidjan, and

---

[216] "From Regional Economic Communities to a Continental Free Trade Area" United Nations Conference on Trade and Development, 12 February 2018, available at: https://unctad.org/en/PublicationsLibrary/webditc2017d1_en.pdf.
[217] Dominic Nsikan, "Top 6 Achievements of the ECOWAS", West African Countries, 2 October 2017, available at: https://www.westafricancountries.com/top-6-achievements-of-the-ecowas/.
[218] Amanda Lucey, "How ECOWAS has got peacebuilding right", ReliefWeb, 1 December 2016, available at: https://reliefweb.int/report/world/how-ecowas-has-got-peacebuilding-right.
[219] Dominic Nsikan, "Top 6 Achievements of the ECOWAS", West African Countries, 2 October 2017, available at: https://www.westafricancountries.com/top-6-achievements-of-the-ecowas/.

terminate at Mile 2 (Eric Moore) in Lagos. Three sections are planned for the construction of this dual three-lane highway: Abidjan (Côte d'Ivoire)–Takoradi (Ghana) (295 km); Takoradi–Akanu (Ghana) (466 km); and Noepe (Togo)–Cotonou (Benin)–Lagos (Nigeria) (320 km). Eight border posts will also be built along the corridor. This project was the largest investment opportunity showcased at the Africa Investment Forum virtual boardrooms held from 15 to 17 March 2022.[220]

ECOWAS has also led to improved communications platforms between countries, facilitating transborder connectivity. Finally, ECOWAS has been particularly successful at ensuring peace and security in the region. It has put tremendous focus on developing its own Conflict Prevention Framework, which the Member States have implemented in order to avoid a rise in conflict in the region.[221] ECOWAS has successfully played a peacekeeping role in Liberia, Guinea–Bissau and Mali, and helped broker the exit of Gambia's long-time leader, Yahya Jammeh.[222] Moreover, the organisation is currently involved in the resolution of the ongoing political crises in Burkina Faso, Guinea and Mali.

When COMESA introduced its free-trade agreement in 2000, trade in the region stood at USD 2.3 billion. By 2014, that number had skyrocketed to USD 22.3 billion, while cross-border investment in manufacturing, infrastructure and services had also grown exponentially.[223] In that same region, the creation of a borderless economy has significantly reduced the cost of doing business. COMESA has also established a number of specialised entities that have, in their own right, created positive change in the region, within their respective fields.[224]

---

[220]   See: "The Africa Investment Forum: catalyzing financing for game-changing Abidjan-Lagos highway project", available at: https://www.afdb.org/en/news-and-events/africa-investment-forum-catalyzing-financing-game-changing-abidjan-lagos-highway-project-50232.

[221]   Amanda Lucey, "How ECOWAS has got peacebuilding right", ReliefWeb, 1 December 2016, available at: https://reliefweb.int/report/world/how-ecowas-has-got-peacebuilding-right.

[222]   Paul D. Williams, "A New African Model of Coercion? Assessing the ECOWAS Mission in The Gambia", Global Observatory, 16 March 2017, available at: https://theglobalobservatory.org/2017/03/ecowas-gambia-barrow-jammeh-african-union/.

[223]   "COMESA at twenty: of the successes, challenges and promises", Addis Standard, 7 April 2015, available at: http://addisstandard.com/comesa-at-twenty-of-the-successes-challenges-and-promises/.

[224]   These include, among others, a clearing house, a monetary institute, an infrastructure fund, a federation of women in business, a leather product institute, a business council, a competition commission and an alliance for commodity trade.

In the case of the EAC,[225] combining knowledge and technologies has had tremendous success in improving transport and communication across borders, allowing for goods to be moved with greater ease. Harmonisation of monetary and fiscal policies has made doing business within this economic bloc more streamlined and efficient. The EAC has also created harmonised tax policies that will facilitate compliance with what are otherwise complex tax laws, allowing businesses to manage domestic taxes more easily.[226] Moreover, the Community has harmonised nearly 1,500 standards, which Member States have made tremendous progress in adopting, and which will further facilitate cross-border business.[227]

The SADC has also made great progress in terms of policy harmonisation, and has successfully shifted all Member States to market-oriented economies.[228] This region has also been more successful than most in expanding its impact by encouraging greater integration on the continent. In June 2015, COMESA, EAC and SADC were successful in forming the Tripartite Free Trade Area (TFTA) on trade in goods.[229] This unprecedented move brings together three of Africa's largest economic communities, who joined forces to further boost trade and economic growth.[230] So far, 22 countries have signed the agreement forming the TFTA, and eight have ratified it. There has been recent commentary that indicates that many countries are waiting until it is better understood what the status of AfCFTA is before ratifying the agreement.[231] This may be a positive point for the AfCFTA, but will diminish the overall successes of the TFTA, which, if ratified in a timely manner, could provide a sound foundation which the AfCFTA can stand on as it is implemented.

---

[225] Reuben Simukoko, "Achievements and Failures of the East African Community" Best of Africa, available at: https://thebestofafrica.org/content/successes-and-failures-of-the-east-african-community.

[226] "Ministry of East African Community and Regional Development", Republic of Kenya, available at: https://meac.go.ke/eac-achievements/.

[227] Ibid.

[228] Paul Baker and Victor Deleplancque, "Achievements, Challenges, and Constraints of Trade Integration in SADC", available at: https://www.tradeeconomics.com/wp-content/uploads/2019/07/Achievements-challenges-and-constrainst-of-trade-integration-in-SADC1-min.pdf.

[229] "From Regional Economic Communities to a Continental Free Trade Area", United Nations Conference on Trade and Development, available at: https://unctad.org/en/PublicationsLibrary/webditc2017d1_en.pdf.

[230] Soamiely Andriamananjara, "Understanding the importance of the Tripartite Free Trade Area", Brookings Institution, 17 June 2015, available at: https://www.brookings.edu/blog/africa-in-focus/2015/06/17/understanding-the-importance-of-the-tripartite-free-trade-area/.

[231] Ibid.

Each African REC has had its own successes. While successes have been varied, and there have also been significant challenges (as will be discussed below), RECs have provided a positive outlook on the prospects of the AfCFTA.

4. A CLOSER LOOK AT THE WEST AFRICAN ECONOMIC AND MONETARY UNION (WAEMU)

Before looking more closely at the challenges faced by African RECs, it is worth pausing to look at one of the most often overlooked economic communities (as demonstrated by its non-inclusion in the African Union's eight "building block" regional economic communities): the West African Economic and Monetary Union (WAEMU). WAEMU is, in many ways, one of the most successful examples of regional integration on the continent. It is not only a free-trade zone, but also one of only four currency unions in the world.[232] Each of the Member States of WAEMU is also a member of ECOWAS, meaning that the free-trade zone created by this body has actually been expanded to a larger region, which, as discussed above, includes both anglophone and francophone countries. WAEMU itself, however, comprises seven francophone countries and one Portuguese- speaking country (Guinea–Bissau).[233] At the same time, all of these countries are also Member States of OHADA, meaning that they have already demonstrated a commitment to the rule of law, and are more attractive to investors due to their harmonised business laws.

WAEMU was established in 1994 by French-speaking countries in West Africa, with the hope of further promoting economic integration in the region.[234] The primary objectives in establishing WAEMU included creating a common market, coordinating policies, and harmonising fiscal policy among neighbouring countries, in an effort to promote security,

---

[232]   Amadou Sy and Mariama Sow, "Four questions on the state of the West African Economic and Monetary Union and implications for other regional economic communities", Brookings Institution, 15 March 2016, available at: https://www.brookings.edu/blog/africa-in-focus/2016/03/15/four-questions-on-the-state-of-the-west-african-economic-and-monetary-union-and-implications-for-other-regional-economic-communities/.

[233]   Benin, Burkina Faso, Côte d'Ivoire, Guinea–Bissau, Mali, Niger, Senegal and Togo.

[234]   Chris Cleverly, "Future of Currency in W. Africa: CFA Franc Collapse and Eco Inadequacy", 13 March 2020, available at: https://cointelegraph.com/news/future-of-currency-in-w-africa-cfa-franc-collapse-and-eco-inadequacy.

sustainability and prosperity.[235] From inception, the common currency of the WAEMU countries was the CFA franc. The franc had been pegged to the euro and backed by an unlimited convertibility guarantee from the French Treasury. The countries, in turn, deposited part of each of their individual foreign exchange reserves with the French Treasury.

On 21 December 2019, France and WAEMU tentatively agreed to rename the CFA franc the "eco", and to change the monetary scheme of the currency by no longer requiring that WAEMU Member States keep 50% of their foreign reserves in the French Treasury.[236] Should this scheme receive final approval, the currency will continue to be pegged against the euro, which has ensured the stability of the currency since its inception. France will also continue to provide a guarantee of unlimited convertibility of the region's currency, as it had done under the original scheme. Experts do not expect these changes to have a major impact on the WAEMU economies.[237] All this said, there have been significant challenges to the implementation of this currency. Namely, the non-WAEMU ECOWAS members have challenged the scheme, leading to a delay in the actual shift of currency, and resulting in questions as to whether the scheme will ultimately be adopted.

The WAEMU bloc of countries shares a common monetary and financial policy, and has unified external tariffs. While many African nations saw a sharp decrease in the value of their currencies during recent global economic crises, the pegged currency of the WAEMU countries has remained stable.[238] At the same time, WAEMU and its ECOWAS partners have an Economic Partnership Agreement with its biggest trading partner, the European Union (EU), and the region has been identified as the EU's most important investment destination in Africa.[239]

---

[235] Ibid.

[236] Payce Madden, "Africa in the news: WAEMU's eco implementation, Sahel security update, and Foresight Africa Launch", Brookings Institution, 18 January 2020, available at: https://www.brookings.edu/blog/africa-in-focus/2020/01/18/africa-in-the-news-waemus-eco-implementation-sahel-security-update-and-foresight-africa-launch/.

[237] Raji Rafiq, "Moody's dim outlook on African Banks", African Business, 2 March 2020, available at: https://africanbusinessmagazine.com/african-banker/moodys-dim-outlook-on-african-banks/.

[238] Most African currencies lost between 20% and 40% of their value. See African Development Bank, "African Economic Outlook 2018", available at: https://www.afdb.org/fileadmin/uploads/afdb/Documents/Publications/African_Economic_Outlook_2018_-_EN.pdf.

[239] "West Africa – Trade Policy", European Commission, available at: https://policy.trade.ec.europa.eu/eu-trade-relationships-country-and-region/countries-and-regions/west-africa_en.

In contrast to many of its non-WAEMU ECOWAS partners, WAEMU countries have seen more steady investment and, until recently, had the largest level of intra-regional exports in sub-Saharan Africa.[240] Sharing a common currency has also allowed WAEMU to better integrate, unlike ECOWAS and other African regional trade communities, in which integration has been a primary challenge.[241] By reducing cross-border transaction costs and operating from shared regulations, WAEMU has seen a somewhat steady increase in intra-regional trade, although informal trading has slowed the full potential of the region.[242] The region has also benefited, albeit perhaps not directly due to its economic union, from relative political stability, compared with other African regions.[243] Moreover, as a direct result of its monetary integration and policies, WAEMU has, according to the International Monetary Fund, experienced "strong growth acceleration since 2012 and, at the same time, has seen macroeconomic stability and investment, improvement in political institutions, improvement in the terms of trade, and [an] increase in productivity".[244]

WAEMU does, however, still suffer from many of the issues holding back Africa as a continent, such as structural weakness, lack of capacity, poor infrastructure and irregular implementation of WAEMU rules and regulations in different Member States.[245] Additionally, several of its members still fall far behind its more successful countries, such as Senegal

---

[240] This has now gone to the SADC.

[241] Alexander Edberg Thorén and Fredrik Azelius, "ECOWAS and WAEMU as Tools for Promoting Export Diversification", 25 May 2016, available at: http://lup.lub.lu.se/luur/download?func=downloadFile&recordOId=8877024&fileOId=8877029.

[242] "Trade Policy Review: Members of the West African Economic and Monetary Union (WAEMU)", Tralac, 26 October 2017, available at: https://www.tralac.org/news/article/12324-trade-policy-review-members-of-the-west-african-economic-and-monetary-union-waemu.html.

[243] However, this stability has recently been challenged in Burkina Faso, Guinea and Mali, where militaries have seized control of power, obliging the respective elected presidents to resign. These coups occurred in 2020 and 2021 in Mali; 2021 in Guinea; and 2022 in Burkina Faso.

[244] See supra note 241. See also Amadou Sy and Mariama Sow, "Four Questions on the state of the West African Economic Monetary Union and implications for other regional economic communities", Brookings Institution, 15 March 2016, available at: https://www.brookings.edu/blog/africa-in-focus/2016/03/15/four-questions-on-the-state-of-the-west-african-economic-and-monetary-union-and-implications-for-other-regional-economic-communities/.

[245] Ibid.

and Côte d'Ivoire,[246] and growth has been seen as disproportionate amongst members. Still, with all of its weaknesses and the fact that some WAEMU countries still suffer from weak governance and a lack of the rule of law, the CFA franc has provided a stable monetary institutional framework.[247] While the benefits of this have played out in different countries in different ways – based on size and political stability, among other aspects – there has been overall stability within the economic bloc.

The stability and success of WAEMU may soon be threatened, however, with the proposed joining of non-WAEMU ECOWAS Member States into the common currency. The original agreement to create a monetary union, the Accra Declaration, was made in 2000. As part of this agreement, the Gambia, Ghana, Guinea, Liberia, Nigeria and Sierra Leone agreed to establish a central bank and create their own monetary union. This union was then to be merged with the WAEMU union, creating one regional currency.[248] This has yet to occur, however the idea behind the establishment of the eco is that the ECOWAS Member States start the process of integration. Nigeria and Ghana, by far the strongest

---

[246] Senegal and Côte d'Ivoire, WAEMU's largest economies, provide strong examples of the benefits of embracing economic integration. Both countries have seen steady growth, with annual growth above 6% for the last four years; numbers higher than almost all other African nations. Both countries have embraced WAEMU regulations and have strived to improve their legal systems at home so as to support the regulations. Both are members of OHADA and, as such, have adopted the OHADA Uniform Acts, making it easier for investors to digest their laws. These two countries have made attracting foreign investment a focus of their political policies, and have been particularly successful in doing so. Public–private partnerships and public-only spending on infrastructure projects have truly set these countries apart from their West African counterparts, with both countries making huge strides in putting in place new roads, railways, buildings, and – in the case of Senegal – a state-of-the-art international airport. In an effort to attract a more diverse field of investment, Senegal and Côte d'Ivoire have extended their traditional relationships with France to other countries, including the United Kingdom, China, India, Turkey and other world players. An eagerness of their governments to acknowledge weaknesses, to embrace regional policies, and to invest state funds into project development have created a greater sense of confidence in both Senegal and Côte d'Ivoire than is seen elsewhere on the continent. While Senegal and Côte d'Ivoire still face the same issues most of the continent faces, in terms of high rates of poverty, weak infrastructure outside of urban areas, and bureaucratic uncertainties, their slow and steady movement forward should be viewed as a model for other countries. Countries should pay particularly close attention to the support being given to regional regulations by the local legal systems.

[247] See *supra* note 241.

[248] Bill Mitchell, "Modern Monetary Theory – Introduction – The Last Colonial Currency: A History of the CFA Franc – Part 3", 8 January 2020, available at: http://bilbo.economicoutlook.net/blog/?p=44038.

non-WAEMU economies in the region, have already provided a laundry list of demands for entry into the eco, demonstrating that, if they join, they will likely dominate the monetary union, probably to the detriment of smaller countries with weaker economies.[249] Some would argue that this would result in similar impacts to those currently being played out in relation to Côte D'Ivoire and Senegal, which have far surpassed the growth of other WAEMU countries; however, the strength of Nigeria, if measured by economic size, dwarves even those countries, and this could have a chilling effect on the region. Fortunately for current WAEMU Members, the non-WAEMU ECOWAS countries continue to drag their feet in moving forward with currency integration, and it is, therefore, unlikely that this will be a pressing issue in the near future. Still, this imbalance of power should be taken into consideration when looking at the future of AfCFTA.

5. STRUGGLES OF REGIONAL ECONOMIC INTEGRATION

For every strength of the African RECs, there has been a plethora of challenges. While the path forward must certainly involve integration, so that African nations can have the strength in numbers necessary to compete on the global scale, the continent must learn from the difficulties currently facing RECs, if the continent is to be successful in the long term. The following subsections highlight some of the most pressing issues impacting on RECs; however, for each REC, there are a host of other issues that could, and should, be analysed as the African Union moves forward in its implementation of the AfCFTA.

The principal challenges currently facing African RECs include, among others, overlapping RECs; poor governance; a lack of political will, coupled with African governments' selective embracing of RECs; lofty goals with little planning on the details; conflicts amongst Member States; and inadequate financing.

5.1. OVERLAPPING RECs

One of the greatest challenges to RECs in Africa is the sheer number of economic communities that exist (the so-called "spaghetti bowl"). This is,

---

249   Ibid.

however, also one of the greatest opportunities for AfCFTA, which seeks to create one continental economic union. As demonstrated above, several African nations are Member States of multiple RECs,[250] which complicates implementation of REC regulations, and frustrates harmonisation, one of the key purposes of each economic community.[251] There is a strong argument to be made that it is actually the number of overlapping economic communities that is most damaging, despite the best intentions of economic integration.

While each REC is different, they all seek, in some capacity, to promote economic integration. This, in turn, means that each REC puts in place its own regulations and policies to promote this objective. At times, overlapping RECs may have contradictory regulations, making it even more difficult for Member States that are party to several economic communities to comply with these regulations.[252] At the same time, an overwhelming majority of African nations lack the capacity and resources to manage the complex web of different regulations. Being a member of several communities often stretches African governments beyond their capabilities, resulting in fragmented implementation of REC policies.[253] Looking forward, if AfCFTA is to be successful, countries will need to dissolve existing RECs or, at the very least, harmonise the AfCFTA and REC regulations.

---

[250] Ombeni N. Mwasha, "The Benefits of Regional Economic Integration for Developing Countries in Africa: A Case of East African Community", (2008) Korea Review of International Studies, pp. 69–92, available at: https://www.semanticscholar.org/paper/The-Benefits-of-Regional-Economic-Integration-for-%3A-Mwasha/18beea4e9968371264a4a0b3a577d657073bde88.

[251] Muhabie Mekonnen Mengistu, "Multiplicity of African Regional Economic Communities and Overlapping Memberships: A Challenge for African Integration", (2015) 3(5) International Journal of Economics, Finance and Management Sciences, p. 417, available at: https://www.researchgate.net/publication/293009606_Multiplicity_of_African_Regional_Economic_Communities_and_Overlapping_Memberships_A_Challenge_for_African_Integration.

[252] Ernest Harsch, "Making African integration a reality", Africa Renewal, September 2002, available at: https://www.un.org/africarenewal/magazine/september-2002/making-african-integration-reality.

[253] Muhabie Mekonnen Mengistu, "Multiplicity of African Regional Economic Communities and Overlapping Memberships: A Challenge for African Integration," (2015) 3(5) International Journal of Economics, Finance and Management Sciences, p. 417, available at: https://www.researchgate.net/publication/293009606_Multiplicity_of_African_Regional_Economic_Communities_and_Overlapping_Memberships_A_Challenge_for_African_Integration.

5.2. POOR GOVERNANCE

Poor governance has long plagued African nations.[254] The same issue also threatens the success of RECs. Constant crises across the continent shift focus away from economic integration and further stretch limited capacity. Political instability, particularly under long-term authoritarian leaders, takes a toll on the ability of RECs to produce real change.[255] Corrupt governments ignore obligations set under RECs, and fail to monitor compliance with REC regulations, which even further undermines the ability of economic communities to create positive change. Respect for human rights, transparency, and peace and security have been proven to be essential for true economic growth, yet many African nations fall short of guaranteeing these things.[256] RECs can only be as strong as their Member States, and the political instability found across the African continent at this time continues to threaten the long-term success of each of Africa's economic communities.

5.3. A LACK OF POLITICAL WILL AND SELECTIVE ADOPTION

In addition to political instability, there is a widespread lack of political will on the part of African governments, even among those that are stable and democratic.[257] Governments on the continent are quick to enter into RECs,

---

[254] See Stephanie Hanson, "Corruption in Sub-Saharan Africa", Council on Foreign Relations, 6 August 2009, available at: https://www.cfr.org/backgrounder/corruption-sub-saharan-africa.

[255] Muhabie Mekonnen Mengistu, "Multiplicity of African Regional Economic Communities and Overlapping Memberships: A Challenge for African Integration", (2015) 3(5) International Journal of Economics, Finance and Management Sciences, p. 417, available at: https://www.researchgate.net/publication/293009606_Multiplicity_of_African_Regional_Economic_Communities_and_Overlapping_Memberships_A_Challenge_for_African_Integration.

[256] Ibid. See also Rodrigo Tavares and Vanessa Tang, "Regional economic integration in Africa: impediments progress?", (2011) 18(2) South African Journal of International Affairs, pp. 217–233, available at: https://www.tandfonline.com/doi/abs/10.1080/1022 0461.2011.588826.

[257] Muhabie Mekonnen Mengistu, "Multiplicity of African Regional Economic Communities and Overlapping Memberships: A Challenge for African Integration", (2015) 3(5) International Journal of Economics, Finance and Management Sciences, p. 417, available at: https://www.researchgate.net/publication/293009606_Multiplicity_of_African_Regional_Economic_Communities_and_Overlapping_Memberships_A_Challenge_for_African_Integration.

as demonstrated by the number of countries that are Member States to multiple RECs, but then fail to put the effort into making them successful. Governments see the favourable aspects of economic communities, particularly the chance to create economic growth, but are not as quick to recognise the internal changes that need to be made in order to create that growth. Moreover, governments pick and choose which regulations they will adopt under domestic law, and which they will ignore.

A strong example of this is provided by the current complications in creating a monetary union in West Africa. While ECOWAS has agreed to form a monetary union, which is to be conjoined with the existing WAEMU monetary union, Member States have dragged their feet for decades in making this integration a reality. The plan for creating this union was first introduced in 1986, and was meant to be implemented in 2000.[258] This date was then pushed back to 2005, then 2010, 2014, 2015, 2020, and now 2027.[259] There is a clear indication that the non-WAEMU Member States will not successfully enter the existing monetary union as long as it fails to comply with the conditions they have set as mandatory.[260] To further complicate the situation, the WAEMU Member States have also demonstrated a hesitancy towards moving from the CFA franc to the newly named eco.

Another example of Member States failing to meet their obligations, thereby threatening the success of the REC, can be seen in CEMAC, where several Member States (who are also Member States of ECCAS) have yet to recognise the Community's required free movement of people regulation.[261] Accordingly, these CEMAC countries are still imposing visas on citizens of other Member States to travel within the region. This poses a real challenge to the success of the economic community in meeting its integration objectives.

---

[258] Bill Mitchell, "Modern Monetary Theory – Introduction – The Last Colonial Currency: A History of the CFA Franc – Part 3", 8 January 2020, available at: http://bilbo.economicoutlook.net/blog/?p=44038.

[259] Ibid.

[260] Emmanuel Pinto Moreira, "From CFA to ECO: Opportunities and Challenges of Economic and Monetary Cooperation in West Africa", 14 September 2021, available at: https://www.policycenter.ma/publications/cfa-eco-opportunities-and-challenges-economic-and-monetary-cooperation-west-africa.

[261] Sylvain Andzongo, "Visa confusion hinders trade, travel in central Africa", Reuters, 12 June 2015, available at: https://www.reuters.com/article/uk-africa-central-trade-idUKKBN0OS0FX20150612.

Across the continent, there is a general lack of political will to mainstream regional commitments and agreements into domestic law, and a lack of the planning which is necessary to ensure the success of the process.[262] As one expert has noted, "[f]ew countries on the continent seem to be prepared for the partial surrender and the pooling of sovereignty, which is critical for the success of any regional integration scheme".[263] The unwillingness of governments to put the obligations of a community above the self-interest of their individual countries has greatly hindered the effectiveness of economic communities.

5.4. LOFTY GOALS WITH LITTLE PLANNING

The objectives of RECs, as described above, set forth lofty goals for Africa's economic communities, shaped primarily around economic integration. RECs on the continent have put a heavy emphasis on trade liberalisation and market integration, which are important goals, but which only have a positive impact if complemented with policies that turn those efforts into development. Member States should be working collectively to promote policies that foster production and help meet the development needs of individual countries within the REC. For example, RECs should be leading development of regional infrastructure to help market integration.

At the same time, RECs need to recognise the realities facing Member States. Regardless of the progress that has been made on the continent, Africa continues to fall behind all other regions in the world in terms of overall development.[264] African states, who are the Member States, are lagging behind in meeting the basic needs of their citizens. Increased trade means nothing if African people are not receiving education, health, labour and other social benefits. Combining efforts among Member

---

262   Mzuski Qobo, "The challenges of regional integration in Africa", ISS Paper 145, June 2007, available at: https://www.files.ethz.ch/isn/98933/PAPER145H.pdf.

263   Muhabie Mekonnen Mengistu, "Multiplicity of African Regional Economic Communities and Overlapping Memberships: A Challenge for African Integration", (2015) 3(5) International Journal of Economics, Finance and Management Sciences, p. 417, available at: https://www.researchgate.net/publication/293009606_Multiplicity_of_African_Regional_Economic_Communities_and_Overlapping_Memberships_A_Challenge_for_African_Integration.

264   André-Michel Essoungou, "Africa's least developed: lands of opportunity", Africa Renewal, August 2011, available at: https://www.un.org/africarenewal/magazine/august-2011/africas-least-developed-lands-opportunity.

States, together with the free movement of goods and people, as well as other positive regulations arising out of economic communities, have the potential to create long-term sustainable growth. Thus far, however, African RECs have fallen short of carrying out the necessary steps to promote this type of development.

5.5. INTERNAL CONFLICTS

Although progress has been made in recent years, the African continent continues to experience a tremendous amount of conflict. The continent has, in recent years, seen a number of bloody civil wars in countries like the Central African Republic, South Sudan, Mali, the Democratic Republic of Congo, Sudan and Burundi, among others.[265] There have also been rising insurgencies of various terrorist groups in Northern Africa and the Sahel region. Additionally, there have been wars between states, including between Ethiopia and Eritrea, and between Morocco and Algeria (known as the Sand War), among others.[266] The Morocco–Algeria dispute over the Western Sahara has rendered the Arab Maghreb Union almost completely ineffective, and ongoing conflict involving the Democratic Republic of Congo led to a substantial delay in the starting up of COMESA. For as long as conflict continues, integration and development in Africa will continue to be hindered, as such conflict curtails economic activities, destroys infrastructure, and constitutes a serious barrier to the flow of trade and investment.[267]

5.6. INADEQUATE FINANCING

Another glaring inadequacy in RECs has been their inability to self-finance. As mentioned above, one of ECOWAS's achievements has been applying a 0.5% tariff rather than the 0% applied in other regions, which has given the REC the ability to finance many of its efforts, including the development of several specialised agencies and institutions. One of the principal intentions of forming RECs is to combine the efforts of several

---

[265] The History Guy, "Current Wars in Africa", available at: https://www.historyguy.com/wars_of_africa_current.html.

[266] Ibid.

[267] "The Economic Consequences of Conflicts", IMF, available at: https://www.elibrary.imf.org/view/book/9781484396865/ch002.xml.

countries, given that some of the independent countries involved are not able to individually fund development efforts. If RECs do not implement policies that will allow them to generate income to fund the necessary actions to promote economic development, they will continue to fall short of meeting their stated objectives.[268]

5.7. OTHER CONSIDERATIONS

In addition to the above-mentioned challenges, African RECs are also facing other issues that will need to be considered as AfCFTA moves forward. For example, RECs have failed to guarantee equal benefits for all members, with larger, more developed countries reaping greater benefits than smaller, less developed countries.[269] The supremacy of certain countries is a feature of each bloc, with economic gains seemingly flowing only to a select few countries on the continent. This leaves smaller or more economically weak countries falling even further behind other Member States. Given the number of small countries on the continent, and the growing economies of wealthier nations, the African Union must cautiously consider this imbalance of impact when implementing the AfCFTA.

Other considerations include inadequate infrastructure, which is hindering development, as well as the lack of skilled human resources in many countries on the continent. Language barriers and differing legal systems may also cause problems in integration. While ECOWAS has largely overcome these barriers, integrating francophone and anglophone countries, and civil and common law systems, doing so across the whole continent may prove to be challenging.

The inability of most African nations to stand out from the crowd and truly attract the outside investment needed to generate measurable economic development means that regional economic integration remains the greatest hope for Africa's successful future. There are few African nations that are capable, based on their own resources, of being self-reliant,

---

[268] See "Assessing Regional Integration in Africa IV: Enhancing Intra-African Trade", United Nations Economic Commission in Africa, May 2010, available at: https://www.unece.org/fileadmin/DAM/trade/TF_JointUNRCsApproach/ECA_IntraAfricanTrade.pdf.

[269] Bill Mitchell, "Modern Monetary Theory – Introduction – The Last Colonial Currency: A History of the CFA Franc – Part 3", 8 January 2020, available at: http://bilbo.economicoutlook.net/blog/?p=44038.

which only adds to the argument that integration is essential. Regardless of the hurdles that stand before them, then, African nations should be, and are, as discussed further in the preceding sections, looking towards more comprehensive and honest engagement in economically integrated blocs. The discussion on the strengths and weaknesses of the existing RECs should be at the heart of the discussion on how Africa can best foster economic growth and greater sustainable development, as it looks to foster greater continental integration. As will be demonstrated in the following chapters, in moving towards such integration, the continent should be paying close attention to the lessons learned in the earliest attempts at legal and economic integration, which have now played out over the course of several decades in each of the RECs discussed in this chapter.

CHAPTER 4

THE AFRICAN LANDSCAPE

The Road to the African Continental Free Trade Area

On 30 May 2019, the African Continental Free Trade Area ("AfCFTA" or the "Agreement") officially entered into force. According to the United Nations Economic Commission for Africa, the AfCFTA will cover a market of 1.2 billion people and a gross domestic product (GDP) of USD 2.5 trillion.[270] The massive economic integration of 53 countries[271] has been predicted to generate as much as USD 35 billion in increased trade between African countries.[272] The AfCFTA will allow African nations to capitalise and build on their collective strengths, by breaking down barriers to the movement of goods, services, people, capital and ideas. This alone is expected to increase the bargaining powers of African nations. At the same time, the Agreement is likely to encourage foreign entry into the continent, by creating a single, more attractive, market.[273] This chapter looks a bit closer at this Agreement, with a particular focus on the dispute settlement mechanisms that exist thereunder.

---

[270] "Africa Continental Free Trade Area – Questions and Answers", United Nations Economic Commission for Africa, available at: https://repository.uneca.org/handle/10855/43253.

[271] On 7 July 2019, President of Nigeria, Muhammadu Buhari signed the Agreement Establishing the African Continental Free Trade Area, thereby adding Africa's largest economy to the Agreement.

[272] Luke Warford, "Africa is Moving Toward a Massive and Important Free Trade Agreement", The Washington Post, 14 July 2016, available at: https://www.washingtonpost.com/news/monkey-cage/wp/2016/07/14/the-7-things-you-need-to-know-about-africas-continental-free-trade-area/?utm_term=.c8c2a586d85d.

[273] Christina Golubski, "Africa in the news: AfCFTA enters into force, South Africa and Senegal tackle climate change, and presidents inaugurated in Nigeria and Malawi", Brookings Institution, 1 June 2019, available at: https://www.brookings.edu/blog/africa-in-focus/2019/06/01/africa-in-the-news-afcfta-enters-into-force-south-africa-and-senegal-tackle-climate-change-and-presidents-inaugurated-in-nigeria-and-malawi/.

The African Union, in 2015, fast-tracked the AfCFTA by putting negotiation of the Agreement at the top of its priorities for the continent. This followed the initial introduction of the idea at the 18th Ordinary Session of the Assembly of Heads of State and Government of the African Union, held in January 2012. During this meeting, a decision to establish a continental free trade area was adopted, putting in motion the negotiation process for this continental document.[274] In an action plan adopted in 2014, titled "Action Plan for Boosting Intra-African Trade and Fast-Tracking the Establishment of a Pan-African Free Trade Area", the African Union expressed concern over Africa's inability to use trade to create sustainable economic growth. The plan states that, "[t]he failure of African trade to serve as a catalyst for sustainable economic growth and poverty alleviation stems partly from its three interrelated basic features: size, structure and direction".[275] The African Union noted that Africa's share of global trade was insignificant, at only 3%. At the same time, trade was heavily concentrated on primary commodities that have slow growth and high price instability. Finally, and perhaps most notably, it referenced the fact that the overwhelming majority of African trade was external, with only 10% of trade on the continent being intra-African.[276] By way of comparison, in 2019 the EU had a share of intra-EU exports of between 50% and 75%. In certain EU countries, the number was above 75%: Hungary (78%), Czechia (79%), Luxembourg (80%) and Slovakia (80%). Only in Ireland (37%) and Cyprus (41%) was the share of intra-EU exports lower than 50%, with extra-EU exports being higher than intra-EU exports.[277] That same year, approximately 60% of Asia's trade was intra-regional.[278] In looking at its own intercontinental trade, the African Union noted that African countries' efforts to negotiate more substantial

---

[274] African Continental Free Trade Area (AfCFTA) Legal Texts and Policy Documents, available at: https://www.tralac.org/resources/our-resources/6730-continental-free-trade-area-cfta.html.

[275] "Action Plan for Boosting Intra-African Trade and Fast-Tracking the Establishment of a Pan-American Free Trade Area", African Union, available at: https://au.int/sites/default/files/newsevents/workingdocuments/27214-wd-cfta_action_plan_ti6174_e_original.pdf.

[276] Ibid.

[277] See "EU trade in goods balance close to €200 bn surplus in 2019", eurostat, 24 March 2020, available at: https://ec.europa.eu/eurostat/documents/2995521/10624801/6-25032020-AP-EN.pdf/c65584e1-c88c-f038-aec1-bd1235c395e1.

[278] UNCTAD Handbook of Statistics 2019, available at: https://unctad.org/system/files/official-document/tdstat44_en.pdf.

trade deals with external state parties and international organisations[279] only bolstered further the need for a continental solution.

The issue of overlapping regional economic communities, with little continual growth found in any of them, has also been noted as a predominant justification for a continental body. As discussed in the previous chapters, the intertwined web of thousands of different regulations, including local, bilateral, regional and multilateral regulations, makes navigating investment in Africa extremely complicated. Recognising this, African states came to the table for AfCFTA ready to harmonise the investment landscape across the continent.

At the same time, the African Union began acknowledging some of the largest hurdles facing investment in Africa, regardless of whether this investment was intra-African or foreign. Investors across the board, from both Africa and abroad, are hesitant to put their money into the continent. Several studies have indicated that the average return on investments in Africa can be as much as two-thirds higher than in leading Asian markets;[280] yet, as noted above, investment in Africa, particularly in sub-Saharan Africa, continues to lag far behind other developing countries. The key question that the African continent is trying to answer by moving towards the AfCFTA, then, is what is holding back investors? Why are the existing regional bodies not attracting greater investment?

1. HURDLES TO AFRICAN INVESTMENT

Several factors add tremendous risk to investing on the African continent, and it is not until African nations begin addressing these issues that investment will begin to flow exponentially. While it is impossible to lump

---

[279] Noting specifically the WTO Doha Round, and the EPA negotiations with the EU, which, at the time of writing, were in a stalemate.

[280] "One was a comprehensive study of the publicly traded companies operating in Africa for the period 2002–07, mostly in the manufacturing and services sectors. It found that these companies' average return on capital was around two-thirds higher than that of comparable companies in China, India, Indonesia, and Vietnam. Another source, on the FDI of US companies, showed that they were getting a higher return on their African investments than on those in other regions. Finally, analysis of a series of surveys of several thousand manufacturing firms around the developing world found that, at the margin, capital investment had a higher return in Africa.": Paul Collier, "The case for investing in Africa", McKinsey and Company, 1 June 2010, available at: https://www.mckinsey.com/featured-insights/middle-east-and-africa/the-case-for-investing-in-africa.

together all 54 African countries, as each is unique, there are common high-level trends that can be identified across the continent.

Top of these issues is institutional weakness. Widespread corruption, a lack of political stability, and problems with rule of law continue to drag countries down, despite reform efforts in many countries. Investors lack confidence in governmental bodies and, as a result, often feel as though their investments will not be adequately protected by African legal systems. This is particularly true in the infrastructure and extractive industry sectors, where corruption has a substantial impact on projects. According to the Organisation for Economic Co-operation and Development (OECD), "half of bribes paid are in industries with the largest spending on infrastructure, namely the extractive (19%), construction (15%) and transportation (15%) sectors".[281] This results in inappropriate project choices, high prices, poor quality, and excessive time and cost overruns,[282] which threaten investments and hinders development.

In addition to these statistics, another major hurdle for African nations is assuring investors that they have turned the corner in reducing corruption. One reason for this is that investors rely on their perceptions, given that real numbers on corruption are nearly non-existent.[283] This reality continues to weigh heavily on the continent. Corruption has been demonstrated to decrease economic growth, and has been found to correlate positively with income inequality.[284] Corruption decreases productivity of resources, by hindering both local and foreign investment.[285] Studies demonstrate that by improving institutional capacity, thereby reducing corruption, African nations could improve attractiveness for investment and, therefore, improve economic growth.[286]

A recent study carried out by PricewaterhouseCoopers (PwC) on corruption in Nigeria, arguably one of Africa's most corrupt countries,

---

[281] Anita Sobjak, "2018 OECD Global Anti-Corruption & Integrity Forum – Corruption Risks in Infrastructure Investments in Sub-Saharan Africa", February 2018, available at: https://www.oecd.org/corruption/integrity-forum/academic-papers/Sobjak.pdf.

[282] Ibid.

[283] Ibid.

[284] Kwabena Gyimah-Brempong, "Corruption, economic growth and income inequality in Africa", (2002) 3 Economics of Governance, pp. 183–209, available at: https://www.usf.edu/arts-sciences/departments/economics/documents/corruption.growth.inequality.africa.econogov.02.pdf.

[285] Ibid.

[286] Ibid. See also Fiza Qureshi, "Revisiting the nexus among foreign direct investment, corruption and growth in developing and developed markets", (2021) 21(1) Borsa Istanbul Review, pp. 80–91, available at: https://www.sciencedirect.com/science/article/pii/S2214845020300405.

and also its largest economy, revealed that corruption in Nigeria "could cost up to 37% of Gross Domestic Products by 2030".[287] This study found that foreign investors are wary of investing in the country, given the unpredictability of doing business where corruption may pop up in various forms. Corruption in Nigeria is found to affect public finances, business investment and the standard of living, thereby impacting on all aspects of the overall Nigerian economy.[288] Corruption has also been found to significantly lower government efficiency, by reducing income and adding to inefficiency in spending. This hampers the country's ability to develop in a meaningful way. Nigeria is but one stark example of how corruption has a substantial impact on the continent as a whole. The country is not unique and, presumably, nor are the impacts corruption has had on its economy.

Political uncertainty on the continent has also led to jittery investors. As noted by the International Development Law Organization, "[i]t is no mere coincidence that the most conflict-prone, insecure countries are also among the poorest".[289] African countries continue to rank lower than countries from other regions in terms of government effectiveness and enforcement of the rule of law, as per the World Bank's "Doing Business" report.[290] Investors in the region have made clear, time and again, that in order to create a more attractive investment environment, African nations must enact stable policies and consistently recognise the rule of law.[291]

Kenya and its political instability, following elections in December 2007, provides an excellent demonstration of how political crises have a negative impact on the economy. Following a contentious election result, wherein Kenya declared a winner of the presidential election amid widespread reports of fraud in the election, the country erupted in protests that lasted two months.[292] In looking at the economic impacts of the political

---

[287] "Impact of Corruption on Nigeria's economy", PricewaterhouseCoopers, available at: https://www.pwc.com/ng/en/press-room/impact-of-corruption-on-nigeria-s-economy.html.
[288] Ibid.
[289] "Africa and the Rule of Law," International Development Law Organization, 18 May 2016, available at: https://www.idlo.int/news/policy-statements/africa-and-rule-law.
[290] "Doing Business in Africa: A Risks, Trends, and Opportunities Roundtable", Brookings Institution, 7 October 2016, available at: https://www.brookings.edu/events/doing-business-in-africa-a-risks-trends-and-opportunities-roundtable-2/.r.
[291] Ibid.
[292] Pascaline Dupas and Jonathan Robinson, "The (hidden) costs of political instability: Evidence from Kenya's 2007 election crisis", (2012) 99 Journal of Development Economics, pp. 314–329, available at: https://web.stanford.edu/~pdupas/Coping_DupasRobinson.pdf.

instability resulting from the election fallout, a Stanford University study found that, "two months of civil conflict in Kenya had a sizeable negative impact on the incomes of a broad range of households, and led to large declines in expenditures and in consumption of necessary items, notably food".[293] Moreover, this conflict was shown to have impacted on the country's trade industries, resulting from disruptions in the operations of local producers, as well as performance issues in exporting firms.[294] One study showed noticeable structural changes in growth-rate trends in EU imports from Kenya, when looking at the cut flower industry, one of Kenya's most important industries.[295] This was the result of the short-term conflict in Kenya. In other countries where political instability and internal conflict are much more prolonged and widespread, the consequences are most certainly more profound.

Creating a more favourable environment for investment will also require African nations to improve domestic judicial systems. Local courts are not often considered competent bodies for resolving complicated disputes involving complex business matters. This only increases investor weariness. Lots of African courts are notorious for corruption and undue interference.[296] In many countries, judges lack the competencies necessary to adequately render decisions, and are politically influenced. This has led investors to question the impartiality of domestic courts, as well as the division of branches in the host states. This hurts Africa's investment prospects. The following chapters of this book will look closely at case studies of existing courts, and will make suggestions for how judicial systems may be improved.

At the same time, African governments have demonstrated more willingness to interfere in the private sector than their counterparts in the developed world. There have also been several high-stakes disputes between private investors and government actors, particularly in the extractive industries, where governments play a vital role in project success. In 2021 alone, 15% of all cases brought to the ICSID involved

---

[293] Ibid.

[294] Andrew Muhammad, Anna E. D'Souza and William Amponsah, "Violence, Political Instability, and International Trade: Evidence from Kenya's Cut Flower Sector", 1 October 2011, available: https://ssrn.com/abstract=1961207.

[295] Ibid.

[296] Charlotte Heyl, "The Judiciary and the Rule of Law in Africa", Oxford Research Encyclopedias, 29 July 2019, available at: https://oxfordre.com/politics/view/10.1093/acrefore/9780190228637.001.0001/acrefore-9780190228637-e-1352.

states from sub-Saharan Africa.[297] Many of these cases involved some of Africa's most lucrative industries, with 29% of ICSID's cases involving the oil, gas and mining industries, and 18% involving electric power and other energy industries.[298] Similar trends can be seen at the International Chamber of Commerce (ICC), where, in 2020, a total of 171 parties from 35 African countries represented 6.8% of all parties. Nigeria (22 parties) and Egypt (13 parties) were the most represented nationalities among sub-Saharan African parties (125) and North African parties (46).[299] In 2019, a total of 188 parties from 33 African countries represented 7.5% of all parties to ICC Arbitration. The most represented nationalities among sub-Saharan African parties (130) and North African parties (58) were Egypt (20), Nigeria (19), Algeria (17), Ivory Coast, (16), South Africa (13), Morocco (11) and Mauritius (10). While the increased use of international arbitration is attractive to investors, as will be further discussed in the following chapters, the increasing number of disputes involving African states has a more negative impact on investors' willingness to enter into the long negotiation processes with governments that inherently come with certain types of projects, particularly in the extractive industries.

As mentioned in previous chapters, and as will be reiterated in the following chapters, a major underlying factor in poor investment is inadequate infrastructure, which makes investment costlier, or even impossible in certain geographic regions.[300] For example, there are often no pre-existing roads, railway tracks or other methods of transportation that can be used to transport extracted resources from point of extraction to shipping ports.[301] Ports themselves are often inadequate or unable to handle large capacities. This, in turn, means that investors looking to invest in certain industries not only need to invest in the target resources or projects,

---

[297]   "The ICSID Caseload – Statistics", Issue 2021-1, International Centre for Settlement of Investment Disputes, available at: https://icsid.worldbank.org/sites/default/files/publications/The%20ICSID%20Caseload%20Statistics%20%282021-1%20Edition%29%20ENG.pdf.

[298]   Ibid.

[299]   "ICC Dispute Resolution Statistics: 2020", available at: https://iccwbo.org/publication/icc-dispute-resolution-statistics-2020/.

[300]   "African Economic Outlook 2018", African Development Bank Group, ch. 3, available at: https://www.afdb.org/fileadmin/uploads/afdb/Documents/Publications/2018AEO/African_Economic_Outlook_2018_-_EN_Chapter3.pdf.

[301]   Barclay Ballard, "Bridging Africa's infrastructure gap", World Finance, 20 April 2018, available at: https://www.worldfinance.com/infrastructure-investment/project-finance/bridging-africas-infrastructure-gap.

but also in at least minimal infrastructure to allow transportation of those resources. This is exactly the case with the Simandou project in Guinea. The success of that project required investors to invest in the development of a port and 650 kilometres of railway lines needed for transportation to Guinea's coast which, has been estimated as costing around USD 23 billion.[302] The same sort of restraints have also hindered the Falémé project in Senegal, another iron mining project. While Senegal's capital, Dakar, does have well-developed ports and highway infrastructure, the mine itself is located extremely far from the city, which has complicated a project that would otherwise be viewed as a tremendous opportunity for profit.[303]

Conditions are changing rapidly in many African countries, but, unfortunately, changes are not always positive. Even seemingly stable countries have fallen to more corrupt governance, or now face internal conflict, or have been hit by drought and other impacts of climate change, setting them back and halting growth. This makes for an uncertain future, and an uncertain future is something that makes investors think twice about putting money into Africa. Not all countries face these particular types of problems; however, there is an unfortunate cloud that hangs over the continent as a whole because of the possible severity of some of these issues in certain countries.

These issues make investing in Africa appear quite the challenge. There are, however, also some growing bright spots, as will be explained in detail over the following pages. In fact, despite these hurdles, there is a sound argument to be made that now is the best ever time to invest in the continent. The enactment of AfCFTA only increases the likelihood of this.

2. THE NEED FOR AFRICA-TO-AFRICA INVESTMENT

Regardless of the importance of FDI in ensuring economic growth in Africa, intra-African investment is of even greater importance. Compared to other regions, Africa's intra-continent investment is lagging

---

[302] Saliou Samb, "Rio Tinto fails to clinch sale of Guinea iron ore project", Reuters, 29 October 2018, available at: https://www.reuters.com/article/us-rio-tinto-deals-chinalco-simandou/rio-tinto-fails-to-clinch-sale-of-guinea-iron-ore-project-idUSKCN1N3010.

[303] Frédéric Maury and Joël Té-Léssia Assoko, "Senegal: le gisement de Falémé, cadeau ou fardeau?", Jeune Afrique, 23 September 2013, available at: https://www.jeuneafrique.com/16514/economie/s-n-gal-le-gisement-de-fal-m-cadeau-ou-fardeau/.

significantly behind. Intra-African exports made up only 18% of the continent's total exports in 2016, compared to 59% intra-Asia exports and 69% intra-Europe exports.[304] In 2015, only 16% of capital investment in Africa came from African countries.[305] To ensure long-term sustainable growth, Africans must invest in Africa.[306]

African countries have recognised the need to diversify their investment opportunities, and have begun to turn to emerging and other developing economies to increase trade and investment in the continent. Over the past decade, trade with the United States has shrunk by more than 60%, and there has also been a decline in trade with the EU, down 5% since 2006.[307] At the same time, trade with India, Indonesia and Russia has doubled,[308] and trade with China surged in 2021 to a new record of USD 254 billion, an impressive USD 67 billion increase from the 2020 total of USD 187 billion.[309] China is now Africa's biggest trading partner, and it has made approximately USD 2 trillion in investments on the continent since 2005.[310] Investment into the continent continues to be concentrated largely in Europe, with 45% of capital investments in Africa coming from Western Europe in 2015. However, the number of FDI projects being carried out by China, India and other Asian markets (including Japan and Indonesia, among others) grew by 11% that same year.[311] These numbers demonstrate that African governments' efforts to amend investment policies

---

[304] Mariama Sow, "Figures of the week: Africa's intra- and extra-regional trade", Brookings Institution, 29 March 2018, available at: https://www.brookings.edu/blog/africa-in-focus/2018/03/29/figures-of-the-week-africas-intra-and-extra-regional-trade/.

[305] "The Africa Investment Report 2016", FDI Intelligence, available at: https://www.camara.es/sites/default/files/publicaciones/the-africa-investment-report-2016.pdf.

[306] Vera Songwe, "Intra-African trade: A path to economic diversification and inclusion", Brookings Institution, Foresight Africa, 11 January 2019, available at: https://www.brookings.edu/research/intra-african-trade-a-path-to-economic-diversification-and-inclusion/.

[307] Mariama Sow, "Figures of the week: Africa's intra-and extra-regional trade", Brookings Institution, 29 March 2018, available at: https://www.brookings.edu/blog/africa-in-focus/2018/03/29/figures-of-the-week-africas-intra-and-extra-regional-trade/.

[308] Ibid.

[309] Eric Olander, "China-Africa Trade in 2021 Amounted to $254 Billion, Breaking an All-Time Record", The China Africa Project, 19 January 2022, available at: https://chinaafricaproject.com/2022/01/19/china-africa-trade-in-2021-amounted-to-254-billion-breaking-an-all-time-record/.

[310] Elliot Smith, "The US-China trade rivalry is underway in Africa, and Washington is playing catch-up", CNBC, 9 October 2019, available at: https://www.cnbc.com/2019/10/09/the-us-china-trade-rivalry-is-underway-in-africa.html.

[311] "The Africa Investment Report 2016", FDI Intelligence, available at: https://www.camara.es/sites/default/files/publicaciones/the-africa-investment-report-2016.pdf.

and enter into a growing number of bilateral trade agreements have been successful in attracting a wider pool of investors.

All of this considered, the number of Africa-to-Africa investments remains almost alarmingly low, and continues to keep the continent from reaching its full potential. African governments must put in place policies that acknowledge the huge potential of intra-continental investment and trade, while demonstrating to African investors the same improvements in rule of law, contractual protections and financial stability that need to be proven to gain the attention of Western investors.

Moreover, to be truly successful, Africa must find a way to keep talent at home, and to capitalise on the vast human capital available continent-wide. The collective population of all 54 African countries is one of the largest regional populations in the world (second only to Asia), and has a maturing and creative youth population that is increasingly eager to make big changes at home. Every year, 12 million young people join the labour market across the continent,[312] and the median age in Africa is only 19.7 years old.[313] Moreover, the world's largest diaspora is demonstrating a growing interest in returning home, in order to utilise the skills they have acquired abroad to develop the countries they feel the most affinity for. One key to a bright future will be African nations' ability to harness this eagerness and take advantage of the intimate familiarity that homegrown talent has with the most important issues holding Africa back.

By creating a more open continental trade bloc, with the AfCFTA, African countries will be able to tap into the natural resources, human capital and knowledge of all of the countries across the continent, allowing for quicker and more robust development. The continental policies being put in place by African countries should encourage job creation across borders, allowing for a greater trickle-down impact, which will, in turn, create the potential for even greater investment as incomes grow. A growing middle class, more educated and innovative than ever before, must be encouraged by sound financial and economic policies to invest on the continent. African businesses must be shown that their investments will be valued and protected as much as, if not more than, outside investments, and that governments are working towards improving the infrastructure

---

[312] "African Economic Outlook 2018", African Development Bank, available at: https://www.afdb.org/fileadmin/uploads/afdb/Documents/Publications/African_Economic_Outlook_2018_-_EN.pdf.

[313] "Population of Africa (2022)", Worldometer, available at: https://www.worldometers.info/world-population/africa-population/.

to allow an easier flow of goods and services from one country to another. One of the primary focuses of the AfCFTA is in providing African investors with such reassurance.

3. RECOGNITION THAT NOT ALL FOREIGN INVESTMENT IS CREATED EQUAL

A surge in recent investment from China highlights the (sometimes dire) consequences of relying solely on foreign investment. As recently as September 2018, China pledged a USD 60 billion package of financial support to Africa, as part of its Belt and Road Initiative (BRI), which is to come from a combination of aid and loans to the continent.[314] This investment will primarily be focused on developing infrastructure. At the same time, China also announced that it would be exempting a portion of the continent's debt.[315] China is actively trying to demonstrate its dedication to the continent. As part of the BRI, China has even opened the China–Africa Joint Arbitration Centre (CAJAC), which will be focused solely on resolving disputes between Chinese and African parties.[316] This court will sit in both Shanghai and Johannesburg. This book will further analyse this new arbitration option in Chapter 5.

There are several acknowledged benefits of China's BRI efforts on the continent.[317] The pledged investment will most certainly bring greater connectivity across the continent, providing the exact thing that Africa needs most: improved infrastructure. This investment will lay the foundation for greater development of other industries, particularly the extractive sectors. For many African nations, China's investment offer is the only offer of financing that has been provided from anywhere in the world. Such investment has the potential to finally link smaller or more

---

[314] This includes USD 20 billion in credit lines, USD 15 billion in grants, interest-free loans and concessional loans, and USD 10 billion in investment financing. See Mariama Sow, "Figures of the Week: Chinese Investment in Africa", Brookings Institution, 6 September 2018, available at: https://www.brookings.edu/blog/africa-in-focus/2018/09/06/figures-of-the-week-chinese-investment-in-africa/.

[315] Prof. Dr Mohamed S Abdel Wahab, "ICSID's Relevance for Africa: A Symbiotic Bond Beyond Time", (2019) 34(2) ICSID Review, pp. 519–541, available at doi:10.1093/icsidreview/siz022.

[316] Ibid.

[317] Paul Nantulya, "Implications for Africa from China's One Belt One Road Strategy", Africa Center for Strategic Studies, 22 March 2019, accessible at: https://africacenter.org/spotlight/implications-for-africa-china-one-belt-one-road-strategy/.

isolated countries to the rest of the continent, which should increase intra-African trade.

For every potential benefit, however, there is a downside. China's investment and continuously growing presence on the continent has increasingly been criticised by economists who believe that they are "debt traps", allowing China to exert control over political decisions on the continent.[318] This is something that is also increasingly alarming other investing countries and development aid donors, particularly Western European countries and the United States, who have expressed concerns over China's willingness to ignore human rights violations, and to avoid abiding by local laws that are in place to protect local workers and economies.

The nature of the investments that China is pouring into the continent is also questionable. In the contractual agreements that result from BRI investment, China holds the power. The contractual provisions are dictated by Chinese law and Chinese terms, which creates an imbalance of power between the Chinese party and the African party. China also tends to rush agreements through without taking into consideration environmental, labour or human rights laws. This results in hastily done work that is more likely to cause damage to the host nation. As described in the next paragraph, China's overlooking of environmental and other local laws has led to catastrophic consequences in many parts of the continent. Other possible issues with BRI investments include corrupt political dealings that lead to corrupt agreements, leaving countries locked into terms that are contrary to their interests, and an overall disregard for quality. Moreover, the terms of agreements with the Chinese government may result in expropriations by the Chinese, in exchange for debt cancellation. African countries should avoid being brought into situations such as that faced by Sri Lanka, where China cancelled USD 8 billion of debt in exchange for China taking control of Sri Lanka's port.[319]

The examples that highlight the issues with Chinese investment in Africa are growing. With respect to environmental damage, there are several significant cases to highlight. In Kenya and Uganda, the development of a railway financed by China cut through national reserves, raising concerns

---

[318]   Mark Klaver and Michael Trebilcock, "Chinese Investment in Africa: Strengthening the balance sheet", gLAWcal, 6 October 2017, available at: http://www.glawcal.org.uk/glawcal-comments/pros-and-cons-of-chinese-investments-in-africa.

[319]   See: Pearl Risberg, "The Give-and-Take of BRI in Africa", New Perspectives in Foreign Policy, Issue 17, 8 April 2019, available at: https://www.csis.org/give-and-take-bri-africa.

for biodiversity in the area.[320] The Chinese-funded Grand Inga Dam in Congo directly threatens biodiversity, and also threatens to cut the water supply for downstream communities.[321] In Cameroon, several projects involving road construction, mining and logging have completely ignored environmental impacts, and have caused havoc in local communities.[322]

Recently, several countries have taken a stand against Chinese investment, including Sierra Leone, Tanzania and Kenya. The Sierra Leone government cancelled plans to build a USD 318 million airport outside of Freetown, citing a lack of transparency in the terms of the agreement.[323] The government stated that it was concerned by an unsustainable level of debt, and had a fear of being pushed into exploitative deals when unable to repay the debt. In 2019, the Tanzanian government suspended a USD 10 billion port project with China, citing "exploitative and awkward" financial terms. That agreement had included a guarantee of 33 years and a lease of 99 years, with no ability to question whoever invested in the port during that time.[324] Neighbouring Kenya also had to stop a USD 2 billion coal plant deal that same year, with the Kenyan courts ordering that the project be halted as a result of inadequate environmental assessments.[325] Democratic African governments appear to be sending China notice that they will not be taken advantage of. That said, the continent still has a number of long-term authoritarian governments who have demonstrated that they will not be so quick to turn away Chinese money.

Investment from China is only one example of how African countries are being constrained by their reliance on foreign investment, loans,

[320] Edith Honan, "Chinese-built railway to cut through national park in Kenya's capital", Reuters, 31 July 2015, available at: https://www.reuters.com/article/kenya-railway-wildlife/chinese-built-railway-to-cut-through-national-park-in-kenyas-capital-idUSL1N10B0OQ20150731.

[321] Jeroen Warner, "The Fantasy of the Grand Inga Hydroelectric Project on the River Congo", MDPI, 26 February 2019, available at: https://www.mdpi.com/2073-4441/11/3/407.

[322] See Amindeh Blaise Atabong, "Cameroon Town's Residents Say Chinese-Run Quarry Damaging their Homes", Epoch Times, 9 June 2019, available at: https://www.theepochtimes.com/cameroon-town-residents-say-chinese-run-quarry-damaging-their-homes_2943839.html.

[323] BBC News, "Mamamah airport: Sierra Leone cancels China-Funded Project", 10 October 2018, available at: https://www.bbc.com/news/world-africa-45809810.

[324] Sophia Yan, "China's ambition dealt blow ahead of G20 as Tanzania and Kenya projects grind to halt", The Telegraph, 27 June 2019, available at: https://www.telegraph.co.uk/news/2019/06/27/tanzania-suspends-10-billion-port-project-new-blow-chinas-belt/.

[325] BBC News, "Kenya halts Lamu coal power project at World Heritage Site", 26 June 2019, available at: https://www.bbc.com/news/world-africa-48771519.

aid and knowledge. Only through increased intra-African trade and investment can African countries truly free themselves from the potential pitfalls involved in accepting outside money regardless of the source. By encouraging internal investment, development of human capital, and sustainable economic practices within the continent, by way of the AfCFTA, African countries will be able to make more profound leaps in their quest for overall economic development.

4. THE AFRICAN CONTINENTAL FREE TRADE AREA

The AfCFTA is meant to be a response to most of the concerns mentioned above. As currently enacted, the Agreement is intended to act as a framework within which further negotiation is to take place. In fact, it comprises three primary frameworks: (i) an overarching Establishment of the African Continental Free Trade Area; (ii) a Protocol on Trade in Goods; and (iii) a Protocol on Trade in Services.[326] Within these frameworks, several topics, including competition, investment and intellectual property, need to be further defined and regulated. Additionally, other matters, such as the movement of people, and dispute settlement (to be discussed at length in the next chapter), will need to be discussed and agreed upon. On these two points, the Protocol to the Treaty Establishing the African Economic Community relating to the Free Movement of Persons, Right of Residence and Right of Establishment, and the Protocol on the Rules and Procedures on the Settlement of Disputes were agreed at the time the AfCFTA was established.

4.1. ESTABLISHMENT OF THE AfCFTA

The first framework, the Establishment of the AfCFTA, covers the following topics: definitions, establishment, objectives, principles and scope, administration and organisation, transparency, continental preferences,

---

[326] Faizel Ismail, "The African Continental Free Trade Area (AfCFTA) and Developmental Regionalism: A Handbook", TIPS (2021), available at: https://www.tips.org.za/research-archive/books/item/4121-the-african-continental-free-trade-area-afcfta-and-developmental-regionalism-a-handbook.

dispute settlement, and final provisions.[327] The key objectives of the Agreement are set forth in Articles 3 and 4. Article 3 sets forth the general objectives of the agreement, which include:

- Creation of a single market for goods, services, facilitated by movement of persons in order to deepen the economic integration of the African continent and in accordance with the Pan African vision of "an integrated, prosperous and peaceful Africa" enshrined in Agenda 2063.
- Creation of a liberalised market for goods and services through successive rounds of negotiations.
- Contribution to the movement of capital and natural persons, and facilitation of investments building on the initiatives and developments in the State Parties and RECs.
- Laying the foundation for the establishment of a Continental Customs Union at a later stage.
- Promoting and attaining sustainable and inclusive socio-economic development, gender equality and structural transformation of the State Parties.
- Enhancing the competitiveness of the economies of State Parties within the continent and the global market.
- Promoting industrial development through diversification and regional value chain development, agricultural development and food security.
- Resolving the challenges of multiple and overlapping memberships and expediting the regional and continental integration processes.[328]

Article 4 then further specifies these primary objectives by providing six specific objectives:

- Progressive elimination of tariffs and non-tariff barriers to trade in goods.
- Progressive liberalisation of trade in services.
- Cooperation in all trade-related areas, including investment, intellectual property rights and competition policy.
- Cooperation on customs matters and the implementation of trade facilitation measures.

---

[327] Agreement Establishing the African Continental Free Trade Area, 21 March 2018 (entered into force 30 May 2019), available at: https://au.int/sites/default/files/treaties/36437-treaty-consolidated_text_on_cfta_-_en.pdf.
[328] Ibid., Art. 3.

- Establishment of a mechanism for the settlement of disputes concerning the rights and obligations of members.
- Establishment and maintenance of an institutional framework for the implementation and administration of the AfCFTA.[329]

Article 5 highlights the 12 "core principles" of the Agreement, some of which appear to contradict one another. The 12 core principles include: an agreement driven by Member States of the African Union; RECs as building blocks for the AfCFTA; variable geometry; flexibility and special and differential treatment; transparency and disclosure of information; preservation of the acquis; MFN treatment; NT; reciprocity; substantial liberalisations; consensus in decision-making; and best practices in RECs, in the State Parties and International Conventions binding the African Union.[330]

Some of these principles, such as reciprocity and MFN, would appear to be in contradiction to one another, and must be further defined by the African Union as it moves forward. Under the most-favoured nation principle, countries are not able to discriminate between their trading partners.[331] Reciprocity provides for mutual concessions to be given between parties. In order for there to be no conflict between these two principles, none of the AfCFTA Member States would be able to have agreements with one another, outside the continent or within, that would contradict the terms of AfCFTA. The MFN principle would require Member States of AfCFTA to provide all countries in the continent (that are party to AfCFTA) with equal trading treatment. This would not be possible if one of the Member States had an agreement – for example, an existing BIT – which required differentiated treatment from that required under AfCFTA. This is just one example of potential conflicting terms under the Agreement that must be worked out. That said, if the intention is to remove the overlapping RECs, these terms could, in fact, accomplish that objective. Regardless, the continent must define its intentions more clearly.

---

[329] Ibid., Art. 4.
[330] Ibid., Art. 5.
[331] "Principles of the trading system", World Trade Organization, available at: https://www.wto.org/english/thewto_e/whatis_e/tif_e/fact2_e.htm. See also Pia Accounci, "Most Favoured Nation Treatment", in Peter Muchlinski, Frederico Ortino and Christopher Schreur (eds.), The Oxford Handbook of International Investment Law, Oxford: OUP, 2008, pp. 363–401.

As demonstrated by these principles, existing regional blocs, previously discussed at length in Chapter 3, will play a key role in shaping the details of the AfCFTA, and will be the building blocks from which the entire Agreement is shaped. This recognises that these blocs have taken huge steps in the right direction, towards improving trade and relationships between African nations, but that, at the same time, the complex web of overlapping regulations, discussed at length throughout this book, must be disentangled. The key to the success of the AfCFTA will be the ability of the African Union to scale up the positive aspects of Africa's RECs, while at the same time harmonising and consolidating the principal features of their governing documents. In so doing, the Union will also have to consider the WTO obligations that African nations are bound by, including the MFN and NT obligations contained therein, ensuring that the final details of the AfCFTA are in line with the governing documents of the WTO.

From an African investor's perspective (and arguably from a foreign investor's perspective as well), there are several key provisions built into the first framework on the Establishment of the AfCFTA which have the potential to be highly favourable. First, the Agreement will lead to the removal of tariff restrictions on intra-African trade.[332] Additionally, the harmonisation introduced by the implementation of the AfCFTA will allow for industrial production to be situated in strategically advantageous countries, and for people and goods to move more freely across borders, which will, in turn, facilitate business. Economists have indicated that freer trade within Africa will lead to increased competition, innovation and prosperity for Africa's people in the long run.[333] At the same time, businesses will be able to benefit from economies of scale and more beneficial value chains.[334] All of these potential benefits have been contemplated, and built into the overarching framework of the Establishment of the AfCFTA.

---

[332] "A Business Guide to the African Continental Free Trade Area Agreement", International Trade Centre, available at: https://cpccaf.org/XCMD.RE9fU2hPQko8MjU+MDAwM DAtMC0wMjgtMDAwMDAwMDAzODA2Mw==.html.

[333] Lemessa Bayissa Gobena, "Power, justice, and trust: A moderated mediation analysis of tax compliance among Ethiopian business owners", (2016) 52 Journal of Economic Psychology, pp. 24–37, available at: sciencedirect.com/science/article/abs/pii/ S0167487015001397.

[334] "A Business Guide to the African Continental Free Trade Area Agreement", International Trade Centre, available at: https://cpccaf.org/XCMD.RE9fU2hPQko8Mj U+MDAwMDAtMC0wMjgtMDAwMDAwMDAzODA2Mw==.html.

4.2.   PROTOCOL ON TRADE IN GOODS

The second framework introduced with the enactment of AfCFTA is the Protocol on Trade in Goods. This Protocol seeks to boost intra-African trade in goods through seven principal objectives, set forth in Article 2:

- Progressive elimination of tariffs.
- Progressive elimination of non-tariff barriers.
- Enhanced efficiency of customs procedures, trade facilitation and transit.
- Enhanced cooperation in the areas of technical barriers to trade and sanitary and phytosanitary measures.
- Development and promotion of regional and continental value chains.
- Enhanced socioeconomic development, diversification and industrialisation across Africa.[335]

The overarching goal of this entire Protocol is to double intra-African trade of goods by 2022, which the African Union intends to do by using a continental customs union.[336] Recent projections demonstrate that, simply by removing tariffs on goods, intra-African trade will increase by somewhere between 15% (USD 50 billion) and 25% (USD 70 billion) by 2040.[337]

Article 4 of the Protocol states that State Parties must apply most-favoured nation treatment, but adds that nothing will preclude them from concluding or maintaining preferential trade arrangements with third parties, so long as they do not impede the objectives of the Protocol.[338] In other words, if existing or future third-party agreements include certain treatment that would be deemed more favourable than that provided under the AfCFTA, African State Parties will have to provide other State Parties with those favourable terms.

---

[335]   Agreement Establishing the African Continental Free Trade Area, Protocol on Trade in Goods, Art. 2, available at: https://au.int/sites/default/files/treaties/36437-treaty-consolidated_text_on_cfta_-_en.pdf.

[336]   "A Business Guide to the African Continental Free Trade Area Agreement", International Trade Centre, available at: https://cpccaf.org/XCMD.RE9fU2hPQko8MjU+MDAwM DAtMC0wMjgtMDAwMDAwMDAzODA2Mw==.html.

[337]   Vera Songwe, "Intra-African Trade: A path to economic diversification and inclusion", Brookings Institution, 11 January 2019, available at: https://www.brookings.edu/research/intra-african-trade-a-path-to-economic-diversification-and-inclusion/.

[338]   Agreement Establishing the African Continental Free Trade Area, Protocol on Trade in Goods, Art. 4.

National treatment is covered in Article 5, which states that:

> [a] State Party shall accord to products imported from other State Parties treatment no less favourable than that accorded to like domestic products of national origin, after the imported products have been cleared by customs. This treatment covers all measures affecting the sale and conditions for sale of such products in accordance with Article III of GATT 1994.[339]

This Article directly demonstrates the AfCFTA's intent to harmonise the terms contained therein with WTO obligations that already exist for most, if not all, of the State Parties.

Arguably one of the most important features of the AfCFTA is Article 6 of the Protocol, which allows for special and differential treatment to be afforded to certain State Parties that have differing levels of economic development.[340] This will allow for special treatment to be given to struggling economies, as agreed by the State Parties. This clause is of great significance given the context of the African continent and the varying levels of economic development across State Parties. If applied equitably and strategically, this provision could be key in promoting sweeping economic development across the continent, not just development concentrated in certain countries.[341]

Part III of the Protocol touches directly on the liberalisation of trade among State Parties. This Part specifies that State Parties are to "progressively eliminate import duties or charges having equivalent effect on goods originating from the territory of any other State Party".[342] Additionally, it states that State Parties should not impose quantitative restrictions on imports from, or exports to, other State Parties.[343] Part III also limits export duties to be paid,[344] requires the elimination of non-tariff barriers,[345] and states that:

> [g]oods shall be eligible for preferential treatment under this Protocol, if they are originating in any of the State Parties in accordance with the criteria and conditions set out in Annex 2 on Rules of Origin, and in accordance with the Appendix to be developed on General and Product Specific Rules.[346]

---

[339] Ibid., Art. 5.
[340] Ibid., Art. 6.
[341] Faizel Ismail, "The African Continental Free Trade Area (AfCFTA) and Developmental Regionalism: A Handbook", TIPS (2021), ch. 3, p. 26.
[342] Agreement Establishing the African Continental Free Trade Area, Protocol on Trade in Goods, Art. 7.
[343] Ibid., Art. 8.
[344] Ibid., Art. 10.
[345] Ibid., Art. 12.
[346] Ibid., Art. 13.

Several key provisions of this Part of the Protocol remain to be ironed out. Chief among these are the tariff concessions that will be provided under the Protocol. Certain issues regarding tariffs under the AfCFTA have been hotly debated among Member States, and have yet to be agreed. These issues include, among others, the proportion of tariff lines to be designated as sensitive or excluded; criteria for designating products as sensitive or excluded; the anti-concentration clause; what role customs unions will play; and, perhaps most importantly, what the actual tariff levels will be.[347]

The remaining provisions of the Protocol set forth the cooperation and trade facilitation that State Parties must commit to in order for the Agreement to be implemented successfully;[348] provide for certain trade remedies such as anti-dumping, and for safeguards;[349] establish certain product standards;[350] and provide for the establishment of certain complementary policies to protect special economic arrangements and infant industries, and to assure transparency under the Agreement.[351] Finally, Part VIII of the Protocol sets forth certain exceptions that are to be applied.

It is important to note that there are three relevant Annexes to the Protocol, which cover the following topics: (i) Customs Cooperation and Mutual Administrative Assistance;[352] (ii) Trade Facilitation;[353] and (iii) Transit.[354]

---

[347] "A Business Guide to the African Continental Free Trade Area Agreement", International Trade Centre, available at: https://cpccaf.org/XCMD.RE9fU2hPQko8Mj U+MDAwMDAtMC0wMjgtMDAwMDAwMDAzODA2Mw==.html.

[348] Agreement Establishing the African Continental Free Trade Area, Protocol on Trade in Goods, Part IV.

[349] Ibid., Part V.

[350] Ibid., Part VI.

[351] Ibid., Part VII.

[352] Annex 3 to the Protocol on Trade in Goods. Annex 3 (Customs Cooperation and Mutual Administrative Assistance) provides a framework for simplification and harmonisation of customs laws and procedures at the continental level, using international standards derived from the World Customs Organization (WCO) and WTO.

[353] Annex 4 to the Protocol on Trade in Goods. The substantive provisions of Annex 4 (Trade Facilitation) are clearly based on the text of the WTO Trade Facilitation Agreement. For example, Art. 1 of the TFA requires that, "[e]ach Member shall promptly publish the following information in a non-discriminatory and easily accessible manner in order to enable governments, traders, and other interested parties to become acquainted with them", followed by a list of information required to be published, including import, export and transit procedures; applied rates of duties

4.3. PROTOCOL ON TRADE IN SERVICES

The WTO, under the GATS, has defined services as being four-pronged, depending on the territorial presence of the supplier and the consumer at the time of the transaction.[355] The GATS itself covers services supplied: (a) from the territory of one Member into the territory of any other Member (Mode 1 – Cross border trade); (b) in the territory of one Member to the service consumer of any other Member (Mode 2 – Consumption abroad); (c) by a service supplier of one Member, through commercial presence in the territory of any other Member (Mode 3 – Commercial presence); and (d) by a service supplier of one Member, through the presence of natural persons of a Member in the territory of any other Member (Mode 4 – Presence of natural persons).[356] Services account for at least 50% of GDP in most African nations, and continue to grow at a more accelerated rate than other industries on the continent.[357] At the same time, intra-African trade of services has, historically, been so low that it could be deemed insignificant.[358] Services, then, and the goal of substantially increasing intra-African trade in services, is a key component of the AfCFTA, as indicated by the inclusion of the third framework to the Agreement: the Protocol on Trade in Services.

---

and taxes; import, export or transit restrictions or prohibitions, etc. In the AfCFTA Annex, Art. 4, para. 1 of Annex 4 (Publication) provides that, "[e]ach State Party shall to the extent possible promptly publish on the internet the following information in a non-discriminatory and easily accessible manner in order to enable governments, traders and other interested State Parties to become acquainted with them", followed by a list that is substantially the same as that provided in Art. 1 of the TFA.

[354] Annex 8 to Protocol on Goods. Annex 8 on Transit is based on the Transports Internationaux Routiers (TIR) Convention (1975). For example, definitions of the term "container" in both Annex 8 and in the TIR Convention are similar, though not identical. This also applies for definitions of the terms "Customs Office of destination", "Customs Office of departure", "Customs Office of entry", "Customs transit", etc. Instead of the TIR Carnet provided in the TIR Convention as a requirement for the provisions to cover transport of goods in transit, the Annex makes provision for the African Union Transit Document.

[355] "Basic Purpose and Concepts: 1.3 Definition of Services Trade and Modes of Supply", World Trade Organization, available at: https://www.wto.org/english/tratop_e/serv_e/cbt_course_e/c1s3p1_e.htm.

[356] Ibid.

[357] "A Business Guide to the African Continental Free Trade Area Agreement", International Trade Centre, available at: https://cpccaf.org/XCMD.RE9fU2hPQko8MjU+MDAwM DAtMC0wMjgtMDAwMDAwMDAzODA2Mw==.html.

[358] Ibid.

The overall objectives of the Protocol on Trade in Services, as stipulated in Article 3 thereof, include the ability of Africa to:

- Enhance competitiveness of services through economies of scale, reduced business costs, enhanced continental market access, and an improved allocation of resources including the development of trade-related infrastructure.
- Promote sustainable development in accordance with the Sustainable Development Goals (SDGs).
- Foster domestic and foreign investment.
- Accelerate efforts on industrial development, to promote the development of regional value chains.
- Progressively liberalise trade in services across the African continent, on the basis of equity, balance and mutual benefit, by eliminating barriers to trade in services.
- Ensure consistency and complementarity between liberalisation of trade in services and the various Annexes in specific services sectors.
- Pursue services trade liberalisation in line with Article V of the GATS by expanding the depth and scope of liberalisation, and increasing, improving and developing the export of services, while fully preserving the right to regulate and to introduce new regulations.
- Promote and enhance common understanding and cooperation in trade in services amongst State Parties, in order to improve the capacity, efficiency and competitiveness of their services markets.
- Promote research and technological advancement in the field of services, to accelerate economic and social development.[359]

Part IV of this Protocol sets forth the general obligations and disciplines. Article 4, as with the Protocol on the Trade in Goods, provides for most-favoured nation treatment, stating that:

> [w]ith respect to any measure covered by this Protocol, each State Party shall, upon entry into force, accord immediately and unconditionally to services and service suppliers of any other State Party treatment no less favourable than that it accords to like services and service suppliers of any Third Party.[360]

---

[359] Agreement Establishing the African Continental Free Trade Area (AfCFTA), 21 March 2018 (entered into force 30 May 2019), Protocol on Trade in Services, Art. 3.
[360] Ibid., Art. 4.

Again, if State Parties have more favourable terms in third-party agreements, they must, under this Protocol, apply such terms to other State Parties.

Article 5 lays forth a number of steps that State Parties must undertake in order to guarantee transparency in relation to services,[361] and Article 6 provides for protection of confidential information.[362] Article 7, as with the equivalent provision on goods, provides for special and differential treatment to be provided to parties, as necessary to "ensure increased and beneficial participation in trade in services by all parties".[363] State Parties are required to issue domestic regulations to put themselves in compliance with the terms of this Protocol, as per Articles 9 and 10.

Article 10 provides for the concept of mutual recognition, which will be essential in ensuring that Africa capitalises on one of its most underutilised greatest potential resources: human capital. This Article states, in part, that:

> [f]or the purposes of the fulfilment, in whole or in part, of its standards or criteria for the authorisation, licensing or certification of services suppliers, and subject to the requirements of paragraph 3 of this Article, a State Party may recognise the education or experience obtained, requirements met, or licenses or certifications granted in another State Party. Such recognition, which may be achieved through harmonisation or otherwise, may be based upon an agreement or arrangement with the State Party concerned or may be accorded autonomously.[364]

This, along with the other terms of this Article, will likely be proven one of the key provisions for meeting Africa's ambitious goals with regard to expansion of trade in services.

Article 11 of the Protocol seeks to limit monopolies and exclusive service suppliers,[365] and Article 12 seeks to end or limit anticompetitive business practices.[366] In an effort to facilitate the cross-border payment and transfer of money, Article 13 of the Protocol provides that, "[e]xcept under the circumstances envisaged in Article 14 of this Protocol, a State Party shall not apply restrictions on international transfers and payments for current transactions relating to its specific commitments".[367] Article 14

---

361 Ibid., Art. 5.
362 Ibid., Art. 7.
363 Ibid.
364 Ibid., Art. 10.
365 Ibid., Art. 11.
366 Ibid., Art. 12.
367 Ibid., Art. 13.

then adds to the protection of payments, setting out certain "restrictions to safeguard the balance of payments".[368]

Following the provision of certain exceptions (in Articles 15, 16 and 17), Part V of the Protocol lays the foundation for "progressive liberalisation", indicating that State Parties are to further negotiate the terms of liberalisation, a central feature of the Protocol. Additionally, Part V provides that services and service suppliers of other State Parties shall be given no less favourable treatment than nationals of any other State Parties with regard to market access.[369] Article 20 then also provides for NT in relation to services.[370]

The final Articles of the Protocol provide for the establishment of certain schedules of specific commitments, and the modification of schedules of specific commitments (Articles 22 and 23, respectively). Moreover, certain Articles lay the grounds for certain "institutional provisions", including terms for consultation and dispute settlement, as well as implementation, monitoring and evaluation, and technical assistance, capacity-building and cooperation.[371]

These foundational Protocols – the Establishment of the African Continental Free Trade Area, the Protocol on Trade in Goods, and the Protocol on Trade in Services – set forth the groundwork of the AfCFTA. As the continent moves towards implementing the Agreement, the details will become more important. African nations must join together to iron out the provisions of the overall Agreement, starting with a focus on some of the key topics. This book will now turn to one of the most pressing of those topics: dispute settlement. The remaining chapters will provide an overview of the current landscape for dispute settlement on the continent, and will assert that Africa must establish its own unique form of dispute settlement as it witnesses the AfCFTA taking effect.

---

[368]   Ibid., Art. 14.
[369]   Ibid., Art. 19.
[370]   Ibid., Art. 20.
[371]   Ibid., Arts. 25, 26 and 27.

CHAPTER 5

EXISTING DISPUTE SETTLEMENT FORUMS

Each type of law previously discussed in Chapter 2 encapsulates a specific type of dispute settlement forum that is to be used in the event that parties to an agreement breach, or are otherwise unable to abide by, their contractual obligations under investment agreements. The AfCFTA, on the other hand, is notably missing a final provision on dispute settlement. As will be further detailed in the following chapters of this book, the Agreement does include a Protocol on the Rules and Procedures on the Settlement of Disputes (the "Protocol"), which closely reflects the current dispute settlement provisions of the WTO.[372]

This Protocol provides for the establishment of a Dispute Settlement Body (DSB) that will have the power to establish Dispute Settlement Panels and an Appellate Body.[373] At the same time, the Protocol provides that the parties may, by mutual agreement, refer disputes to arbitration, bypassing the DSB. However, the Protocol does not specify the details of either the DSB or the arbitration option, including where, and under what rules, disputes will be settled using either of these mechanisms. The African Union has made clear that the Protocol is to be further developed by Member States, now that the Agreement has been enacted. This leaves several questions open, but also presents an opportunity for Africa to

---

[372] Feleke Habtamu Zeleke, "African Continental Free Trade Area (AfCFTA): A Corner Stone for Pan-Africanism and Dispute Settlement Mechanisms" Addis Ababa University, School of Law, Ethiopia, available at: https://www.academia.edu/84632188/African_Continental_Free_Trade_Area_AfCFTA_A_Corner_Stone_for_Pan_Africanism_and_Dispute_Settlement_Mechanisms.

[373] These bodies are to be composed of experts in both law and international trade, who will be independent from member states' governments. See Olabisi D. Akinkugbe, "Dispute Settlement Under the African Continental Free Trade Area Agreement: A Preliminary Assessment", (2020) 28 (Supplement) African Journal of International and Comparative Law, pp. 138–158, available at: https://ssrn.com/abstract=3403745 or http://dx.doi.org/10.2139/ssrn.3403745.

shape its own future in investment arbitration. To do so, however, the continent must move swiftly to consider what possibilities exist for dispute settlement under the AfCFTA.

Before delving into what AfCFTA should consider, it is important to look at the forums currently used under existing investment law. These will be discussed in this chapter, and the mechanisms used for dispute settlement will be discussed in the next chapter. Generally speaking, the options for dispute settlement forums include domestic courts, regional arbitration centres and international arbitration centres.[374] This chapter will look closely at the positives and negatives of each of these forums, from the perspective of both African nations and foreign investors.

1. DOMESTIC COURTS

When there is no specific law on the books dictating otherwise, local disputes are resolved in local courts. Everyday business in a country, by locals or foreigners, is governed by local law. Every country on the continent then has local domestic courts that will resolve business-related disputes in the same way that they will resolve disputes between citizens. The sizes and capacities of these courts vary dramatically from country to country. So, too, does the knowledge of local judges with regard to business-related matters. In those countries where there is an authoritarian government, the independence of the judiciary is most certainly in question. In other, more established, democracies, there are robust court systems, which are able to have a strong influence over business practices within the country.

One of the key benefits of utilising domestic courts, from the perspective of African nations, is the tremendous understanding of local context that these courts inherently have. As part of the local legal system, domestic courts are inarguably in the best position to understand the political, economic and legal context that underlies investment in the country. They are able to render decisions that take into consideration the legitimate needs of the local population and weigh the need for foreign investment with the rights of local populations. There is also an indisputable affordability and convenience to these courts, in the eyes of African nations and local investors. Costs associated with filing claims in

---

[374] Kwadwo Sarkodie and Joseph Otoo, "The rise and rise of arbitration in Africa", African Law and Business, 5 April 2018, available at: https://www.africanlawbusiness.com/news/8105-the-rise-and-rise-of-arbitration-in-africa.

local courts are nearly always reasonable, and there is no need to send legal teams on lengthy foreign trips to argue cases. As business flourishes on the continent, it is presumed that local courts will also develop their understanding of business-related matters and their repository of business law precedents. In many African jurisdictions, steps have been taken to set up special commercial courts dedicated to adjudicating on business disputes, so as to speed up the process, and to make it more tailored to both foreign and local investors' expectations. According to "Doing Business" data issued by the World Bank:

> in the 20 Sub-Saharan African economies that have introduced commercial courts or sections since 2005 – namely Benin, Burkina Faso, Cameroon, Côte d'Ivoire, Ethiopia, Ghana, Guinea, Guinea–Bissau, Lesotho, Liberia, Malawi, Mauritius, Mozambique, Niger, Rwanda, Senegal, the Seychelles, Sierra Leone, South Africa and Togo – the average time to resolve the standardized case measured by Doing Business was reduced by more than two months. In Côte d'Ivoire, the reduction was more than eight months. In 2011, resolving a commercial dispute in Abidjan took 770 days. In 2013, after the creation of a specialized commercial court, it took only 585 days. Today, it takes 525 days.[375]

Some courts on the continent, such as South Africa's Constitutional Court, are seen as beacons of hope, with their strong, equitable judgments. However, even with all of the above-mentioned benefits for local parties, including African states themselves, the inexperience, lack of capacity and corruption of domestic courts in most African countries cannot be overstated. With few exceptions,[376] African courts have a long history of weak judges, a lack of resources, inexperience in handling complex matters, and, above all, corruption. Complaints abound of slow, lengthy processes that do not result in any clear outcome.[377] Perhaps one of the greatest examples of this is the enforcement of contracts. The World Bank's "Doing Business" report has, year after year, highlighted the length of

---

[375] Doing Business, Subnational Studies, "Enforcing Contracts", available at: https://subnational.doingbusiness.org/en/data/exploretopics/enforcing-contracts/good-practices.

[376] Mauritius, for example, is well known for the strength of its investment courts. See "An overview of judicial review in parts of Africa", Hogan Lovells, July 2017, available at: https://www.hoganlovells.com/en/publications/an-overview-of-judicial-review-in-parts-of-africa.

[377] "Why justice in Africa is slow and unfair", The Economist, 1 June 2017, available at https://www.economist.com/middle-east-and-africa/2017/07/01/why-justice-in-africa-is-slow-and-unfair.

time it takes to enforce contracts as one of sub-Saharan Africa's weakest business features. The time it takes to enforce a contract through courts in sub-Saharan Africa is, in many countries, double that of other regions.[378] This same report has also consistently highlighted weak judicial systems as a key factor that deters business in sub-Saharan Africa. These weak systems are said to deter businesses, due not only to long enforcement times, but also to corrupt processes, poor case management, and high costs for poor-quality results.[379]

The judges holding up some of the above-mentioned processes have been found to delay cases where the parties do not provide bribes. In fact, bribery and corruption have, historically, crippled judicial systems in Africa.[380] In Benin, 90 judges were sentenced to jail for corruption. For similar reasons, judges were sanctioned in Ghana.[381] These examples demonstrate a rare case of a country cracking down on corruption on a grand scale, arresting judges for corruption. For every country where such a crackdown has occurred, there are a handful of other countries where corruption among judges continues to hinder judicial practices.

Inept domestic courts have proven to frustrate even local investors. Foreign investors, in most cases, will outright reject local courts. The lack of capacity previously highlighted is not the only concern of foreign investors. Domestic courts also have a perceived bias towards local parties, and are considered more easily manipulated by local parties, who are savvier with local systems. Most multinational corporations, when negotiating transactions on the continent, will insist that disputes be brought outside of the relevant country; most typically, this will be outside the continent entirely, in neutral international dispute settlement bodies.

Perhaps the greatest concern of foreign investors, even greater than the concerns mentioned above, is that domestic courts are seen as lacking

---

[378] "Doing Business: Region Profile Sub-Saharan Africa", The World Bank, 2020, available at: https://www.doingbusiness.org/content/dam/doingBusiness/media/Profiles/Regional/DB2020/SSA.pdf.

[379] Ibid.

[380] "Why justice in Africa is slow and unfair", The Economist, 1 June 2017, available at https://www.economist.com/middle-east-and-africa/2017/07/01/why-justice-in-africa-is-slow-and-unfair.

[381] Apollinaire Kouton, "Droits-Benin: Des juges condamnés pour corruption à la prison ferme, une leçon pour tout le pays", Inter Press Service News Agency, 8 June 2004, available at: http://ipsnews.net/francais/2004/06/08/droits-benin-des-juges-condamnes-pour-corruption-a-la-prison-ferme-unelecon-pour-tout-le-pays/. Dasmani Laary, "22 Ghanaian judges suspended over corruption scandal", The Africa Report, 10 September 2015, available at: https://www.theafricareport.com/2596/22-ghanaian-judges-suspended-over-corruption-scandal/.

the business knowledge necessary to consider complex investments. As previously discussed, foreign investment in Africa, while growing steadily in recent years, is still a relatively new phenomenon. At the same time, an overwhelming majority of investment disputes have, for decades, been brought to international, or at the very least foreign, forums. This, in turn, means that domestic African courts have little experience (at times, likely none) of handling complex business matters of the nature that may arise as a result of FDI. A local judge who has never heard a case involving transborder transactions or – also likely – has never worked in private business transactions, is unlikely to have the capacity necessary to issue a sound ruling on these types of matters. In Senegal, for instance, where there has been an established commercial court since 2017, several actors and investors have complained about the lack of experience of judges in the court. Most of the judges in the Senegalese court have only minimal experience of, or training for, handling commercial cases, and, as a result, more than 50% of judgments have been overturned on appeal.

Concerns with the state of the rule of law in individual countries only adds to the reluctance of foreign investors to rely on host states' governments to protect their contractual obligations. This is especially true when the state is a party to an agreement. Foreign investors demonstrate this concern by pushing to have stabilisation clauses (including freezing clauses, intangibility clauses, economic equilibrium clauses, allocation of burden clauses and hybrid clauses) included in their agreements.[382] This is further demonstrated by the desire to have full agreements, or at least certain provisions (i.e. dispute settlement), governed by bilateral and international treaties. Demonstrating that domestic courts can handle investment disputes requires demonstrating that the rule of law is protected and supported within the country, which is not an easy thing to do in all cases.

Even considering the concerns against domestic courts, there is a growing argument that countries should stop relying so heavily on international tribunals (to be discussed in the following pages), and should instead turn back to domestic courts. According to a recent study, there are two prominent arguments as to why the world should look more

---

[382] For a broad description of these types of clauses, see Jola Gjuzi, "Stabilization Clauses in International Investment Law: A Sustainable Development Approach", ch. 2, Cham: Springer International Publishing, 2018, available at: https://www.springerprofessional.de/en/meaning-evolution-rationale-sources-and-typology-of-stabilizatio/16314714.

closely at domestic courts: (i) the international system often ignores the fact that courts that offer adequate justice to foreign investors do exist; and (ii) domestic investors are not able to benefit from international arbitration, which creates an inequality in the system between domestic and foreign investors.[383] As will be demonstrated in Chapter 7, certain Western countries, including Australia, the EU and the United States, have all recently expressed a desire to scale back international arbitration, including a move away from ISDS, in an effort to better protect domestic investors. There should be no reason why African nations, particularly those with reputable domestic courts, should not be making the same argument. That said, as will be argued further in the following chapters, the best option for the continent, considering the varying capacities of domestic courts, is a continental tribunal, which combines the respective strengths of a domestic judicial system and the international system.

2. INTERNATIONAL TRIBUNALS

The most-used dispute settlement forum, particularly where non-African investors are party to an agreement, is international investment arbitration. Most bilateral investment agreements between African and non-African countries (as well as intra-Africa agreements) include international arbitration provisions that allow for investment disputes to be brought before an international arbitral tribunal. The international system arose in the 1960s, at the same time that the first BITs were being agreed, culminating in the enactment of the International Centre for Settlement of Investment Disputes Convention, in 1965.[384] International arbitration allows for a Contracting Party to bring a claim against the national of another Contracting Party, which, as previously discussed, does not allow for domestic investors to bring a claim under this system.[385] The purposes of establishing this type of system were threefold, and include: (i) attracting foreign investment, by allowing for a direct means of enforcement of

---

[383]   Gabrielle Kaufmann-Kohler Michele Potestà, "Investor-State Dispute Settlement and National Courts. Current Framework and Reform Options", European Yearbook of International Economic Law, Cham: Springer, 2020.

[384]   Ibid.

[385]   Ibid.

international disputes on the part of international investors; (ii) depoliticising disputes; and (iii) allowing foreign investors an alternative to domestic courts.[386]

The most commonly selected institutions devoted to international investment dispute settlement include the ICC and the ICSID. The UNCITRAL Arbitration Rules are commonly used to govern arbitrations not heard by these two institutions, which both have their own rules and procedures. Other notable international arbitration institutions include the London Court of International Arbitration (LCIA), the International Centre for Dispute Resolution (ICDR), the Hong Kong International Arbitration Centre (HKIAC) and the Singapore International Arbitration Centre (SIAC). The following pages will provide greater detail on the two most-used bodies, and will highlight Africa's relations with each.

2.1. INTERNATIONAL CENTRE FOR SETTLEMENT OF INVESTMENT DISPUTES (ICSID)

The ICSID Convention is a "multilateral treaty formulated by the Executive Directors of the World Bank to further the Bank's objective of promoting international investment".[387] This self-described independent, depoliticised institution allows for dispute settlement through conciliation, arbitration or fact-finding procedures.[388] The minister of justice of Nigeria, at the time that the ICSID Convention was being negotiated, remarked that the aim of the ICSID system was to "strike a balance between the interests of investors and those of developing countries".[389] The ICSID system is intended to ensure that final judgments of the tribunal receive the same treatment as judgments from national courts, and has at its core the intention of providing the full effect as that rendered by a national court and treaty rights to all parties. One hundred and sixty-three states are party to the

---

386   Ibid.
387   Lucy Reed, Jan Paulsson and Nigel Blackaby, "Guide to ICSID Arbitration", Alphen aan den Rijn: Wolters Kluwer Law and Business, 2010. See also "About ICSID", International Centre for Settlement of Investment Disputes, available at: https://icsid. worldbank.org/en/Pages/about/default.aspx.
388   Ibid.
389   Mek Kinnear and Paul Jean Le Cannu, "Concluding Remarks: ICSID and African States Leading International Investment Law Reform", (2019) 34(2) ICSID Review, pp. 542–551, available at: doi:10.1093/icsidreview/siz026.

ICSID Convention, and have accepted its rules of arbitration, which are also widely respected by private investors.[390]

African states were some of the first and strongest supporters of the ICSID system. In fact, out of the 20 instruments of ratification required for the ICSID Convention to enter into force, 15 came from African states.[391] It is also worth mentioning that the first request for arbitration registered before ICSID was against an African state.[392] Since this first case, African countries have accounted for 15% of all ICSID cases, or 115 out of 768 total cases.[393] The ICSID has, increasingly, been used in recent years to resolve disputes involving Africa. In 2020, 10% of all cases brought to the ICSID involved states from sub-Saharan Africa.[394] These cases largely involved some of Africa's most lucrative industries, with 30% of ICSID's cases involving the oil and mining industries, and 20% involving electric power and other energy industries.[395] As demonstrated by these numbers, investors in Africa have demonstrated their appreciation for the ICSID's wealth of experience in handling complex investment matters.

The cases that have been brought to the ICSID Tribunal against African nations have also helped build the experience of the tribunal, allowing it to issue landmark cases on several novel issues.[396] Some examples of

---

[390] The rules for arbitration and mediation were amended on 21 March 2022 to further reduce the time and cost of cases, including mandatory time frames for rendering orders and awards. New expedited arbitration rules are also now available, which would cut case times in half when adopted by parties. These came into effect on 1 July 2022. See https://icsid.worldbank.org/news-and-events/communiques/icsid-administrative-council-approves-amendment-icsid-rules#:~:text=The%20ICSID%20rules%20for%20arbitration,half%20when%20adopted%20by%20parties.

[391] Uche Ewelukwa Ofodile, "African States, Investor-State Arbitration and the ICSID Dispute Resolution System: Continuities, Changes and Challenges", (2019) 34(2) ICSID Review, pp. 296–364, available at: doi:10.1093/icsidreview/siz031.

[392] *Holiday Inns SA and others v. Morocco*, ICSID Case No. ARB/72/1. See Pierre Lalive, "The First 'World Bank' Arbitration (*Holiday Inns v. Morocco*) – Some Legal Problems", (1980) 51(1) British Yearbook of International Law, pp. 123–162, available at: https://doi.org/10.1093/bybil/51.1.123.

[393] "The ICSID Caseload – Statistics", Issue 2020-2, International Centre for Settlement of Investment Disputes, 2020, available at: https://icsid.worldbank.org/sites/default/files/publications/The%20ICSID%20Caseload%20Statistics%20%282020-2%20Edition%29%20ENG.pdf.

[394] Ibid.

[395] Ibid.

[396] Benoit Lebars, "The Evolution of Investment Arbitration in Africa", Global Arbitration Review, May 2018, available at: https://globalarbitrationreview.com/review/the-middle-eastern-and-african-arbitration-review/2018/article/the-evolution-of-investment-arbitration-in-africa.

these cases include *Salini Costruttori SpA and Italstrade SpA v. Kingdom of Morocco*, in which the tribunal ruled that, "[t]he jurisdiction of the Centre shall extend to any legal dispute arising directly out of an investment, between a Contracting State … and a national of another Contracting State, which the parties to the dispute consent in writing to submit to the Centre", as indicated in Article 25(1) of the ICSID Convention;[397] *Southern Pacific Properties (Middle East) Limited v. the Arab Republic of Egypt*, in which the tribunal ruled on whether it can assert jurisdiction on the basis of a host country's investment law;[398] and the *Menzies v. Senegal* case, in which the tribunal ruled on whether a claimant can rely on the MFN clause in the GATS to access more favourable ISDS provisions in other BITs.[399] African nations have also been brought into several cases involving the fair and equitable treatment obligation set forth in various BITs. These cases have revolved primarily around domestic policies that have been put in place in an effort to protect domestic interests, but which have been challenged by investors as contrary to their interests. These types of cases are perhaps one of the greatest frustrations African nations have with the international dispute resolution system. This and other issues with the ICSID system will be discussed further in the following chapters.

In recent years, the ICSID system has been undergoing a comprehensive review and amendment process. The current amendment process, launched in 2016, is centred around two pillars: (i) a participative and transparent working method that involves all Member States and stakeholders; and (ii) proposals that are designed to broaden the choice of methods, achieve greater efficiency, maintain the balance between investors and states, strengthen the processes for avoiding conflict of interest, and increase the transparency of proceedings.[400] Member States and stakeholders have presented various ideas for improving the ICSID system. This has resulted in the adoption, on 21 March 2022, of the new rules and regulations, which come into effect on 1 July 2022. These include the new Institution Rules (2022 Institution Rules) and the new rules on conciliation (2022 Conciliation Rules) and arbitration (2022 Arbitration Rules), in addition

---

[397] *Salini Costruttori SpA and Italstrade SpA v. Kingdom of Morocco*, ICSID Case No. ARB/00/4, Decision on Jurisdiction (16 July 2001).

[398] *Southern Pacific Properties (Middle East) Limited v. Arab Republic of Egypt*, ICSID Case No. ARB/84/3, Award (20 May 1992).

[399] *Menzies v. Senegal*, ICSID Case No. ARB/15/21, Award (5 August 2016).

[400] See: ICSID Rules and Regulations Amendment, ICSID/15/Rev. 3 July 2022, available at: https://icsid.worldbank.org/resources/rules-amendments.

to its new set of rules for its Additional Facility (2022 Additional Facility) Proceedings), and the new Administrative and Financial Regulations (2022 Administrative and Financial Regulations).[401]

2.2. INTERNATIONAL CHAMBER OF COMMERCE INTERNATIONAL COURT OF ARBITRATION

The other most reputable and widely used international arbitration institution is the ICC International Court of Arbitration. This body resolves disputes arising out of international commercial and business activities through arbitration. According to the ICC itself, "more than half of all arbitration disputes worldwide" are brought to its Court of Arbitration.[402] The Court "supervises and administers the arbitration process, while disputes are decided by arbitrators who are either selected by the parties or directly appointed by the court".[403] The ICC has its own Rules of Arbitration, which govern the procedural matters of arbitration brought before it.[404] This Court sits in Paris, but has the capacity to hear cases in its offices in New York, Hong Kong, Singapore, Panama and Tunisia, or anywhere else in the world the parties to the case agree to.

In 2019, the ICC heard 946 new cases. This is the most cases the ICC Court has ever registered, with the exception of 2016, when a collective dispute led to 135 related small-claim cases.[405] Of these 2019 cases, a total of 171 parties from 35 African countries represented 6.8% of all parties. Nigeria (22 parties) and Egypt (13 parties) were the most represented nationalities among the African parties.[406]

In 2018, the ICC announced the creation of an Africa Commission to coordinate its expanding range of activities and growth on the continent.[407] Representatives from sub-Saharan Africa have been invited to serve on this body, which will focus on training, awareness and outreach activities.[408]

---

[401] Ibid.
[402] "ICC releases 2019 Dispute Resolution statistics", available at: https://iccwbo.org/media-wall/news-speeches/icc-releases-2019-dispute-resolution-statistics/.
[403] Ibid.
[404] An amended version of these rules entered in force on 1 January 2021.
[405] "ICC releases 2019 Dispute Resolution statistics", available at: https://iccwbo.org/media-wall/news-speeches/icc-releases-2019-dispute-resolution-statistics/.
[406] Ibid.
[407] ICC, "ICC Court to launch Africa Commission", Paris, 19 July 2018, available at: https://iccwbo.org/media-wall/news-speeches/icc-court-launch-africa-commission/.
[408] Ibid.

In 2020, the ICC Court appointed a Regional Director for Africa to work closely with the ICC Africa Commission towards developing ICC activities, and raising awareness of ICC dispute resolution services within sub-Saharan countries. This new role acknowledges the ICC's efforts to expand the pool of qualified African practitioners who may act in the many ongoing and future disputes arising in the region.[409]

The ICC has expressed its desire to work closely with the ICC Belt and Road Commission while implementing this Africa Commission.[410] The former Commission is focused on Chinese investment in the continent, which, as mentioned previously, is growing exponentially.[411] These efforts to focus more closely on the needs of the continent, as with the efforts of the ICSID, reflect the growing influence of African nations on the international arbitration system.

Each of the different international arbitration institutions – not only the ICC and ICSID, but each of the other above-mentioned institutions – has its own benefits. Collectively, these forums offer the most experience in handling complex business transactions, in what are seemingly neutral tribunals. The combined experience of these institutions and their recognition of the importance of expanding their own understandings and competencies with regard to African-specific transactions are why these institutions have, for some time now, been the most favoured options for settling investment disputes. These forums are also particularly favoured by foreign investors, who are familiar with their rules and regulations, and have faith in their capacities. This is particularly true of companies that operate all over the world, which appreciate the ability to move easily from one region to another. There is also a perceived neutrality to these bodies, which only builds investor confidence in them, and the arbitrators are seen as well-versed in the complex business matters that often lead to disputes in a globalised world. Investors in Africa who are from Europe or the United States also appreciate the ability to have disputes resolved outside of the African continent, which is done in nearly all cases involving African parties and international arbitration.[412]

---

[409] See *supra* note 407.

[410] Zachary Mollengarden, "'One-Stop' Dispute Resolution on the Belt and Road: Toward an International Commercial Court with Chinese Characteristics", (2019) 36(1) Pacific Basin Law Journal, pp. 65–111, available at: https://escholarship.org/content/qt43q7s46n/qt43q7s46n.pdf?t=pm8ts1.

[411] Ibid.

[412] Andrew Mizner, "The future is now for African arbitration", Commercial Dispute Resolution, 23 May 2019, available at: https://www.cdr-news.com/categories/arbitration-and-adr/9573-the-future-is-now-for-african-arbitration.

Regardless of their favourability with foreign investors, international arbitration tribunals have become increasingly unfavourable to many developing nations, particularly African states. While these tribunals do have tremendous experience in handling complex business disputes, African governments have long complained that their processes are overly burdensome, and biased towards foreign investors. Several African leaders have argued that these tribunals play into the desire of foreign companies to influence or even restrict domestic policy, by allowing their claims to overshadow the underlying needs of the countries themselves.[413] The claims brought by foreign investors, while often based in breach of contract, have been seen as overlooking environmental, social, health, labour and other matters of public interest within countries.[414]

At the same time, the arbitration rules of these institutions typically provide for party selection of arbitrators, which makes the process unpredictable. The list of arbitrators available for these proceedings are often stocked full of arbitrators with substantial experience working in Europe and/or the United States, but few who have experience in Africa.[415] While the rules of these institutions allow for the selection of the location for arbitral proceedings, the influence of foreign investors in negotiating investment agreements often results in cities in the northern hemisphere being chosen, none of which are the most convenient seats for African parties. There is also an uneven power dynamic in this process, which typically leads African nations to hire external counsel from reputable international law firms, so that they may be perceived as having the same standing as their counterparts and jurists.[416] The resources, both financial

---

[413] Emmanuel T. Laryea and Oladapo O. Fabusuyi, "Africanisation of international investment law for sustainable development: challenges", (2021) 20(1) Journal of International Trade Law and Policy, pp. 42–64, available at: https://doi.org/10.1108/JITLP-06-2020-0039.

[414] Christiane Gerstetter and Nils Meyer-Ohlendorf, "Investor-State Dispute Settlement Under TTIP – A Risk for Environmental Regulation?", Heinrich Böll Stiftung TTIP Series, 31 December 2013, available at SSRN: https://ssrn.com/abstract=2416450.

[415] "Domestic and International Arbitration: Perspectives from African Arbitration Practitioners", SOAS Arbitration in Africa Survey, 2020, available at: https://eprints.soas.ac.uk/33162/1/2020%20Arbitration%20in%20Africa%20Survey%20Report%20 30.06.2020.pdf.

[416] Won Kidane, "The Culture of Investment Arbitration: An African Perspective", (2019) 34(2) ICSID Review – Foreign Investment Law Journal, pp. 411–433, available at: https://doi.org/10.1093/icsidreview/siz027.

and otherwise, needed to argue investment cases in front of international tribunals are draining on African parties. Moreover, the cultural differences between Western systems and African judiciaries are stark and leaves African nations, almost immediately, with a disadvantage in these Western-centric processes. At times, this has led to seemingly unjust decisions being rendered against African states, who are then required to pay damages, sometimes of huge amounts.[417] The latest example is an ad hoc award rendered in 2017 against Nigeria, granting an investor USD 9.6 billion in damages, a sum that amounts to 20% of the country's foreign reserves.[418]

In addition to these frustrations, the cost of international arbitration is one of the key sticking points for African countries. Not only do these countries generally have to expend resources on attorneys, travelling to the location of the court, and the fees of the tribunals themselves, the judgments rendered in these international tribunals can be seen as almost crippling to smaller economies on the continent. For example, in 2015, the Gambia, one of Africa's smallest countries, with a total GDP of around USD 2 billion,[419] was ordered by an ICSID Arbitral Tribunal to pay USD 24 million to Astron Corporation Limited, a large multinational mining company.[420] Awards like this are contradictory to the development needs of the continent, and demonstrate a disconnect between international tribunals and African investment.

Considering both the crucial role that African nations had in getting the international arbitration system up and running, and the fact that many of the ICSID and ICC landmark cases involved African parties,

---

[417] See *World Duty Free v. Kenya*, ICSID Case No. ARB/00/7, Award (4 October 2006), available at: https://www.italaw.com/cases/documents/3281. See Won Kidane, ibid.

[418] See *Process and Industrial Developments Ltd. v. The Ministry of Petroleum Resources of the Federal Republic of Nigeria*, Final Award, 31 January 2017, available at: https://jusmundi.com/en/document/decision/en-process-and-industrial-developments-ltd-v-the-ministry-of-petroleum-resources-of-the-federal-republic-of-nigeria-final-award-tuesday-31st-january-2017. See, on the same topic, Oludara Akanmidu, "How Nigeria got hit with a $9.6 billion gas deal judgment debt in a UK court", Quartz Africa, 17 September 2019, available at: https://qz.com/africa/1710707/how-nigeria-got-hit-with-a-9-6-billion-judgment-debt-in-the-uk/.

[419] "The Gambia", The World Bank, available at: https://data.worldbank.org/country/gambia-the.

[420] See *Carnegie Minerals (Gambia) Limited v. Republic of the Gambia*, ICSID Case No. ARB/09/19, available at: https://jusmundi.com/en/document/decision/en-carnegie-minerals-gambia-limited-v-republic-of-the-gambia-decision-on-jurisdiction-and-merits-monday-29th-september-2014#decision_11752.

there is a strong argument to be made that the concerns of African nations should be more honestly considered as the international system develops.[421] For their part, African nations should assert their importance, and demand that systems be better suited to meeting their needs, as some of the most frequent "customers". At the same time, Africa should consider the strengths and weaknesses of the international tribunal system when creating its own system under the AfCFTA. This will be discussed further, at length, in the following chapters.

3. REGIONAL TRIBUNALS

The final category of tribunal, lying between international arbitration and domestic courts, consists of regional arbitration institutions and regional courts. While there has been a growing number of regional arbitration centres on the continent in recent years, these have had varying levels of success.[422]

The OHADA CCJA is amongst those that are worth considering. One of OHADA's most attractive accomplishments is not just its Uniform Acts, as previously discussed in Chapter 3, but rather the establishment of the CCJA. This court of 13 judges provides advice on proposed Uniform Acts, and serves as a court of cassation. This court is seen as superior to national courts in matters pertaining to the Uniform Acts, and allows cases to be presented by either party or a national judge. Moreover, the CCJA Arbitration Centre facilitates and oversees arbitrations on matters related to the Uniform Acts, and any other matters referred to it. This serves to add greater scrutiny of the impartiality of arbitration tribunals, reducing the possibility of corruption, and adding greater legitimacy to dispute resolution. In creating this security, CCJA is building investors' confidence that their investments will be protected. This court still has a hill to climb in building its reputation and legitimacy to a point where it is trusted as

---

[421] See Olabisi D. Akinkugbe, "Reverse Contributors? African State Parties, ICSID and the Development of International Investment Law", (2019) 34(2) ICSID Review, pp. 434–454, available at: doi:10.1093/icsidreview/siz010.

[422] Markus Bockenforde, Babacar Kante, Yuhniwo Ngenge and H. Kwasi Prempeh, "Judicial Review Systems in West Africa: A Comparative Analysis", International Institute for Democracy and Electoral Assistance (2016), available at: https://www.idea.int/sites/default/files/publications/judicial-review-systems-in-west-africa.pdf.

much as more established centres such as the ICC and ICSID, but it is making strides in the right direction.[423]

In 2017, the CCJA amended its Arbitration Act, as well as the CCJA Rules, making these more attractive and efficient. These amendments were intended to put the CCJA better in line with its international counterparts, particularly the ICC, allowing it to become more globally competitive. Among other changes, the amended Act now specifically states that an arbitration may be initiated on the basis of an investment-related instrument. This means that disputes arising from the growing number of investment treaties entered into by Member States may be brought to the CCJA, allowing for African settlement of the disputes rather than settlement by international tribunals. Additionally, this new Act puts in place mechanisms for the parties to a dispute to resolve an issue amongst themselves before resorting to a formal arbitration proceeding. This amendment puts the tribunal in line with international standards, creates a more effective process, and gives parties an opportunity to avoid the costly and time-consuming process inherent to any dispute settlement.[424]

The CCJA is not the only example of a regional bloc working to build confidence in Africa's dispute resolution capabilities. In 2008, the ECOWAS Member States enacted the ECOWAS Supplementary Act on Investments, placing an emphasis on the importance of investment in meeting development goals.[425] This Act grants the Community of ECOWAS the competence to regulate foreign investment. That said, it is uncertain to what extent this REC is able to use its existing Court of Justice. This Court was established in 1991 by Protocol A/P.l/7/91 on the Community Court of justice signed on 6 July 1991, and sits in Abuja, Nigeria. As of 2005, private individuals are able to access this Court directly, opening it up from State Party disputes only.[426] According to Article 9 of the Protocol, this judicial

[423] Babatunde Fagbayibo, "Towards the harmonisation of laws in Africa: is OHADA the way to go?", (2009) 42(3)The Comparative and International Law Journal of Southern Africa, pp. 309–322, available at: https://www.jstor.org/stable/23253105?seq=1#page_scan_tab_contents.

[424] See Mouhamed Kebe, "The Attractiveness of the New OHADA Arbitration Act", Geni & Kebe SCP, 13 December 2018, available at: https://www.lexology.com/library/detail.aspx?g=680f77e3-1b8c-4327-87c1-183a7abc45f4.

[425] Matthew Happold, "Investor-State Dispute Settlement using the ECOWAS Court of Justice: An Analysis and Some Proposals", (2019) 34(2) ICSID Review, pp. 496–518, available at: doi:10.1093/icsidreview/siz028.

[426] Ibid.

body is able to hear four categories of disputes: (i) disputes arising under Community law; (ii) human rights violations that occur in the Member States; (iii) arbitrations, until such time an arbitral tribunal is established; and (iv) any matter provided in an agreement where the parties provide that the Court shall settle disputes thereunder.[427]

Based on this, it would be presumed that this Court has the capacity to hear investment disputes arising under the 2008 Supplementary Act; however, the reach of the Court's jurisdiction to non-Member State parties (i.e. foreign investors) remains an open question. Foreign investors have used the human rights capabilities of the Court to challenge actions by Member States that they perceive to be contrary to their rights, given that such aggrievements occurred in Member States and, therefore, fall under the jurisdiction of the Court.[428] In a very recent case brought by an investor against Guinea, the Court emphasised its jurisdiction to rule on any breach of a State Party of its obligations to comply with fundamental rights.[429] The Court has, however, ruled that corporate bodies cannot bring human rights claims under the applicable human rights provision of the Protocol (10(b) of the Court's Protocol).[430] Other decisions, however, have held that all citizens of Member States, including all entities, may bring human rights claims.[431] In other words, the ECOWAS Court's own jurisprudence

---

[427] Protocol A/P.l/7/91 on the Community Court of justice signed on 6 July 1991, available at: http://www.courtecowas.org/wp-content/uploads/2018/11/Protocol_AP1791_ENG.pdf.

[428] See *OAO Netyanaya Kompaniya Yukos v. Russia*, App no. 14902/04 (ECtHR, 31 July 2014).

[429] See *Ibrahima Kassus Diuoubate & K ENERGIE S.A. v. Guinea*, Judgment, 9 July 2020, ECW/CCJ/JUD/14/20, available at: http://www.courtecowas.org/wp-content/uploads/2020/09/ARRÊT-ECW_CCJ_JUD_14_20.pdf; https://www.africa-energy.com/article/guinea-ecowas-court-orders-payout-k-energie.

[430] See *Ocean King Nig Ltd v. Republic of Senegal*, Judgment, 8 July 2011, ECW/CCJ/JUD/07/11. In this case, however, in holding that corporations could not bring claims under the human rights provision, the ECOWAS Court also found that, "the Applicant was complaining, inter-alia, of a denial of the right to fair hearing which is a fundamental right, open to any party who is affected by a tribunal's decision. That right is not dependent on human rights, and for that reason a party who has such a complaint of denial of fair hearing should not be thrown out of a court without first being heard. That was sufficient justification for this Court to embark upon hearing this application in the first place. Being a Member State of the Community, the defendant owes an obligation to every ECOWAS citizen or entity to ensure fair hearing within its territory, failing which this Court will have the right to entertain an application by an aggrieved party, even if it is based on the Court's inherent jurisdiction."

[431] See ECW/CCJ/APP/24/17, [2019] ECOWASCJ 3; Judgment, 6 February 2019, para. 72, available at: https://africanlii.org/ecowas/judgment/ecowas-community-court-justice/2019/3.

questions the scope of its jurisdiction and ability to render meaningful decisions in investment-related disputes. While this Court could build on Africa's experience in investment-related matters, particularly given the strength of the ECOWAS itself, it has a tremendous amount of work to do to prove its legitimacy.

In addition to regional blocs seeking to expand their dispute settlement capabilities, more and more individual countries are starting to recognise that arbitration is the most effective means of dispute settlement in the world, and one of the best ways to build investor confidence. This is demonstrated by extensive efforts to establish and support new and existing arbitral tribunals, as well as the inclusion of strong arbitration language in BITs. This growing willingness to utilise arbitration also demonstrates increasing acknowledgement, by African states, that arbitration can also serve to protect their interests as much as it protects the rights of investors. Several individual countries have established, or are in the process of establishing, national arbitration centres that can serve as the primary dispute resolution body in their respective countries and, in many cases, within the larger regions in which they are located. These countries have acknowledged weaknesses in their own judicial systems, and the inability of local courts to handle complex business disputes. They have also openly stated the importance of a strengthened arbitration regime in increasing investment, particularly FDI.

In Rwanda, the government, faced with a large backlog of cases, passed a robust arbitration law in 2008, establishing the Kigali International Arbitration Centre (KIAC). Straight away, the government committed substantial funding to KIAC, building a state-of-the-art facility, putting in place alternative dispute resolution training programmes to build the capacity of arbitrators, and instilling in local judges the importance of arbitration. This court has largely been successful, and is among the top reasons why Rwanda is currently second on the World Bank's "Ease of Doing Business" rankings for Africa.

The Cairo Regional Centre for International Commercial Arbitration is also a reputable arbitration centre, and the oldest one in Africa. The African Development Bank has recognised it as one of the best arbitration centres across the African continent and elsewhere.[432]

---

[432]   See The Cairo Regional Centre for International Commercial Arbitration, available at: https://globalarbitrationreview.com/organisation/the-cairo-regional-centre-international-commercial-arbitration-crcica.

Mauritius, the top African country in the "Ease of Doing Business" rankings, is host to several arbitral institutions, and has long been the chosen jurisdiction for African arbitration. Ghana and Kenya have recently put greater effort into improving their already comparatively well-established arbitration centres, which have improved along with the economies of those countries. More recently, Mauritania rewrote the rules for the Mauritania Chamber of Commerce and Industry's Arbitration and Mediation Centre, so that they better align with international standards and may be more attractive to foreign investors. Another bold example of a successful arbitration centre created by strong national policy is the Casablanca International Mediation and Arbitration Centre (CIMAC). This newly established tribunal merges several predecessor arbitral institutions, and is supported by Casablanca Finance City, an African business hub established by Morocco to serve as the leading financial centre in Africa. CIMAC has already proven that it will provide a sound option for dispute resolution on the continent, even in its early years, and has attracted the attention of some of the world's leaders in arbitration. These centres are attracting the attention of other African nations, who have, in some cases, begun to consider African dispute settlement bodies when choosing the forums for resolving their conflicts.

That said, these arbitration centres, as well as others established on the continent, still face a long road ahead to becoming widely recognised on the world stage. Investors, particularly foreign investors, still prefer, in most cases, to choose European or American arbitration centres to resolve disputes that arise. Still, efforts to build the capacity of these local centres are important – even crucial – in building confidence in investing in the continent. A little progress in building cases and demonstrating oversight of processes will, over time, lead to more substantial recognition of these centres. In building the reputations of these centres, countries are also building the confidence of investors.

4. DISPUTE SETTLEMENT UNDER THE AfCFTA

The enactment of the AfCFTA marks a historic opportunity for the African continent, and a chance for African nations to put in place a sound dispute settlement system that is more equitable, and better meets the development objectives of the continent, than the more ad hoc system that has been used to date. A comprehensive system that covers any and all matters pertaining to the three foundational protocols of the Agreement will be one of the keys to ensuring that the AfCFTA as a whole is successfully implemented in such a way that it promotes growth and investment in Africa.

In a first step towards creating a uniform dispute settlement system for the continent, the enacted version of the AfCFTA included a Protocol on Rules and Procedures on the Settlement of Disputes (the "Dispute Settlement Protocol").[433] While this Dispute Settlement Protocol sets forth a basic framework for dispute settlement under the Agreement, which in large part mirrors that of the WTO, it leaves several holes that must be filled if there is to be a clear and effective procedure. The following paragraphs highlight some of the key provisions of the AfCFTA as they pertain to the skeleton forum envisioned under the Dispute Settlement Protocol. In the chapters that follow, this book will then explore the current landscape of dispute settlement across Africa, and set forth the author's position on what the future of dispute settlement on the continent should look like.

Unlike the Protocols on goods and services, the Dispute Settlement Protocol's objective is short and straightforward. Article 2 states that the purpose is to "ensure that the dispute settlement process is transparent, accountable, fair, predictable and consistent with the provisions of the Agreement".[434] Article 3 then specifies that the scope of the Dispute Settlement Protocol covers disputes that arise between State Parties, concerning their rights and obligations under the provisions of the Agreement.[435] The essential role of the Dispute Settlement Protocol is highlighted in Article 4 ("General Provisions"), which provides, in part, that:

> [t]he dispute settlement mechanism of the AfCFTA is a central element in providing security and predictability to the regional trading system. The dispute settlement mechanism shall preserve the rights and obligations of State Parties under the Agreement and clarify the existing provisions of the Agreement in accordance with customary rules of interpretation of public international law.[436]

---

[433] Agreement Establishing the African Continental Free Trade Area (AfCFTA), 21 March 2018 (entered into force 30 May 2019), available at: https://au.int/sites/default/files/treaties/36437-treaty-consolidated_text_on_cfta_-_en.pdf.

[434] Ibid., Dispute Settlement Protocol, Art. 2, available at: https://au.int/sites/default/files/treaties/36437-treaty-consolidated_text_on_cfta_-_en.pdf.

[435] Ibid., Art. 3.

[436] Ibid., Art. 4.

Article 5 is one of the key provisions of the Dispute Settlement Protocol because it establishes what is referred to as the DSB. The DSB is to be comprised of representatives of the State Parties, and shall have the authority to:

- Establish Dispute Settlement Panels and an Appellate Body.
- Adopt Panel and Appellate Body reports.
- Maintain surveillance of implementation of rulings and recommendations of the Panels and Appellate Body.
- Authorise the suspension of concessions and other obligations under the Agreement.[437]

According to Article 5, the DSB is to have a chairperson, and shall determine the procedures that such individual must follow. The DSB is to meet as often as necessary, and take decisions by consensus.[438]

Article 6 sets forth the procedure to be followed for dispute settlement, and is, therefore, worth noting in its entirety here. This Article states that:

1. Where a dispute arises between or among the State Parties, in the first instance, recourse shall be had to consultations, with a view to finding an amicable resolution to the dispute.
2. Where an amicable resolution is not achieved, any party to the dispute shall, after notifying the other parties to the dispute, refer the matter to the DSB, through the Chairperson and request for the establishment of a Dispute Settlement Panel, (hereinafter referred to as the "Panel") for purposes of settling the dispute.
3. The DSB shall adopt Rules of Procedure for the selection of the Panel, including the issues of conduct, to ensure impartiality.
4. The Panel shall set in motion the process of a formal resolution of the dispute as provided for in this Protocol and the parties to the dispute shall, in good faith, observe in a timely manner, any directions, rulings and stipulations that may be given to them by the Panel in relation to procedural matters and shall make their submissions, arguments and rebuttals in a format prescribed by the Panel.
5. The DSB shall make its determination of the matter and its decision shall be final and binding on the parties to a dispute.

---

[437] Ibid., Art. 5.
[438] Ibid.

6.   Where the parties to a dispute consider it expedient to have recourse
     to arbitration as the first dispute settlement avenue, the parties to a
     dispute may proceed with arbitration as provided for in Article 27 of
     this Protocol.[439]

Following on from the first step in this procedure, Article 7 provides that
State Parties should engage in consultations to resolve disputes amicably.
This Article provides a procedure for a State Party to bring disputes to
the attention of another State Party.[440] The two states must notify the DSB
of the request for consultation, and the parties must then respond within
the applicable deadlines provided in the Article. All consultations are to
be confidential and without prejudice. When disputes are not resolved by
way of consultation, they may be referred to the DSB. The Article further
provides for expediency of processes in certain circumstances, and allows
for the joinder of third parties, in certain circumstances. Article 8 adds
to Article 7, by providing that State Parties to a dispute "may, at any time,
voluntarily undertake good offices, conciliation, or mediation".[441]

Articles 9 to 19 of the Dispute Settlement Protocol set forth the
basic procedures for when disputes are not resolved amicably through
conciliation. In such cases, a Panel shall be established. The composition
of this Panel, as described in Article 10, mirrors that of international
arbitration tribunals, in that the individuals that sit on the body are selected
from a roster of experts, with each party having the opportunity to select
the individuals they would like to have sitting on the Panel. Individuals
from the countries who are party to the dispute will not be allowed to sit on
the Panel. When no decision can be reached on the members of the Panel,
the matter is referred to the DSB.[442]

The purpose of the Panel, as indicated in Articles 11 and 12, is to
assist the DSB in discharging its responsibilities.[443] The procedures of
the Panel are provided for in Article 15, supplemented by Articles 13 and
14. The latter two Articles dictate the terms of third parties being joined
to a dispute, and multi-party disputes, respectively. Panels have five
months to render a report (one and a half months in cases of urgency),
which can be extended for up to a further four months, in accordance

---

[439]   Ibid., Art. 6.
[440]   Ibid., Art. 7.
[441]   Ibid., Art. 8.
[442]   Ibid., Art. 10.
[443]   Ibid., Art. 12.

with Article 15. Certain specifications as to the right of the Panel to seek information (Article 16) and the requirement that the Panel's deliberations be confidential (Article 17) are briefly detailed.

The process for the Panel's compilation of its report is stipulated in Article 18. At the conclusion of its Report, the Panel is to circulate the Report to the State Parties, who, according to Article 19, will have 20 days to express their written objections to the report to the DSB. The State Parties will then have the opportunity to participate in the DSB's consideration of the Report. If neither party expresses its intent to appeal, the DSB must consider, adopt and sign the Report within 60 days.[444]

Appeals are governed by Articles 20 to 23 of the Protocol. According to Article 20, the DSB is to establish a standing Appellate Body composed of seven people, three of whom shall serve on any one case.[445] Further stipulations as to the composition of the Appellate Body are also provided in Article 20. Articles 21 and 22 then set forth the procedures for appeals, indicating that only parties to the dispute have the opportunity to appeal (not third parties, as per Article 21), and that the actual working procedures for the Appellate Body are to be drawn up by the body itself, in consultation with the DSB. According to Article 23, once the Panel or Appellate Body concludes that a measure is inconsistent with the Agreement, it "recommends that the State Party concerned bring the measure into conformity with the Agreement".[446]

The final Articles of the Dispute Settlement Protocol discuss post-decision procedures, indicating that State Parties are to comply promptly with recommendations and rulings of the DSB.[447] When Parties do not comply with their obligations under the rulings and recommendations of the DSB, temporary compensation, and suspension of concessions or other obligations, may be available.[448] The wording of Article 25, which governs "Compensation and the Suspension of Concessions or any other Obligations" almost directly addresses one of African nations' biggest complaints against international arbitration: that the exorbitant awards rendered are crippling on African states, and do not meet the breaches for which they are awarded. So, too, does Article 26, which provides that costs are to be borne equally by the parties.

---

[444]   Ibid., Art. 19.
[445]   Ibid., Art. 20.
[446]   Ibid., Art. 23.
[447]   Ibid., Art. 24.
[448]   Ibid., Art. 25.

The weakest Article of the entire Dispute Settlement Protocol is Article 27, titled "Arbitration", which puts into question the effectiveness of the Protocol. This Article states that, "[p]arties to a dispute may resort to arbitration subject to their mutual agreement and shall agree on the procedures to be used in the arbitration proceedings".[449] It then further elaborates that, "[p]arties to a dispute who may have referred a dispute for arbitration pursuant to this Article shall not simultaneously refer the same matter to the DSB".[450] In other words, after setting forth, in great detail, a dispute settlement process that at least begins to address some of the greatest concerns that African nations have had with international investment arbitration, the AfCFTA's Dispute Settlement Protocol then allows for State Parties to completely sidestep the entire process and opt for arbitration, without clearly defined rules and procedures. Herein lies the predominant problem with the Dispute Settlement Protocol, and the reason why it is absolutely essential for the African Union to better establish a clearer process for dispute settlement on the African continent.[451]

The author's recommendation for how the continent should go about addressing this issue is set forth at length in Chapter 8 of this book.

---

[449] Ibid., Art. 27.

[450] Ibid.

[451] Katrin Khulmann and Akinyi Lisa Agutu, "The African Continental Free Trade Area: Toward a New Legal Model for Trade and Development", (2020) 51 Georgetown Journal of International Law, pp. 753–808, available at: https://www.law.georgetown.edu/international-law-journal/wp-content/uploads/sites/21/2020/11/THE-AFRICAN-CONTINENTAL-FREE-TRADE-AREA.-TOWARD-A-NEW-LEGAL-MODEL-FOR-TRADE-AND-DEVELOPMENT.pdf.

CHAPTER 6

MECHANISMS FOR DISPUTE SETTLEMENT

Equally as important as the type of forum used in investment dispute settlement is the mechanism for dispute settlement. The two primary options discussed here are state-to-state dispute settlement, which encompasses the principle of diplomatic espousal, and ISDS, which encompasses the Calvo Doctrine. This chapter will discuss the fundamental aspects of both mechanisms, including the positives and negatives of each, from the perspective of developing states and foreign investors carrying out business in said states.

1. STATE-TO-STATE DISPUTE SETTLEMENT

State-to-state dispute settlement was, for a long time, the only means of resolving disputes that arose between an individual of one state, regardless of whether or not he or she was a state actor, and an individual of a foreign state, or that state itself. The principle of diplomatic espousal – the underlying principle giving rise to state-to-state dispute settlement – enshrines the idea that individuals with claims against a foreign country should rely on their home state to utilise diplomatic means to resolve the dispute with the foreign state. This was one of the primary principles of international law before the implementation of human and individual rights and was centred around the belief that only states were involved in international matters and, therefore, only states had rights by and between other states. Traditional international law, in other words, did not confer rights on individuals, regardless of nationality, and, therefore, individuals were unable to sue or be sued under international law.[452] Instead,

---

[452]   Sung Teak Kim, "Adjudicating Violations of International Law: Defining the Scope of Jurisdiction under the Alien Tort Statute – *Trajano v. Marcos*", (1994) 27(2) Cornell International Law Journal.

individuals had to rely on the intervention of their home governments to be heard.

It is important to note here that the state-to-state settlement mechanism relied heavily on the understanding that individuals with claims against a state, or other individuals from another host state, would first need to exhaust all domestic remedies before raising their claim to the international level.[453] According to the International Law Commission, this principle is still applicable within the realm of diplomatic protection. In 2006, that body, in its Draft Articles on Diplomatic Protection, stated that a state "may not bring an international claim in respect of an injury to a national … before the injured person has … exhausted all local remedies".[454] This is important to note at this point, as it stands in stark contrast to the ISDS mechanism that will be discussed in the following pages, which has given rise to a great deal of angst among African nations.

The state-to-state system has changed over time as individuals have gained additional individual rights. This shift dates back to some of the earliest jurisprudence of the Permanent Court of International Justice, which held in its 1928 decision in the *Danzig Railway Officials* case that:

> [i]t may be readily admitted that according to a well-established principle of international law, the agreement being an international agreement, cannot as such create direct rights and obligations for private individuals. But it cannot be disputed that, the very object of an international agreement according to the intention of contracting parties, may be the adoption by the parties, of some definite rules creating individual rights and obligations, enforceable by the national courts.[455]

Regardless, state-to-state dispute settlement continued to be the only mechanism permitted for international disputes throughout the first half of the twentieth century. It was not until 1969, in a BIT between Chad and

---

[453] Gabrielle Kaufmann-Kohler Michele Potestà, "Investor-State Dispute Settlement and National Courts. Current Framework and Reform Options", European Yearbook of International Economic Law, Cham: Springer, 2020.

[454] International Law Commission (2006), "Draft Articles on Diplomatic Protection", Official Records of the General Assembly, Sixty-first Session, Supplement No. 10, UN Doc. A/6/10, Art.14(1).

[455] *Jurisdiction of the Courts of Danzig* (Advisory Opinion) (1928) P.C.T. Ser. B, No. 15 pp. 17–18.

Italy, that ISDS (to be discussed later) was introduced as an alternative mechanism.[456]

State-to-state dispute settlement, as with ISDS, follows the same internationally accepted rules of arbitration[457] as are used in any other form of investor dispute. This includes the selection of arbitrators. Typically there are three arbitrators, one selected by each party, and the third by mutual agreement of the parties.[458] General procedural matters, including rules on submissions, the structure of claims, etc. follow a similar structure as well. State-to-state disputes are almost always brought to either the International Court of Justice or regional courts.

One of the key advantages of state-to-state dispute settlement, from the perspective of states, is the ability of states to insert matters of public interest into their arguments. In the case of developing countries, this allows states to better consider their development needs, without direct challenges from foreign investors, who may view legitimate development objectives as contrary to potential profit. Additionally, this mechanism gives states more control over events in their countries, as well as their international relations. States can, ultimately, decide whether or not to bring claims, and to what extent they will push these claims, weighing the needs and wants of individual investors against their own country's needs, and allowing for diplomatic considerations to play a leading role. From the point of view of investors, having states involved raises the importance of a claim, increasing the likelihood that the counterparty state will participate.

That said, state-to-state dispute settlement is viewed as more unfavourable to foreign investors, given that the decision to proceed with dispute settlement is, ultimately, out of their hands. One of the clearest indications that this system is not a favourite of corporations is the increasing number of cases being brought by corporations under ISDS provisions, wherein the corporation itself can determine whether a dispute moves forward, with a possibility for huge gains. "Corporations are

---

456   Nathalie Bernasconi-Osterwalder, "IISD Best Practices Series: State–State Dispute Settlement in Investment Treaties", IISD, October 2014, available at: https://www.iisd.org/sites/default/files/publications/best-practices-state-state-dispute-settlement-investment-treaties.pdf.

457   Following the model rules of the United Nations Commission on International Trade Law (UNCITRAL).

458   Nathalie Bernasconi-Osterwalder, "IISD Best Practices Series: State–State Dispute Settlement in Investment Treaties", IISD, October 2014, available at: https://www.iisd.org/sites/default/files/publications/best-practices-state-state-dispute-settlement-investment-treaties.pdf.

increasingly using investment and trade agreements – specifically, the investor-state dispute settlement provisions in them – to bring opportunistic cases in arbitral courts, circumventing decisions states deem in their best interest".[459] This places greater power in the hands of investors than they would otherwise have under the state-to-state mechanism. As will be discussed further in the following pages, ISDS allows investors to protect their investments by allowing them to bring claims against a state which breaches its contractual obligations. Little regard is given to the public interest reasons underlying said breach. In state-to-state dispute settlement, investors must rely on their own country to defend their rights. In so doing, their home country will weigh several factors, including their political relationship with the other country, and the possible benefits it may be able to get from bringing a claim. It may also weigh other considerations, such as the time and resources necessary to commit to seeing a case through to its conclusion.

A state, under this mechanism, is able to decide whether or not it even brings a claim at all. For obvious reasons, then, this mechanism is not preferred by investors, as it largely takes the decision-making power out of their hands. Under this mechanism, states are able to bring cases for various reasons, including (i) as the home state of an investor, to enforce diplomatic protection; (ii) to seek interpretation on an investment treaty; and/or (iii) to request declaratory relief, seeking a determination that the treaty has been breached by a specific act.[460] As with any dispute, a state must weigh different considerations when determining whether to bring a claim, including cost, resources needed, and diplomatic relations.

Certain limitations on state-to-state dispute settlement are stipulated in the ICSID Convention. Article 27 of that Convention states that:

[n]o Contracting State shall give diplomatic protection, or bring an international claim, in respect of a dispute which one of its nationals and another Contracting State shall have consented to submit or shall have submitted to arbitration

---

Manuel Perez-Rocha, "When Corporations Sue Governments", The New York Times, 3 December 2014, available at: https://www.nytimes.com/2014/12/04/opinion/when-corporations-sue-governments.html.
460 Nathalie Bernasconi-Osterwalder, "IISD Best Practices Series, State–State Dispute Settlement in Investment Treaties", International Institute for Sustainable Development, October 2014, available at: https://www.iisd.org/system/files/publications/best-practices-state-state-dispute-settlement-investment-treaties.pdf.

under this Convention unless such other Contracting State shall have failed to abide by and comply with the award rendered in such dispute.[461]

This Article further provides that diplomatic protection shall not include informal diplomatic exchanges for "the sole purpose of facilitating a settlement of a dispute."[462] This, then, calls into question the interplay between ISDS and state-to-state dispute settlement when the two appear together in the same investment treaty, which is becoming more frequent.[463]

Only a handful of state-to-state disputes have been brought under investment treaties: the two most notable include a case between Italy and Cuba, brought on behalf of Italian investors for diplomatic protection, and another between Mexico and the United States, wherein Mexico claimed that the United States was violating the treaty between them. In *Mexico v. the United States*, there was no investor involved, and Mexico was seeking only declaratory confirmation of the treaty violation.[464] In the *Republic of Italy v. The Republic of Cuba*, Italy brought a claim for diplomatic protection on behalf of 16 different Italian companies, under the Italy–Cuba BIT, in the first-ever publicly known state-to-state dispute settlement under a BIT.[465] In addition to the diplomatic protection claim Italy brought on behalf of its investors, it also brought a direct claim to defend its own substantive rights. Ultimately, the tribunal dismissed all of Italy's claims on the merits, or due to jurisdictional conflict.[466] However, the tribunal did find that an investor's home country could bring a claim under an investment agreement using state-to-state dispute settlement, even if the same treaty allows for ISDS as well, so long as the investor had neither

---

[461] ICSID Convention, Regulations and Rules, International Centre for Settlement of Investment Disputes, Washington D.C., 2003, Art. 27, available at: https://icsid. worldbank.org/sites/default/files/ICSID%20Convention%20English.pdf.

[462] Ibid.

[463] Nathalie Bernasconi-Osterwalder, "IISD Best Practices Series, State–State Dispute Settlement in Investment Treaties", International Institute for Sustainable Development, October 2014, available at: https://www.iisd.org/system/files/publications/best-practices-state-state-dispute-settlement-investment-treaties.pdf.

[464] Ibid.

[465] Michele Potestá, *"Republic of Italy v. Republic of Cuba,"* (2012) 106(2) American Journal of International Law, pp. 341–347, doi:10.5305/amerjintelaw.106.2.0341, available at: https://www.cambridge.org/core/journals/american-journal-of-international-law/article/republic-of-italy-v-republic-of-cuba/15DAB44D01A94E1ABBD4E17E1F2358DF.

[466] Nathalie Bernasconi-Osterwalder, "IISD Best Practices Series, State–State Dispute Settlement in Investment Treaties", International Institute for Sustainable Development, October 2014, available at: https://www.iisd.org/system/files/publications/best-practices-state-state-dispute-settlement-investment-treaties.pdf.

consented to arbitrate with the host state nor submitted the dispute to ISDS arbitration.[467] In rendering this decision, the tribunal relied on *CMS v. Argentina*, an ISDS case where the tribunal had held that diplomatic protection is complementary to ISDS.[468] Despite these cases, however, there have been very few cases brought using state-to-state dispute settlement under an investment agreement, which makes it difficult to know exactly how the relationship between state-to-state dispute settlement and ISDS may play out in the future, as countries start considering what role each mechanism should play in their new investment agreements.

African nations appear to be eyeing a shift back to state-to-state dispute settlement. In the case of South Africa, for example, as mentioned in past chapters, the country has terminated its BITs that allow for ISDS, and has essentially pushed the country back towards the state-to-state mechanism, by way of domestic law and enforcement. Other courts in Africa have their own means for handling state-to-state disputes. Several regional bodies, for example, have built in the possibility of disputes being referred for settlement, or for an advisory opinion where necessary. The Investment Agreement for the COMESA Common Investment Area, for example, refers cases either to arbitration, or to the COMESA Court of Justice itself.[469] ECOWAS also allows for the ECOWAS Court of Justice to act as an advisory body, as well as a tribunal for resolving contentious disputes.[470] Certain states are showing signs of moving towards re-embracing state-to-state dispute settlement, while other states are slower to make such a dramatic shift. One common trend across the continent is that there are indications that countries are growing tired of the alternative mechanism, ISDS, which also comes with its own positives and negatives. This alternative mechanism is discussed at length in the following pages.

---

[467]   Ibid.

[468]   Fiona Marshall, "*CMS Gas Transmission Co. v. Republic of Argentina*, ICSID Case No. ARB/01/8", Investment Treaty News, 18 October 2018, available at: https://www.iisd.org/itn/2018/10/18/cms-v-argentina/.

[469]   Investment Agreement for the COMESA Common Investment Area: Common Market for Eastern and Southern Africa, signed 23 May 2007, available at: https://www.comesa.int/wp-content/uploads/2020/10/English-Revised-Investment-agreement-for-the-CCIA-28.09.17-FINAL-after-Adoption-for-signing.pdf.

[470]   ECOWAS Supplementary Protocol A/SP.1/01/05 Amending the Preamble and Articles 1, 2, 9 and 30 of Protocol A/P.1/7/91 Relating to the Community Court of Justice and Article 4 Paragraph 1 of the English Version of Said Protocol, available at: http://ecowas.akomantoso.com/_lang/fr/doc/_iri/akn/ecowas/statement/protocol/2005-01-19/A_SP.1_01_05/eng@/!main.

2. INVESTOR-STATE DISPUTE SETTLEMENT

The underlying doctrine in ISDS is the Calvo Doctrine, which enshrines the idea that foreign nationals who hold property or carry out business in a foreign country, and who have claims against a foreign state, should bring their claims directly against the foreign state, rather than seeking diplomatic intervention. This doctrine was first developed in 1868 by Carlos Calvo, a diplomat from Argentina.[471] The doctrine was intended to set forth international rules on how countries can exercise authority over aliens in their country, to be binding on all nations. The core principle of the doctrine is that aliens should not be entitled to any rights or privileges not accorded to nationals, and since nationals are only permitted to bring claims to domestic courts or regulatory bodies, then aliens should be required to do the same, and not rely on state intervention.[472] This doctrine then began to be incorporated into international investment agreements as a distinct provision that provided for ISDS as the dispute settlement mechanism.

As mentioned briefly above, as individuals began to gain greater rights under international law, there began to be a stronger argument that individuals making foreign investments should be able to bring claims directly against the states where their investments were, much as was envisioned in the Calvo Doctrine. Therein arose the idea for ISDS, which places a great amount of power back with individuals. As globalisation began to grow, so too did the number of BITs. Under these BITs, investors began entering foreign markets in greater numbers. Individual investors found themselves entering into direct agreements with state parties, under governing BITs. This direct investor and state relationship therefore strengthened the argument that ISDS is necessary, by demonstrating that the state-to-state mechanism, which relied on diplomatic protection, was limited in scope and ability.[473]

When states began to introduce ISDS into BITs as the governing dispute settlement mechanism,[474] the stated purpose was to protect investors from

---

[471] Patrick Juillard, "Calvo doctrine/Calvo clause", in Rüdiger Wolfrum (ed.), Max Planck Encyclopedia of Public International Law, Oxford: Oxford Public International Law, 2012, vol. i, pp. 1086 et seq. 31.

[472] Ibid.

[473] Andrew Newcombe and Lluis Paradell, "Law and Practice of Investment Treaties: Standard of Treatment Chapter 1, Historical Development of Investment Treaty Law", Kluwer Law International, 9 April 2009, available at: https://papers.ssrn.com/sol3/papers.cfm?abstract_id=1375600.

[474] The BIT concluded between Indonesia and the Netherlands in 1968 was the first to include an ISDS mechanism. See ibid., p. 44. See also: Dr Ahmad Ali Ghouri,

being targeted by the governments of states where they operated. The United States, for example, has stated that its reason for including ISDS in international agreements is to provide Americans investing abroad with freedom from discrimination, protection against uncompensated seizure of property, protection against denial of justice, and the right to transfer capital.[475] Ultimately, ISDS bestows certain legal privileges on foreign investors, allowing them to sue host governments for failing to live up to their contractual agreements. The original leading perspective on this was that ISDS is a way of protecting the rule of law by holding governments accountable for their obligations under international and private agreements.[476] Whether or not this is accurate is hotly debated, and will be discussed at length below, and in the following chapters.

ISDS is governed by international rules of arbitration, particularly – in the majority of cases – the Convention on Settlement of International Investment Disputes (ICSID Convention) or – also frequently used – the UNCITRAL Arbitration Rules. The International Chamber of Commerce and its arbitration rules, which are, in most ways, the same as the ICSID rules, are also commonly chosen procedures in international investment disputes. These same rules are also most often followed in state-to-state arbitration, when conducted at the international level.

From an investor's perspective, ISDS is highly favourable over state-to-state dispute settlement. This mechanism gives investors control over the procedure and allows them to bring any claim they feel is justified and necessary from their business perspective. Investors do not have the same diplomatic restraints that states do, and are able to think of cases solely in terms of how they impact their projects. For this reason, ISDS is also seen as less politicised than state-to-state dispute settlement.[477] In most cases,

---

"The Evolution of Bilateral Investment Treaties, Investment Treaty Arbitration and International Investment Law" (2011) 14(6) International Arbitration Law Review, pp. 189–204, available at SSRN: https://ssrn.com/abstract=1970561.

[475] "ISDS: Important Questions and Answers", Office of the United States Trade Representative, March 2015, available at: https://ustr.gov/about-us/policy-offices/press-office/blog/2015/march/isds-important-questions-and-answers.

[476] Lise Johnson, Lisa Sachs, Brooke Güven and Jesse Coleman, "Costs and Benefits of Investment Treaties", Columbia Center on Sustainable Investment, Policy Paper, March 2018, available at: http://ccsi.columbia.edu/files/2018/04/07-Columbia-IIA-investor-policy-briefing-ENG-mr.pdf.

[477] Lise Johnson, Brooke Skartved Güven and Jesse Coleman, "Investor-State Dispute Settlement: What are we Trying to Achieve? Does ISDS Get us There?", Columbia Center on Sustainable Investment, 11 December 2017, available at: http://ccsi.columbia.edu/2017/12/11/investor-state-dispute-settlement-what-are-we-trying-to-achieve-does-isds-get-us-there/.

investors also have the advantage of relying on international systems, without having to utilise or understand local courts or laws. While this is less the case in ISDS proceedings carried out at the regional level in regional courts or tribunals, the large majority of cases continue to be brought before one of the predominant international arbitration tribunals, and even regional tribunals tend to echo the rules and regulations of the larger international bodies with which many foreign investors have become accustomed. Finally, in considering the benefits of ISDS, from an investors' point of view, this mechanism is believed to be (and, in most cases, has proven to be) better at providing compensation for harm caused to investors in the course of carrying out projects in a foreign country. Overall, the common belief has, historically, since the rise of ISDS, been that investors look at ISDS as a means of protecting their investments, making them more likely to enter into new markets, particularly in parts of the world they would not normally consider, due to a perceived (or real) failure to protect contracts.[478]

From the perspective of states, ISDS has taken the burden off the home countries of investors, which would otherwise have to argue on behalf of private citizens, and has removed the inherently politicised decision of deciding whether or not to bring a case. Developed nations, especially those with the largest number of foreign investors, have asserted that ISDS creates a fair and transparent process that is grounded in established legal principles.[479] While this view of ISDS has shifted somewhat in recent years, with more and more challenges to the system arising, even in developed nations[480] (as will be discussed in the next chapter), the fact remains that ISDS is not generally harmful to countries like the United States or European countries. Many of these countries have economies built on the idea that the government should not be involved in business. This falls right in line with the primary purpose of ISDS.

At this point, it is important to pause and consider the cultural connotations incorporated into the international arbitration system.

---

[478] Jason Yackee, "New Trade Agreements Don't Need ISDS", Cato Institute, 19 May 2015, available at: https://www.cato-unbound.org/2015/05/19/jason-yackee/new-trade-agreements-dont-need-isds.

[479] "The Facts on Investor-State Dispute Settlement", Office of the United States Trade Representative, March 2014, available at: https://ustr.gov/about-us/policy-offices/press-office/blog/2014/March/Facts-Investor-State%20Dispute-Settlement-Safeguarding-Public-Interest-Protecting-Investors.

[480] "Case Studies: Investor-State Attacks on Public Interest Policies", Public Citizen, available at https://www.citizen.org/wp-content/uploads/egregious-investor-state-attacks-case-studies_4-1.pdf.

The New York Convention, the ICSID Convention, the UNCITRAL, and all other international arbitration agreements, have been developed around "western legal systems."[481] As pointed out by one expert, in his comprehensive study of the culture of arbitration in Africa, even though they had consented to the process establishing international arbitration, "Africans had to acquire working knowledge of the rules, and acclimate better to the Eurocentric cultures of the institutions ... This meant decades of struggle to adjust and rebuild systems and institutions of their own."[482] In addition to complicating processes, the system has also resulted in African nations needing to rely on external counsel, most often from Western countries, which has only further disadvantaged the African nations. The culture of international arbitration has, in and of itself, had a negative impact on developing countries, particularly African countries, by providing Western countries with an unfair advantage.[483]

While there is a list of other criticisms of this mechanism, both investors and states do agree on one benefit, which led to the almost global switch from diplomatic espousal to the Calvo Doctrine in the first place. As the use of ISDS has increased over the last decades, states (both developing and developed) and investors viewed ISDS as stronger in promoting the rule of law than state-to-state dispute settlement. As has previously been mentioned in this chapter, the idea behind this was that ISDS allows investors to put a check on states, most specifically when they are seen as overstepping their bounds.[484] Proponents of this argument argue that ISDS helps bring otherwise hesitant investors to markets they would otherwise avoid because of their poor legal systems.[485] At the same time, at the advent of individual rights taking centre stage in international law,

---

[481] Won Kidane, "The Culture of Investment Arbitration: An African Perspective", (2019) 34(2) ICSID Review – Foreign Investment Law Journal, pp. 411–433, available at: https://doi.org/10.1093/icsidreview/siz027.

[482] Ibid.

[483] See Emilia Onyema, "2020 Arbitration in Africa Survey Report", 30 June 2020, available at: https://eprints.soas.ac.uk/33162/1/2020%20Arbitration%20in%20Africa%20Survey%20Report%2030.06.2020.pdf. On the relevance of cultural considerations in arbitration, see Mouhamed Kebe, "La culture juridique de l'Arbitre est très importante", LJA OHADA, no. 1, 2019, available at: http://www.ohada.com/content/newsletters/5388/LJA_n00_15mars2020.pdf.

[484] "ISDS: Important Questions and Answers", Office of the United States Trade Representative, March 2015, available at: https://ustr.gov/about-us/policy-offices/press-office/blog/2015/march/isds-important-questions-and-answers.

[485] Tim R. Samples, "Winning and Losing in Investor–State Dispute Settlement", (2019) 56(1) American Business Law Journal, pp. 115–175, doi:10.1111/ablj.12136, available at: https://onlinelibrary.wiley.com/doi/10.1111/ablj.12136.

ISDS was seen as even further protecting the rights of individual citizens around the globe.

There are questions as to whether this mechanism is actually accomplishing the goal of strengthening the rule of law. Perhaps because of the cultural imbalance discussed previously, or more likely because of their position in the world, developed countries tend to have fewer issues when challenged through the ISDS process. During the Obama administration, the United States Trade Representative proudly stated that, "[a]s a country that plays by the rules and respects the rule of law, the United States has never lost an ISDS case".[486] While this may sound commendable, it also demonstrates one of the key criticisms that African and other developing nations have had of the ISDS: it is a mechanism that inherently and outwardly favours wealthier states and private investors. In other words, the potential that ISDS may reward those countries that abide by the rule of law, which would be a positive aspect of the mechanism, has been quashed by the reality that it actually hurts those countries that do not have Western-modelled judicial systems.

Thousands of BITs later, and years into the ISDS revolution, perhaps the strongest criticism of the mechanism is that it has, in fact, had the opposite impact on the rule of law than proponents had predicted. Skeptics – some long-time, some new – argue that ISDS in fact weakens the rule of law by giving rights exclusively to investors, allowing domestic legal systems to be circumvented, and democratically elected governments to be challenged.[487] There is an argument to be made that ISDS is, in actuality, creating a dual legal system where privileged companies with substantial resources are able to challenge even the most important and well-intentioned policies of host governments.[488] Host governments may actually be pushed to support the needs of foreign investors over the needs of their own citizens, which few could deny runs contrary to the rule of law. As will be further demonstrated in the next chapter, several countries – especially developing countries – have begun to argue that it is precisely in

---

[486]   "The Investor-State Dispute Settlement Mechanism: An Examination of Benefits and Costs", Cato Institute, 20 May 2014, available at: https://www.cato.org/events/investor-state-dispute-settlement-mechanism-examination-benefits-costs.

[487]   Ibid.

[488]   Lise Johnson, Brooke Skartved Güven and Jesse Coleman, "Investor-State Dispute Settlement: What are we Trying to Achieve? Does ISDS Get us There?", 11 December 2017, available at: http://ccsi.columbia.edu/2017/12/11/investor-state-dispute-settlement-what-are-we-trying-to-achieve-does-isds-get-us-there/.

the interests of protecting the rule of law that countries should reconsider ISDS as their dispute settlement mechanism of choice.

Some of the loudest critics of ISDS have been developing nations. Not only has ISDS struggled, in the eyes of many developing nations' governments, to attract greater foreign investment by demonstrating a strong rule of law, but these states believe it has gone a step further by impeding their national sovereignty. African and Latin American countries have been brought into more claims by foreign investors than countries anywhere else in the world.[489] Many of these governments have expressed concerns about the ability of foreign investors to bring claims challenging legitimate policy decisions aimed at promoting sustainable development.[490] Countries have seen challenges to environmental, labour, and tax laws that may have had a negative impact on investors, but which are essential to protecting the basic liberties of their citizenry. The impact that ISDS decisions have had, and could have, on African nations, in particular, is further explained in Chapter 7; however, this is a growing concern across the developing world. There is even an argument that the ability of major multinational companies from the world's largest economies to challenge and be successful in challenging, the development policies of third-world economies are continuing the same repression originally seen during colonisation.

The other major issue is the almost suffocating impact on developing nations that the amount of resources needed to argue an ISDS case, and the financial implications of huge judgments, are having on developing countries.[491] Many African nations have expressed frustrations over the fact that arguing a case at an international tribunal is extremely costly and time-consuming. Not only are large amounts of financial resources expended, but so too are human resources, which many countries have little to expend. This burden is even greater when the counterparty in a

---

[489] "The Current State and Future of International Arbitration: Regional Perspectives," IBA Arb 40 Subcommittee, International Bar Association, August 2015, available at: https://cvdvn.files.wordpress.com/2018/10/int-arbitration-report-2015.pdf.

[490] See *Philip Morris Brands Sàrl v. Oriental Rep. of Uruguay*, ICSID Case No. ARB/10/7, Award (8 July 2016). See also Samson L. Sempasa, "Obstacles to International Commercial Arbitration in African Countries", (1992) 41(2) International and Comparative Law Quarterly, pp. 387–413, doi:10.1093/iclqaj/41.2.387.

[491] Diana Rosert, "The Stakes are High: A review of the financial costs of investment treaty arbitration", International Institute for Sustainable Development, July 2014, available at: https://www.iisd.org/sites/default/files/publications/stakes-are-high-review-financial-costs-investment-treaty-arbitration.pdf.

claim is a well-represented (typically by the top attorneys and law firms in the world) multinational corporation with seemingly unlimited resources. Further, the often-gigantic judgments handed down in favour of multinational corporations can be crippling to governments that have extremely tight budgets, to begin with. The case of the Gambia, discussed previously,[492] is an excellent example of this. The "elephant in the room" question that must be asked of ISDS, then, is how requiring a developing country to pay damages to an extremely rich corporation will in any way promote the sustainable development that developed countries often state as a top global priority.

This very question, along with several other considerations, has led many countries to begin questioning ISDS, and whether this is the best mechanism for global dispute settlement, or whether there should be a return to diplomatic espousal and state-to-state dispute resolution. The following chapter looks closely at how world views appear to be shifting, and what this means for the future of dispute settlement in international investment.

---

[492]   See *supra* n 420.

CHAPTER 7

A GLOBAL SHIFT

Investor-state dispute settlement (ISDS) came to the centre of the world stage during the negotiations for the Trans-Pacific Partnership Agreement (TPP), held between 2008 and 2015.[493] The TPP, had the United States remained a party,[494] would have been the largest trade agreement in the world. This agreement would have shifted US focus to Asia, joining the other partners to the pact: Brunei, Chile, New Zealand, Singapore, Vietnam, Peru, Canada, Japan, Malaysia and Mexico.[495] Given the massive scope of this agreement, and the number of prominent countries participating in the negotiations, the TPP gained significant press attention and became more mainstream in conversation than most other trade agreements. At the forefront of the heated debates involving this agreement was its ISDS provision. These debates, featuring strong arguments as to why ISDS should no longer be included in trade agreements, came amid a growing worldwide trend away from ISDS.

While the TPP may be at the centre of current worldwide discussion, due to its prominence in the news, there are several prominent trade agreements around the world that laid the foundation for this newer agreement. In North America, the North American Free Trade Agreement, between Canada, Mexico and the United States, was a landmark agreement that came into effect in 1994. This agreement created an explosion of trade

---

[493] Tania Voon and Elizabeth Sheargold, "The Trans-Pacific Partnership", (2016) 5(2) British Journal of American Legal Studies, pp. 341–370, doi: https://doi.org/10.1515/bjals-2016-0012.

[494] President Donald Trump withdrew the US from this agreement in 2017, shortly after becoming president. See Mireya Solís, "Trump withdrawing from the Trans-Pacific Partnership", Brookings Institution, 24 March 2017, available at: https://www.brookings.edu/blog/unpacked/2017/03/24/trump-withdrawing-from-the-trans-pacific-partnership/.

[495] These parties continue to negotiate this agreement, following US withdrawal. It is now called the Comprehensive and Progressive Agreement for Trans-Pacific Partnership.

between the countries, and greatly integrated the three economies.[496] However, it met with a mixed reaction in the US, the largest economy of the parties to the agreement. This agreement once again came to the forefront of discussion, very much at the same time as the TPP, with US President Trump promising to abolish the agreement when he first came to office in 2016. This led to renewed negotiations on the agreement, and the rise of the new version of the agreement, known as the United States–Mexico–Canada Agreement (USMCA).

The world's oldest and most established economic community is the European Economic Community, now the EU, which was created after the Second World War. Twenty-seven countries are now party to the EU, which is now more expansive than just an economic union. The EU is now a sophisticated organisation of policy bodies as well, with specific regulations governing everything from climate and the environment to health and security, and from justice to migration.[497] This union paved the way for nearly all of its successors, and has played an important role in demonstrating the possibilities of integration on the global stage.

In addition to these more prominent trade agreements, nearly every region in the world also has smaller economic and, in some circumstances, political unions. In Latin America, for example, Mercosur is a four-country common market made up of Argentina, Brazil, Paraguay and Uruguay, and the Pacific Alliance brings together the economies of Chile, Colombia, Peru and Mexico.[498] In Asia, in addition to the TPP, there exists the Association of Southeast Asian Nations (ASEAN), which brings together a large number of countries, including Brunei Darussalam, Cambodia, Indonesia, Lao PDR, Malaysia, Myanmar, Philippines, Singapore, Thailand and Vietnam.[499] ASEAN also has several agreements, known as "plus one agreements", wherein the economic bloc has entered into an agreement with another major country in the region, such as China, Japan or India.

[496] Andrew Chatzky, James McBride and Mohammed Aly Sergie, "NAFTA and the USMCA: Weighing the Impact of North American Trade", Council on Foreign Relations, 1 July 2020, available at: https://www.cfr.org/backgrounder/naftas-economic-impact.
[497] "The European Union: What it is and what it does", European Commission, available at: https://op.europa.eu/webpub/com/eu-what-it-is/en/.
[498] Andrew Thompson, "Who Is Free Trade Really For in Latin America?", World Politics Review, 23 September 2019, available at: https://www.worldpoliticsreview.com/articles/28209/who-is-free-trade-really-for-in-latin-america#:~:text=By%20size%20and%20economic%20importance,and%20the%20Pacific%20Alliance%2C%20a.
[499] ASEAN Member States, available at: https://asean.org/member-states/.

Then, in Africa, there is a long list of economic blocs, as discussed extensively in Chapter 3.

As with TPP, each of these regions has a unique approach to ISDS, with the topic of whether ISDS should be continued becoming an important topic of conversation in the global discussion on trade blocs.[500] This system has been widely criticised for creating an uneven power dynamic between states and investors, which has left states in a vulnerable position, unable to defend some of their most important public interest decisions. As a result, various solutions have been proposed in different regions of the world, in regard to ISDS. This chapter looks closely at each region, looking at how perceptions appear to be shifting, starting with the TPP.

1. TRANS-PACIFIC PARTNERSHIP AGREEMENT

1.1. HISTORY

The idea for the TPP first arose in 2005, when a group of countries, known as the Pacific Rim countries, entered into a massive trade agreement.[501] The original parties to that agreement were Brunei, Chile, New Zealand, and Singapore. In 2008, the then President of the United States, George W. Bush, expressed interest in having his country begin conversations with this group, which then sparked Australia, Vietnam, and Peru to join the conversation on expanding the agreement.[502] Later, Canada, Japan, Malaysia and Mexico also joined, bringing the total number of countries interested in forming a Trans-Pacific Partnership to 12.[503] These countries covered approximately one-third of all global trade, producing 40% of global economic output.[504] A successful agreement between them, therefore, would have constituted the biggest trade agreement in the world.

---

[500] Umar Ghori, "Investment Court System or 'Regional' Dispute Settlement?: The Uncertain Future of Investor-state Dispute Settlement", (2018) 30(1) Bond Law Review, pp. 83–117, available at: http://www.austlii.edu.au/au/journals/BondLawRw/2018/7.pdf.

[501] James McBride, Andrew Chatzky and Anshu Siripurapu, "What's Next for the Trans-Pacific Partnership (TPP)?", Council on Foreign Relations, available at: https://www.cfr.org/backgrounder/what-trans-pacific-partnership-tpp.

[502] Ibid.

[503] Ibid.

[504] John A. Powell, Elsadig Elsheikh and Hossein Ayazi, "The Trans-Pacific Partnership: Corporations before People and Democracy", Haas Institute, University of California Berkeley, May 2016, available at: https://escholarship.org/content/qt3b62p6v0/qt3b62 p6v0_noSplash_5ebb097cb314dfeff25a61915c831820.pdf?t=qc4v1u.

This group of 12 nations continued to negotiate the agreement for nearly a decade, with the new Obama administration in the US showing a keen interest in executing a final agreement, despite some pushback in the country's Congress, and pushback internally in several other countries, including Japan, one of the strongest economies participating in negotiations. In total, the agreement went through 19 rounds of negotiations before a final agreement was released in October 2015.[505] On 4 February 2016, the 12 countries signed the Trans-Pacific Partnership, thereby leaving its fate to the internal ratification processes of its various members.[506] The idea of the agreement was that it could serve as a "docking" agreement, allowing the possibility for other countries that agreed to its terms to join later.

The agreement, as signed, met with substantial pushback from individual state parties, particularly the US. President Trump, who came to power in the US a year after the agreement was signed, was a staunch opponent of the agreement. He criticised it as pushing manufacturing jobs overseas, increasing the US's trade deficit, and failing to address currency manipulation.[507] Members of Congress from both sides also agreed with this analysis, which would eventually lead to the failure of the agreement in the US. On 23 January 2017, only days after coming to power, President Trump signed an executive order withdrawing the US from the agreement.[508] In other countries, including Australia and Canada, domestic trade unions also opposed the agreement as giving too much power to global corporations. The primary concern amongst these countries was that jobs would be able to be moved to countries that were party to the agreement that had lower wages and perhaps less rigid labour standards, which would, in turn, hurt industry in more developed countries.[509]

---

[505] James McBride, Andrew Chatzky and Anshu Siripurapu, "What's Next for the Trans-Pacific Partnership (TPP)?", Council on Foreign Relations, available at: https://www.cfr.org/backgrounder/what-trans-pacific-partnership-tpp.

[506] John A. Powell, Elsadig Elsheikh and Hossein Ayazi, "The Trans-Pacific Partnership: Corporations before People and Democracy", Haas Institute, University of California Berkeley, available at: https://escholarship.org/content/qt3b62p6v0/qt3b62p6v0_noSplash_5ebb097cb314dfeff25a61915c831820.pdf?t=qc4v1u.

[507] James McBride, Andrew Chatzky and Anshu Siripurapu, "What's Next for the Trans-Pacific Partnership (TPP)?", Council on Foreign Relations, available at: https://www.cfr.org/backgrounder/what-trans-pacific-partnership-tpp.

[508] Mireya Solís, "Trump withdrawing from the Trans-Pacific Partnership", Brookings Institution, 24 March 2017, available at: https://www.brookings.edu/blog/unpacked/2017/03/24/trump-withdrawing-from-the-trans-pacific-partnership/.

[509] James McBride, Andrew Chatzky and Anshu Siripurapu, "What's Next for the Trans-Pacific Partnership (TPP)?", Council on Foreign Relations, available at: https://www.cfr.org/backgrounder/what-trans-pacific-partnership-tpp.

Despite these opponents, the other 11 parties to the TPP, without the US, moved forward in negotiating the agreement. In March 2018, these remaining parties were able to sign the Comprehensive and Progressive Agreement for Trans-Pacific Partnership (CPTPP).[510] This new agreement was rapidly ratified in a majority of countries and entered into force on 30 December 2018. This was, in large part, due to the removal of certain provisions that had been pushed by the US, including the removal of several of the intellectual property rights provisions, which many Member States had opposed.[511] The ISDS provision remained in the agreement, but became more limited in scope, as discussed below. These provisional changes were noted as mere suspensions of the provisions, leaving room for the provisions to be added again, should the US decide it wanted to rejoin the agreement. Now that the US is no longer party to the agreement, notable changes have begun to occur, including China showing interest in the agreement; this is something the US feared, but is a move which would exponentially expand the agreement's scope and dominance in global trade.[512]

1.2. OVERVIEW OF THE AGREEMENT'S PRIMARY CLAUSES

The TPP consisted of 30 chapters that, together, aimed to create a fully integrated economic area with established, consistent rules for global investment.[513] Several of the agreement's largest parties, particularly the US, viewed the agreement as a means of limiting Chinese influence in the world.[514] The agreement has five key features: (i) comprehensive market access; (ii) a regional approach to commitments; (iii) addressing new trade challenges; (iv) inclusive trade; and (v) a platform for regional integration.[515]

---

[510] Ibid.

[511] Ibid.

[512] Lavender Au and Benjamin Wilhelp, "China Once Feared the U.S.-Led TPP. Now It's Trying to Join the CPTPP", World Politics Review, 25 November 2020, available at: https://www.worldpoliticsreview.com/trend-lines/29249/china-once-feared-the-u-s-led-tpp-now-it-s-trying-to-join-the-cptpp.

[513] See "Text of the Trans-Pacific Partnership", New Zealand Foreign Affairs & Trade, available at: https://www.mfat.govt.nz/en/about-us/who-we-are/treaties/trans-pacific-partnership-agreement-tpp/text-of-the-trans-pacific-partnership.

[514] James McBride, Andrew Chatzky and Anshu Siripurapu, "What's Next for the Trans-Pacific Partnership (TPP)?", Council on Foreign Relations, available at: https://www.cfr.org/backgrounder/what-trans-pacific-partnership-tpp.

[515] "Summary of the Trans-Pacific Partnership Agreement", available at: http://www.sice.oas.org/TPD/TPP/Negotiations/Summary_TPP_October_2015_e.pdf.

One of the most important and prominent provisions was the elimination or reduction of tariffs, found in Chapters 2 and 3 of the agreement. The TPP lowered tariffs on a range of different goods, including the most prominent goods traded between the countries, such as automotive and agricultural goods.[516] Chapter 3 focused specifically on textiles and apparel, two prominent industries in the countries. Another important feature is the liberalisation of trade in services, found in Chapter 10, which removed restrictions on cross-border services. This provision also added protection for several key industries, including retail, communications, entertainment and finance, which were protected by new rules under the agreement.[517] The investment provisions found in Chapter 9 were aimed particularly at opening markets up to foreign investment among members. The investor-state dispute settlement provision, to be discussed at length below, was included in this Chapter.[518]

The agreement also specifically set out guidelines for e-commerce and intellectual property protections. In many ways, the e-commerce provision found in Chapter 14 of the agreement was a landmark provision, in that it was the first regional deal to include comprehensive rules on digital commerce, and envisioned a trade area where information could flow freely across borders without an investor having to move all their technologies to the target country.[519] The intellectual property provisions, while not unlike those in other trade agreements, allowed for expansive protections of intellectual property, including on prescription drugs and medications, which was a controversial inclusion in the agreement.

Chapters 19 and 20, covering labour and environment, respectively, set higher standards for labour and environmental protections than other global trade agreements.[520] These protections included allowing unions to be formed, prohibitions on child and forced labour, improved workplace conditions, and a wide range of environmental protections. Other chapters in the TPP covered everything from transparency and anti-corruption to

---

[516] James McBride, Andrew Chatzky and Anshu Siripurapu, "What's Next for the Trans-Pacific Partnership (TPP)?", Council on Foreign Relations, available at: https://www.cfr.org/backgrounder/what-trans-pacific-partnership-tpp.

[517] Ibid.

[518] "Summary of the Trans-Pacific Partnership Agreement", available at: http://www.sice.oas.org/TPD/TPP/Negotiations/Summary_TPP_October_2015_e.pdf.

[519] James McBride, Andrew Chatzky and Anshu Siripurapu, "What's Next for the Trans-Pacific Partnership (TPP)?", Council on Foreign Relations, available at: https://www.cfr.org/backgrounder/what-trans-pacific-partnership-tpp.

[520] "Summary of the Trans-Pacific Partnership Agreement", available at: http://www.sice.oas.org/TPD/TPP/Negotiations/Summary_TPP_October_2015_e.pdf.

regulatory coherence, and from competitiveness and business facilitation to rules governing small and medium-sized enterprises.[521] Finally, the dispute settlement provisions, contained in Chapter 28, set forth processes aimed at allowing parties to expeditiously address disputes, with a focus on resolving disputes amicably through alternative dispute resolution mechanisms.[522] Disputes that could not be resolved through alternative dispute mechanisms could then be brought to a panel, similar to an arbitration tribunal, for resolution. One of the unique features of this agreement was the ability for trade retaliation (for example, the suspension of benefits) to be used against parties found not to have complied with their obligations, which goes much further than other trade agreements in providing some recourse for non-compliance.[523]

1.3.   ISDS UNDER THE AGREEMENT

The US's Obama administration was a firm supporter of ISDS, which some have found surprising. In line with its often-criticised support for this mechanism,[524] the administration supported having ISDS included in the TPP, but was met with strong resistance from liberal Democrats in the country. Prominent senator Elizabeth Warren, for example, stood strongly against the administration, stating in no unclear manner her disdain of ISDS, which she viewed as "lacking checks and balances and as an attack on regulatory sovereignty".[525]

The US White House, and other proponents of ISDS among the TPP parties, pointed to several safeguards that had been built into the agreement, in order to demonstrate that the ISDS provisions in the agreement would not be like the standard ISDS provisions that had been built into BITs and other international trade agreements for decades. The TPP, as finalised (before the US withdrew), included several exceptions that limited the scope of ISDS in the agreement. The agreement also

---

[521]   For a complete summary of each Chapter of the TPP, see ibid.

[522]   Ibid.

[523]   Ibid.

[524]   Ezra Klein, "What the most controversial part of Obama's trade deal really does", Vox, 10 November 2015, available at: https://www.vox.com/2015/11/10/9698698/tpp-investor-state-dispute-settlement.

[525]   Todd Tucker, "The TPP has a provision many love to hate: ISDS. What is it, and why does it matter?", Washington Post, 6 October 2015, available at: https://www.washingtonpost.com/.

provided that there must be more than an alleged breach of an obligation in the agreement for ISDS to be activated. The investor had to prove that it had incurred loss or damage as a result of the alleged breach, meaning that there had to be a causal link between the two.[526] The TPP also allowed for an expedited review in favour of host states, which allowed for frivolous or otherwise unmeritorious claims to be dismissed.[527] Moreover, it set out certain protections, including confirming that government action to implement legitimate measures, such as those relating to public health, safety and the environment, would not qualify as expropriation.[528] In an effort to create more transparent procedures, the TPP- specific arbitration procedural rules provided for open and public hearings that allowed expert testimony.[529] Many would deem the protections provided for in the TPP as revolutionary, given that it was the first time that a major international trade agreement had sought to set strong boundaries in relation to ISDS.

Opponents of the TPP, however, presented strong arguments that the provisions in the agreement were not enough, and that ISDS should not be used at all as a dispute settlement mechanism. They argued that, regardless of the protections provided under the TPP, investors would still be able to use other BITs to which Member States were party, to circumvent the limitations provided under the TPP.[530] They also pointed to the ability of investors to choose to have claims heard at a private arbitral

---

[526] The World Bank, "Comparative gap analysis: Indonesia's current obligations under international investment agreements (IIAs) vs. the obligations under the investment chapter of the Transpacific Partnership Agreement (TPP)," available at: https://documents1.worldbank.org/curated/en/202111540822026864/pdf/Comparative-Gap-Analysis-Indonesia-s-Current-Obligations-Under-International-Investment-Agreements-IIAs-vs-The-Obligations-Under-the-Investment-Chapter-of-the-Trans-Pacific-Partnership-Agreement-TPP.pdf.

[527] Ibid. See also Lixiao Fu, "Legal review on investor-state dispute settlement under TPP" (2017) 2 Research on Modern Higher Education, pp. 155–161, 10.24104/rmhe/2017.02.02003, available at: https://www.researchgate.net/publication/314219390_Legal_review_on_investor-state_dispute_settlement_under_TPP.

[528] See, James Roberts, Ted Bromund and Riddhi Dasgupta, "Straight Talk on the ISDS Provisions in the Trans-Pacific Partnership", The Heritage Foundation Issue Brief, No. 4564, 17 May 2016, available at: http://report.heritage.org/ib4564.

[529] Ibid. See also Ko-Yung Tung, "Investor-State Dispute Settlement under the Trans-Pacific Partnership", (2015) 23(1) California International Law Journal, pp. 19–25, available at: https://media2.mofo.com/documents/150800investorstatedisputesettlement.pdf.

[530] Todd Tucker, "The TPP has a provision many love to hate: ISDS. What is it, and why does it matter?", Washington Post, 6 October 2015, available at: https://www.washingtonpost.com/.

centre, with lower transparency requirements, rather than at the ICSID, where the unique procedural rules provided for under the TPP would be respected.[531] More generally, opponents still did not believe that the TPP ISDS protections went far enough to guarantee sovereignty and protection of democratically elected governments.[532]

Given that the TPP did not itself become law, it is impossible to know exactly how this debate would have ended. However, the newly signed – and in most cases ratified – CPTPP, which involves most of the same parties and terms as the original TPP, does include ISDS and continues to face some of the same pushback as the agreement originally negotiated. The most developed countries in the agreement, including New Zealand, Australia, Canada, and Japan, have been active in pushing a positive message on the benefits of ISDS, including a code of conduct of arbitrators, which was included in the enacted agreement.[533]

Under the CPTPP, despite the pushback in the opposite direction, ISDS is still included. That said, the CPTPP goes beyond what was envisioned in the original TPP agreement, limiting ISDS to claims that are related to the investment chapter of the agreement, as well as limited clauses in the financial services chapter. The agreement has also built several safeguards to better protect governments' rights to regulate, with the objective of limiting corporate abuse of systems by using ISDS. These safeguards include the ability for a tribunal to throw out frivolous claims; limits on monetary awards, including on punitive damages; a statute of limitations that reduces the amount of time in which a claim can be brought; and requirements that investors waive their rights to bring other legal proceedings against a state.[534] The agreement also includes rules requiring greater transparency in proceedings. Moreover, investors must follow the procedures referred to in the dispute settlement chapter, as discussed above, which require that alternative dispute mechanisms be utilised prior to a claim being brought

---

[531] Ibid.

[532] See James Roberts, Ted Bromund and Riddhi Dasgupta, "Straight Talk on the ISDS Provisions in the Trans-Pacific Partnership", The Heritage Foundation Issue Brief, No. 4564, 17 May 2016, available at: http://report.heritage.org/ib4564.

[533] See "CPTPP: Investor-State Dispute Settlement", Australian Government Department of Foreign Affairs and Trade, available at: https://www.dfat.gov.au/trade/agreements/in-force/cptpp/official-documents/Pages/official-documents. See also "Trans-Pacific Partnership Investment and ISDS" New Zealand Government, available at: https://tpp.mfat.govt.nz/assets/docs/TPP_factsheet_Investment.pdf.

[534] "Investment and ISDS", New Zealand Foreign Affairs and Trade, available at: https://www.mfat.govt.nz/en/trade/free-trade-agreements/free-trade-agreements-in-force/cptpp/understanding-cptpp/investment-and-isds/.

to an arbitration tribunal. As the agreement is still relatively new, little precedent has thus far been established. That said, this agreement will be an important one for other regions to look to in the future, as other trade agreements are renegotiated or initiated, particularly as the question of ISDS remains the centre of attention in many countries.

2.   NORTH AMERICA AND USMCA

Another hotly debated and highly publicised international trade agreement is the North American Free Trade Agreement (NAFTA), which has now been replaced by the USMCA.

2.1.   HISTORY

The NAFTA was first envisioned in 1990, when US President George H.W. Bush and Mexican President Carlos Salinas de Gortari first began talks on the agreement. In 1991, Canada joined the talks, even though Canada and the US had signed a bilateral free trade agreement in 1988.[535] The initial agreement between Canada and the US was itself considered a landmark agreement, and the most comprehensive trade agreement of its kind at the time, and many of the terms incorporated into this agreement were later incorporated into NAFTA.[536] The agreement, among other things, eliminated tariffs, tightened rules of origin, provided NT, and provided for a binding binational panel to resolve disputes arising under the agreement.[537] At the same time as Canada and the US were negotiating their deal, Mexico was, on its own, attempting to liberalise its trade, and to move away from the statist economy that had carried it into a severe debt crisis in the 1980s.[538]

All of these pre-agreement efforts created an ideal opening for NAFTA negotiations, which would bring together the strengths of the Canada–US

---

[535]   "The rocky history of NAFTA", Reuters, 1 September 2017, available at: https://www.reuters.com/article/us-trade-nafta-timeline/the-rocky-history-of-nafta-idUSKCN1BC5IL.

[536]   M. Angeles Villareal and Ian F. Fergusson, "The North American Free Trade Agreement (NAFTA)", CRS Report R42965, Washington DC: Congressional Research Service, 16 April 2015, available at: http://digitalcommons.ilr.cornell.edu/key_workplace/1411/.

[537]   Ibid.

[538]   Ibid.

trade agreement, and capitalise on the work Mexico had been putting into better promoting trade. Negotiations continued until 1992, when the three countries signed the agreement, in Bush's last year in office. It was not until November 1993, however, that the US Congress ratified the agreement, and President Clinton signed it into law shortly thereafter. The agreement officially came into effect on 1 January 1994, creating the then-largest free trade area in the world.[539]

The start of NAFTA was more than rocky. In Mexico, the agreement caused a huge backlash, leading to the Maya Indian Zapatista guerrillas' declaration of war against the Mexican government, which resulted in days of fighting, and the death of dozens.[540] Later, in 1999, huge protests against the agreement took place in Seattle, in the US. These protests were not only against the agreement itself, but against globalisation in general. The protestors were worried about unsafe imports and labour rights, and angry about capitalism in general.[541] Criticism of NAFTA has continued since its inception, with the loudest criticism of the agreement coming from Donald Trump.

On 19 July 2016, then presidential candidate Donald Trump called NAFTA the "worst trade deal ever", setting in motion the start of a complete renegotiation of the agreement.[542] While several indicators demonstrate that NAFTA has largely been a successful agreement, President Trump and opponents of the agreement were adamant that it be renegotiated. Mexico and Canada are the US's largest trading partners, and the US depends heavily on these countries to provide intermediate goods necessary for production.[543] At the same time, the numbers cited by opponents of the agreement as reasons for withdrawing, including decreased jobs in the US and an increased national deficit, have been demonstrated not to be

---

[539]   Ibid.
[540]   "The rocky history of NAFTA", Reuters, 1 September 2017, available at: https://www.reuters.com/article/us-trade-nafta-timeline/the-rocky-history-of-nafta-idUSKCN1BC5IL.
[541]   Noah Smith, "The Dark Side of Globalization: Why Seattle's 1999 Protesters Were Right", The Atlantic, 6 January 2014, available at: https://www.theatlantic.com/business/archive/2014/01/the-dark-side-of-globalization-why-seattles-1999-protesters-were-right/282831/.
[542]   "The rocky history of NAFTA", Reuters, 1 September 2017, available at: https://www.reuters.com/article/us-trade-nafta-timeline/the-rocky-history-of-nafta-idUSKCN1BC5IL.
[543]   Amanda Waldron, "NAFTA renegotiation: Separating fact from fiction", Brookings Institution, 17 August 2017, available at: https://www.brookings.edu/blog/brookings-now/2017/08/17/nafta-renegotiation-separating-fact-from-fiction/.

attributable to the agreement, but rather to changes in technology, and the modernisation of systems.[544] Regardless, on 16 August 2017, talks began between the three parties to NAFTA to renegotiate the Agreement, in an effort that was said to be focused on modernising the relationship between the partners. This process ended on 24 April 2020, when the three parties concluded the internal processes for the agreement to be enacted.[545] On 1 July 2020, the first day of the third month following that notification, the USMCA officially entered into force, as per Paragraph 2 of the Protocol.[546] The US has indicated, however, that it will not begin enforcing the agreement until 2021.[547]

2.2. OVERVIEW OF NAFTA'S PRIMARY PROVISIONS

Perhaps the most notable feature of NAFTA was that it gradually eliminated all tariffs, as well as most non-tariff barriers, on goods and services, over a period of 15 years.[548] This change had the greatest impact on certain key industries, including the textiles, apparel, automotive and agricultural industries. All duties on textiles and apparel goods were phased out under the agreement, which allowed for a greater flow of these goods across borders. The change that caused the biggest stir in the US was NAFTA phasing out Mexico's auto decree, which had been quite restrictive.[549] This was, however, subject to rules of origin requirements. This change has, over time, led to a move of the US car industry to Mexico, which has caused tremendous pushback from the country's automobile industry unions. Agriculture was the only section not negotiated trilaterally; instead, three separate agreements were signed between each pair of parties.[550] Each of

---

[544]   Ibid.

[545]   "Entry into Force of the United States–Mexico–Canada Agreement", Press Statement of Michael R. Pompeo, Secretary of State of the United States, 1 July 2020, available at: https://ee.usembassy.gov/2020-07-02-5/.

[546]   Eleanor Wragg, "USMCA enters into force, sort of", Global Trade Review, 1 July 2020, available at: https://www.gtreview.com/news/americas/usmca-enters-into-force-sort-of/.

[547]   The enforcement started in the US on 1 January 2021. See, ArentFox Schiff, "Wait Is Over: USMCA Border Enforcement Begins" 5 January 2021, available at: https://www.afslaw.com/perspectives/alerts/wait-over-usmca-border-enforcement-begins.

[548]   M. Angeles Villareal and Ian F. Fergusson, "The North American Free Trade Agreement (NAFTA)", CRS Report R42965, Washington DC: Congressional Research Service, 16 April 2015, available at: http://digitalcommons.ilr.cornell.edu/key_workplace/1411/.

[549]   Ibid.

[550]   Ibid.

these changes led to a steady shift in trade in these industries during the time NAFTA was in force.

NAFTA also created internationally agreed principles on government regulation of trade in services, building on foundations that had been established in the Canada–US agreement, and which had been discussed at the international level.[551] These principles allowed for service providers to be given certain protections, which allowed for non-discriminatory treatment, cross-border sales and entry, investment, and access to information, among others.[552] NAFTA also established certain standards for health, safety and industry, which had never before been enforced among the countries. Each country agreed to establish national standards for inspections, increasing the speed of export-product inspections and certifications.[553] The agreement also put in place certain supplemental agreements aimed at protecting workers, and avoiding the potential for countries to move production abroad in order to avoid worker health and safety regulations.[554]

The dispute settlement provision of NAFTA was one of the most novel components of the agreement. The agreement sets forth a complex system of dispute settlement that altogether provides for five distinct dispute resolution procedures. Chapter 11, which governs foreign investment, provides for investor-state dispute resolution, which will be discussed at length below.[555] Chapter 19 allows for actions of administrative agencies that are contrary to the antidumping and countervailing duties contained in the agreement to be appealed to a binational panel review, bypassing domestic judicial review.[556] The agreement itself may be interpreted or enforced under Chapter 20 thereof, which sets forth dispute settlement mechanisms that mimic those of the WTO, and allow for government-to-government claims to be brought.[557] Additional specifications for financial services are set out in Chapter 14, and the supplemental agreements for labour and environment set forth their own procedures for challenging

---

[551]   Ibid.

[552]   Ibid.

[553]   "North American Free Trade Agreement (NAFTA)", Corporate Finance Institute, 7 April 2020, available at: https://corporatefinanceinstitute.com/resources/knowledge/economics/north-american-free-trade-agreement-nafta/.

[554]   Ibid.

[555]   Jerry L. Lai, "A Tale of Two Treaties: A Study of NAFTA and the USMCA's Investor-State Dispute Settlement Mechanisms", (2021) 35 Emory Int'l L. Rev. 259, available at: https://scholarlycommons.law.emory.edu/eilr/vol35/iss2/3.

[556]   Ibid.

[557]   Ibid.

labour and environmental violations, respectively. These provisions contain a mix of state-to-state dispute settlement and ISDS, which creates a unique system for dispute settlement that allows different provisions to be challenged in different ways. The impacts of this will be further discussed below.

2.3. NOTABLE NAFTA CASES

Before looking more closely at the ISDS and other dispute settlement elements of NAFTA, as well as how these provisions may be changing under the USMCA, the box below explores the most notable cases that were brought under NAFTA. Each of these cases has influenced, in some way, discussions on the agreement, and demonstrated how the dispute settlement provisions contained in NAFTA became some of the most hotly debated elements leading to the negotiation of USMCA.

Notable Cases Under NAFTA[558]

Ethyl Corporation v. The Government of Canada[559]

- Case type: International Investment Agreement
- Applicable arbitration rules: UNCITRAL (1976)
- Investment treaty: NAFTA
- Applicable legal instruments: NAFTA
- Award on Jurisdiction dated 24 June 1998

A Virginia-based chemical company challenged Canada on its ban of MMT, a toxic chemical that has been found to have negative impacts on health and the environment. Ethyl sued Canada under the dispute settlement provision of NAFTA, for USD 251 million in damages. Following a negative ruling by the NAFTA panel on an objection raised by Canada, Canada settled and paid Ethyl USD 13 million in legal fees and damages.

---

[558] William L. Owen, "Investment Arbitration under NAFTA Chapter 11: A Threat to Sovereignty of Member States?", (2015) 39 Canada–United States Law Journal, pp. 55–67, available at: https://scholarlycommons.law.case.edu/cgi/viewcontent.cgi?article=2488&context=cuslj.
[559] *Ethyl Corporation v. The Government of Canada*, available at: https://investmentpolicy.unctad.org/investment-dispute-settlement/cases/16/ethyl-v-canada.

Metalclad Corporation v. Mexico[560]

- Case type: International Investment Agreement
- Applicable arbitration rules: ICSID Additional Facility
- Investment treaty: NAFTA
- Applicable legal instruments: NAFTA
- Award dated 30 August 2000

Metalclad, a California-based corporation that carried out transfer of hazardous waste, contaminated the waste site with 55,000 drums (20,000 tons) of toxic and potentially explosive waste. The company then attempted to construct a new toxic waste facility, but this was shut down before operation, by the municipality of Guadalcazar, for not obtaining the proper permits. The company sued Mexico under NAFTA, claiming that the actions of the municipality amounted to expropriation, and that it did not receive fair and equitable treatment. The NAFTA tribunal, operating under ICSID, awarded USD 16,685,000 in damages to Metalclad.

S.D. Myers, Inc. v. Government of Canada[561]

- Case type: International Investment Agreement
- Applicable arbitration rules: UNCITRAL (1976)
- Investment treaty: NAFTA
- Applicable legal instruments: NAFTA
- Final Award (concerning the apportionment of costs between the Disputing Parties) dated 30 December 2002
- Dissenting Opinion of Professor Bryan P. Schwartz concerning the apportionment of costs between the Disputing Parties (Final Award)
- Partial Award dated 13 November 2000 (Merits)
- Second Partial Award dated 2 December 2002 (Damages)

S.D. Myers, an Ohio-based waste treatment company, sued Canada for USD 20 million to cover lost profits from a ban by Canada of PCBs

---

[560] *Metalclad Corporation v. Mexico*, available at: https://investmentpolicy.unctad.org/investment-dispute-settlement/cases/17/metalclad-v-mexico.
[561] *S.D. Myers, Inc. v. Government of Canada*, available at: https://investmentpolicy.unctad.org/investment-dispute-settlement/cases/20/myers-v-canada.

(toxic chemicals that are to be limited as hazardous material by the Basel Convention) over the 16-month period that the ban was in place. The company claimed that Canada had violated the NT provisions of NAFTA. The NAFTA tribunal ruled against Canada, finding that, while it had legitimate reasons for limiting PCBs, it must still adhere to its obligations under NAFTA.

Loewen Group, Inc. and Raymond L. Loewen v. United States of America, ICSID Case No. ARB(AF)/98/3[562]

- Case type: International Investment Agreement
- Applicable arbitration rules: ICSID Additional Facility
- Investment treaty: NAFTA
- Applicable legal instruments: NAFTA
- Decision on Hearing of Respondent's Objection to Competence and Jurisdiction dated 5 January 2001
- Award dated 26 June 2003

Loewen is a Canadian-based funeral home conglomerate. After aggressively seeking to acquire over 1,000 funeral homes in the US, it was sued in a Mississippi state court by a local businessman who claimed the company's practices were unlawful, anticompetitive and predatory. The jury in the Mississippi case ruled against the company, and in favour of the small business owner. The company then filed a suit against the US, demanding USD 725 million in compensation, arguing that the amount it was ordered to pay by the state court (which it never paid in full) violated its investor rights under NAFTA. What is most notable about this case is that the NAFTA panel agreed to hear the case, saying that it had jurisdiction regardless of whether a local court was involved.

Other Important Cases

- *Pope and Talbot v. Canada*
- *Mondev v. United States*
- *UPS v. Canadian Postal Service*
- *ADF Group v. Buy America*
- *Methanex v. United States*

---

[562] *Loewen Group, Inc. and Raymond L. Loewen v. United States of America*, available at: https://investmentpolicy.unctad.org/investment-dispute-settlement/cases/24/loewen-v-usa.

2.4. ISDS UNDER NAFTA

The ISDS provision of NAFTA, established in Chapter 11 thereof, came after years of the US challenging Mexico's adherence to the Calvo Doctrine and state-to-state dispute settlement. This provision allows foreign investors to utilise arbitration to enforce the most substantive provisions of the agreement, including MFN treatment, freedom from export or local content performance requirements, and the right to make financial transfers.[563] The arbitration utilised under this provision follows international standards, allowing for dispute settlement under the ICSID Convention, where the investor's country and the host country are parties to this Convention, and for dispute settlement under the UNCITRAL rules, for all cases. Under the agreement, none of these mechanisms are required, and investors may also opt for cases to be brought before domestic courts.[564]

NAFTA is, arguably, what put ISDS at the forefront of worldwide dispute settlement.[565] It was not until American companies began bringing claims under NAFTA, against Canada, that international arbitration really took off. US companies challenged Canada 26 times (out of a total of 27 cases brought against Canada under the agreement), more often than not for what may be considered by many as logical and necessary protections enacted by Canada, such as challenging a ban on certain products due to health and environmental risks and denying permits for environmentally unsound projects.[566] As a result, Canada has challenged the ISDS provision under NAFTA, arguing during the negotiations of the USMCA that ISDS should no longer be permitted.

2.5. CHANGES IN THE USMCA PROVISIONS

The introduction of the USMCA changes the landscape for trade regulation in North America. The new version of the agreement contains several

---

[563] David Gantz, "Addressing Dispute Resolution Institutions in a NAFTA Renegotiation", Rice University's Baker Institute for Public Policy, April 2018, available at: https://www.bakerinstitute.org/media/files/files/fa4d9adf/mex-pub-nafta-040218-1.pdf.
[564] Ibid.
[565] Nathalie Bernasconi-Osterwalder, "USMCA Curbs How Much Investors Can Sue Countries – Sort Of", International Institute for Sustainable Development, 2 October 2018, available at: https://www.iisd.org/library/usmca-investors.
[566] Ibid.

changes that the three Member States hope will further enhance trade between them. More than anything, the new agreement updates what had become dated provisions of the initial agreement. The new agreement, for example, has built in substantial labour protections for workers in Mexico that were not found in the initial agreement.[567] These new regulations allow workers to organise and bargain collectively, allow for violations of labour law to be punishable by the cancellation of shipments, and bar all products made by forced labour from importation.[568] The agreement also reduces the protections that drug companies were given under NAFTA, in an effort to better protect consumers, but at the same time adds certain benefits for these companies.[569] To this end, the USMCA puts in place a ten-year protection against generic biologics and increases the length of time that copyrights are valid from 50 to 70 years.[570]

Across various industries, the new agreement makes efforts to keep jobs and production in North America, in an attempt to keep companies from turning to Europe or Asia for production needs. For example, in order to qualify for zero tariffs under the USMCA, vehicle makers must demonstrate that 75% of a vehicle's content was produced in North America, a notable increase from the 62.5% required under NAFTA.[571] Moreover, the vehicle maker must demonstrate that 40 to 45% of the parts for the vehicle were made in high-wage factories and that 70% of steel and aluminium included in the vehicles was melted and poured in North America.[572] Certain provisions included in the new agreement aim to streamline processes. For example, exporters will no longer be required to complete formal certifications of origin, and the de minimis rate for low-valued goods to enter each country has also increased.[573]

Perhaps the biggest change in the entire USMCA is the changes it has made to NAFTA's dispute settlement provisions. The new agreement is somewhat unique in that the actual ISDS provisions will differ depending on which states are involved. Between Canada and the US, ISDS will no

---

[567] Ana Swanson and Jim Tankersley, "Trump Just Signed the U.S.M.C.A. Here's What's in the New NAFTA", The New York Times, 1 July 2020, available at: https://www.nytimes.com/2020/01/29/business/economy/usmca-deal.html.
[568] Ibid.
[569] Eleanor Wragg, "USMCA enters into force, sort of", Global Trade Review, 1 July 2020, available at: https://www.gtreview.com/news/americas/usmca-enters-into-force-sort-of/.
[570] Ibid.
[571] Ibid.
[572] Ibid.
[573] Ibid.

longer be permitted. US or Canadian (as history has demonstrated, typically US) investors will now have to bring their claims under the agreement directly to local courts.[574] Between Mexico and the US, however, an annex to the USMCA dictates that ISDS will still be the mechanism utilised, but only in matters pertaining to expropriation and non-discrimination.[575] Additionally, similarly to what was included in the TPP, investors from these two countries, when operating in the other country, will have an obligation to first try and resolve disputes using direct negotiation, before bringing a claim to an arbitration tribunal.[576] Interestingly, the relationship between Canada and Mexico will be regulated by the CPTPP (discussed above), as both countries are party to that agreement.

What makes these new developments in North America most significant is that the pioneering region, when it comes to ISDS, is now, at least in part, turning its back on the practice. The question then arises as to whether this will – particularly now the USMCA has been enacted – spur a global movement away from ISDS, as was the case towards ISDS after the enactment of NAFTA. It will also be important to monitor developments on the new agreement, particularly amid growing tensions between the three countries under the current administrations in each country.

3.   EUROPE

3.1.   INVESTMENT AGREEMENTS IN EUROPE AND THE IMPACT OF THE LISBON TREATY

BITs originated in Europe, with the first BIT involving a European country, having been concluded between the Federal Republic of Germany and Pakistan in 1959.[577] Since that time, the continent has spearheaded the

---

[574]   Ibid.

[575]   Martin Valasek, Alison Fitzgerald and Jenna Anen de Jong, "Major changes for investor-state dispute settlement in new United States–Mexico–Canada Agreement", October 2018, available at: https://www.nortonrosefulbright.com/en/knowledge/publications/91d41adf/major-changes-for-investor-state-dispute-settlement-in-new-united-states-mexico-canada-agreement.

[576]   Nathalie Bernasconi-Osterwalder, "USMCA Curbs How Much Investors Can Sue Countries – Sort of", International Institute for Sustainable Development, 2 October 2018, available at: https://www.iisd.org/library/usmca-investors.

[577]   Carrie E. Anderer, "Bilateral Investment Treaties and the EU Legal Order: Implications of the Lisbon Treaty", (2010) 35(3) Brooklyn Journal of International Law, pp. 851–882, available at: https://brooklynworks.brooklaw.edu/cgi/viewcontent.cgi?article=1152&context=bjil.

world's increase in the usage of BITs, and has largely championed the rights of investors. This expansion of the use of BITs in Europe has continued since the inception of this practice, even as the EU itself continued to expand as one of the world's largest, and arguably most well-established, trade blocs. Collectively, Member States had entered into 1,400 BITs by 2009.[578] As the Union began to expand into Eastern and Central Europe, where many BITs had been executed between the EU and the new Member States, there arose an uncertainty regarding the legal order between conflicting agreements.[579]

The Lisbon Treaty, which entered into force in 2009, was an effort to create greater cohesion among legal agreements on the continent. This international agreement between EU Member States amended the sources of EU law.[580] The most notable provision of this law, as it pertains to BITs, is one that transfers competence over FDI from Member States to the EU, bringing it under the EU's Common Commercial Policy.[581] What this means is that international investment policy is now set at the EU level, including regulation of investment liberalism, post-establishment treatment standards and investment protection.[582] Through this agreement, Europe is seeking to create its own unique model for international investment agreements.[583] The implementation of this law, given the complexity of laws in the EU, and the mix of national and international agreements, has proven quite complicated.

The EU has gone about constructing continental investment law in much the same way as it had previously constructed laws on market access,

---

[578] Catherine Titi, "International Investment Law and the European Union: Towards a New Generation of International Investment Agreements", (2015) 26(3) European Journal of International Law, pp. 639–661, available at: http://www.ejil.org/pdfs/26/3/2598.pdf.

[579] Carrie E. Anderer, "Bilateral Investment Treaties and the EU Legal Order: Implications of the Lisbon Treaty", (2010) 35(3) Brooklyn Journal of International Law, pp. 851–882, available at: https://brooklynworks.brooklaw.edu/cgi/viewcontent.cgi?article=1152&context=bjil.

[580] Ibid.

[581] Ibid.

[582] Robert Basedow, "A Legal History of the EU's International Investment Policy", (2016) 17(5) Journal of World Investment and Trade, pp. 743–772, available at: http://eprints.lse.ac.uk/86423/1/Basedow_Legal%20history_2018.pdf.

[583] Catherine Titi, "International Investment Law and the European Union: Towards a New Generation of International Investment Agreements", (2015) 26(3) The European Journal of International Law, pp. 639–661, available at: http://www.ejil.org/pdfs/26/3/2598.pdf.

something that has been within the Union's competency (as opposed to that of individual Member States) for quite some time. What this means is that the European Commission, charged with constructing continental-level laws and policy, has put tremendous focus on the protection of human rights, including labour and environmental rights, as well as on a state's right to regulate.[584] According to Article 205 of the Treaty on the Functioning of the European Union (TFEU), the EU has a constitutional obligation to comply with the principles that guide its external action, including democracy, human rights, sustainable development, the preservation and improvement of the environment, sustainable management of natural global resources, and the guiding principles of the Charter of the United Nations.[585] In the opinion of the Commission, this means that Member States must be given the ability to establish domestic policies. This position has also been supported by the European Parliament. In most cases, the Commission has sought to add an investment chapter into existing trade agreements, rather than to construct stand-alone agreements, although in some cases the investment chapter is intended to serve as a stand-alone document.[586]

Following the Lisbon Treaty, the EU has continued to negotiate agreements on an individual basis, and has not yet established a single model investment agreement. This runs contrary to the practice prior to this treaty, whereby individual countries such as Germany and the Netherlands established model agreements using best practices. The EU has indicated that it intends to deploy certain tactics and strategies when negotiating with developing countries, and another standard when it negotiates with developed nations, which may explain why it has not yet established a single model agreement.[587] The EU has, however, put in place certain standards in all of the agreements it has negotiated thus far.[588] This includes a provision that the terms of the investment agreements are "without prejudice to the right of the EU and the Member States to adopt and enforce measures

---

[584]   Ibid.
[585]   Ibid.
[586]   Ibid. One example of the investment chapter being separated from the other provisions of the free trade agreement is the EU–Singapore Free Trade Agreement (FTA), which concluded as an investment chapter-free FTA.
[587]   Ibid.
[588]   Stephen Woolcock, "EU Trade and Investment Policymaking after the Lisbon Treaty", (2010) 45(1) Intereconomics, pp. 22–25, available at: https://www.intereconomics.eu/contents/year/2010/number/1/article/eu-trade-and-investment-policymaking-after-the-lisbon-treaty.html.

necessary to pursue legitimate public policy objectives".[589] The agreements also stress fair and equitable treatment. Whether these terms will eventually be incorporated into a model agreement for investment remains unknown. What is already certain is that the EU is leading the way with a new vision of the investment agreement.

3.2. THE EVOLUTION OF ISDS IN EUROPE

With the expansive number of BITs entered into by EU Member States from the 1960s until the Lisbon Treaty, the continent's individual countries have been party to a substantial number of investment arbitrations. As late as 2012, EU Member States were party to 60% of the world's total number of investment arbitrations.[590] These cases were brought under the traditional BIT ISDS model. The box below highlights some of the most notable cases brought against EU Member States under the ISDS language included in the continent's numerous BITs.[591]

Notable Cases in Europe[592]

Renewable Energy Cases against Spain

In 2007 Spain implemented several incentive measures to boost its renewable energy sector with the purpose of incentivising investment in renewable energy. In 2010, Spain amended most of these measures, which led to approximately 40 arbitral claims on the ground that it violated the FET provision contained in Article 10(1) of the Energy Charter Treaty (ECT).[593]

---

[589] Catherine Titi, "International Investment Law and the European Union: Towards a New Generation of International Investment Agreements", (2015) 26(3) The European Journal of International Law, pp. 639–661, available at: http://www.ejil.org/pdfs/26/3/2598.pdf.

[590] Ibid.

[591] Carrie E. Anderer, "Bilateral Investment Treaties and the EU Legal Order: Implications of the Lisbon Treaty", (2010) 35(3) Brooklyn Journal of International Law, pp. 851–882, available at: https://brooklynworks.brooklaw.edu/cgi/viewcontent.cgi?article=1152&context=bjil.

[592] "Fact Sheet on Intra-European Union Investor-State Arbitration Cases", International Investment Agreements, UNCTAD, December 2018, available at: https://unctad.org/en/PublicationsLibrary/diaepcb2018d7_en.pdf.

[593] See, Amélie Noilhac, "Renewable energy investment cases against Spain and the quest for regulatory consistency" QIL, 14 June 2020, available at: http://www.qil-qdi.org/renewable-energy-investment-cases-against-spain-and-the-quest-for-regulatory-consistency/.

Blusun S.A., Jean-Pierre Lecorcier and Michael Stein v. Italian Republic, ICSID Case No. ARB/14/3[594]

- Case type: International Investment Agreement
- Applicable arbitration rules: ICSID Convention – Arbitration Rules
- Investment treaty: ECT
- Applicable legal instruments: ECT
- Award dated 27 December 2016

Challenging legislative Acts placing certain restrictions on the use of agricultural land for solar plants, and amending the rules on "feed-in tariffs".

Poštová banka, a.s. and Istrokapital SE v. Hellenic Republic, ICSID Case No. ARB/13/8[595]

- Case type: International Investment Agreement
- Applicable arbitration rules: ICSID
- Investment treaty: Cyprus-Greece BIT, Greece-Slovakia BIT
- Applicable legal instruments: Cyprus-Greece BIT, Greece-Slovakia BIT
- Award dated 9 April 2015

Challenging legislation concerning the restructuring of government bond obligations.

Antaris Solar GmbH and Dr. Michael Göde v. Czech Republic, PCA Case No. 2014-01[596]

- Case type: International Investment Agreement
- Applicable arbitration rules: UNCITRAL (1976)

---

[594] *Blusun S.A., Jean-Pierre Lecorcier and Michael Stein v. Italian Republic,* ICSID Case No. ARB/14/3, available at: https://investmentpolicy.unctad.org/investment-dispute-settlement/cases/575/blusun-v-italy.

[595] *Poštová banka, a.s. and Istrokapital SE v. Hellenic Republic,* ICSID Case No. ARB/13/8, available at: https://investmentpolicy.unctad.org/investment-dispute-settlement/cases/551/po-tov-banka-and-istrokapital-v-greece.

[596] *Antaris Solar GmbH and Dr. Michael Göde v. The Czech Republic,* PCA Case No. 2014-01, available at: https://investmentpolicy.unctad.org/investment-dispute-settlement/cases/558/antaris-and-g-de-v-czech-republic.

- Investment treaty: ECT, Czech Republic-Germany BIT (1990)
- Applicable legal instruments: ECT (1994), Czech Republic-Germany BIT (1990)
- Award dated 2 May 2018

Challenging abrogation of tax incentives and introduction of a levy on solar energy producers.

European American Investment Bank AG v. The Slovak Republic, PCA Case No. 2010-17[597]

- Case type: International Investment Agreement
- Applicable arbitration rules: UNCITRAL (1976)
- Investment treaty: Austria-Slovak Republic BIT
- Applicable legal instruments: Austria-Slovak Republic BIT
- Award on Jurisdiction dated 22 October 2012
- Second Award on Jurisdiction dated 4 June 2014
- Award on Costs dated 20 August 2014

Challenging legislation prohibiting private health insurance companies from distributing profits and requiring them to reinvest all such profits in the provision of public healthcare.

AES Summit Generation Limited and AES-Tisza Erömü Kft. v. Republic of Hungary (II), ICSID Case No. ARB/07/22[598]

- Case type: International Investment Agreement
- Applicable arbitration rules: ICSID
- Investment treaty: ECT
- Applicable legal instruments: ECT
- Award dated 23 September 2010

Challenging legislation introducing regulated prices for electrical energy.

---

[597] *European American Investment Bank AG v. The Slovak Republic*, PCA Case No. 2010-17, available at: https://investmentpolicy.unctad.org/investment-dispute-settlement/cases/357/euram-bank-v-slovakia.

[598] *AES Summit Generation Limited and AES-Tisza Erömü Kft. v. Republic of Hungary (II)*, ICSID Case No. ARB/07/22, available at: https://investmentpolicy.unctad.org/investment-dispute-settlement/cases/279/aes-v-hungary-ii-.

Ioan Micula, Viorel Micula, S.C. European Food S.A, S.C. Starmill S.R.L. and S.C. Multipack S.R.L. v. Romania (I), ICSID Case No. ARB/05/20

- Case type: International Investment Agreement
- Applicable arbitration rules: ICSID Convention – Arbitration Rules
- Investment treaty: Romania-Sweden BIT
- Applicable legal instruments: Romania-Sweden BIT
- Final Award dated 11 December 2013

Ioan Micula, Viorel Micula and others v. Romania (II), ICSID Case No. ARB/14/29

- Case type: International Investment Agreement
- Applicable arbitration rules: ICSID
- Investment treaty: Romania-Sweden BIT
- Applicable legal instruments: Romania-Sweden BIT
- Final Award dated 5 March 2020

Challenging legislation revoking the majority of incentives previously granted to investors in the country's "disfavoured" regions.

EDF (Services) Limited v. Republic of Romania, ICSID Case No. ARB/05/13

- Case type: International Investment Agreement
- Applicable arbitration rules: ICSID
- Investment treaty: Romania-United Kingdom BIT
- Applicable legal instruments: Romania-United Kingdom BIT
- Award dated 8 October 2009

Challenging legislation abolishing duty-free activities at airports.

Eastern Sugar B.V. (Netherlands) v. The Czech Republic, SCC Case No. 088/2004

- Case type: International Investment Agreement
- Applicable arbitration rules: UNCITRAL (1976)
- Investment treaty: Czech Republic-Netherlands BIT
- Applicable legal instruments: Czech Republic-Netherlands BIT
- Final Award dated 12 April 2007

Challenging legislation concerning quotas for the production of sugar.

Following the enactment of the Lisbon Treaty, the world of international arbitration, and particularly dispute settlement, has become quite complicated. Of particular difficulty is the question as to the relationship between the BITs that had been entered into between Member States, on the one hand, and EU treaties, on the other.[599] To resolve this situation, the European Commission has, in certain circumstances, required that Member States terminate the BITs between them. One example of this is the *Micula* case, which concerned compensation to be paid by Romania to Swedish investors, under the Sweden–Romania BIT.[600] This compensation would, however, have constituted illegal state aid under EU law, thereby highlighting the potential conflict between EU law and BITs. The Commission required Romania to not enforce the BIT, and required the two countries to terminate the agreement altogether.

Outside of the EU, there has also been discussion on what the future of ISDS under BITs should look like. While, as previously discussed, the EU has acknowledged and embraced the importance of states having sovereignty to implement internal policies that protect domestic rights, more recent EU agreements have actually continued to embrace ISDS. This may be seen by some as running contrary to the protections the Union is putting into new investment agreements. In defending the inclusion of ISDS in recent agreements, the European Commission has argued that there needs to be an effective ISDS structure included in agreements, otherwise there is a risk of discouraging investors and lowering the attractiveness of an economy as an investment destination.[601] At the same time, however, the European Parliament has argued that the decision to include ISDS in a new investment agreement must be made on a case-by-case basis, and considering the circumstances giving rise to that agreement.[602]

Under this perception, the EU has demonstrated an express interest in improving the ISDS system. Some of the proposed changes that the EU has raised at the international level include the need for greater transparency in the system, the prevention of investors from engaging in multiple or frivolous claims, and the need to introduce a code of conduct

---

[599] Tahmina Sahibli, "The relationship of EU Law and bilateral investment treaties", 2015, available at: https://www.diva-portal.org/smash/get/diva2:903370/fulltext01.pdf.

[600] Ibid.

[601] Catherine Titi, "International Investment Law and the European Union: Towards a New Generation of International Investment Agreements", (2015) 26(3) The European Journal of International Law, pp. 639–661, available at: http://www.ejil.org/pdfs/26/3/2598.pdf.

[602] Ibid.

for arbitrators.[603] The EU brought these desires to the negotiation of its most important trade agreement, thus far, since the Lisbon Treaty – the Canada–EU Comprehensive Economic and Trade Agreement (CETA) – and, until talks were halted, had the same intention of incorporating these terms in the US–EU Transatlantic Trade and Investment Partnership (TTIP).[604]

The CETA has demonstrated a clear break from the traditional ISDS model used in BITs, and serves as a model for Europe's intended moves forward with ISDS. This agreement sets forth full transparency of proceedings and clear investment protection standards.[605] At the same time, this agreement aims to move towards the establishment of a permanent multilateral investment court.[606] Under the agreement, investor-state disputes will be heard by a permanent tribunal, composed of independent and publicly appointed members of a first-instance tribunal, and then, later, by an appellate court. This "CETA Tribunal" will be composed of 15 members.[607] The procedural rules mimic those of the WTO on dispute settlement and create a new model for resolving disputes. The EU has indicated that this model of a specific dispute settlement body for resolving disputes under this agreement is one step forward in advocating for the establishment of a multilateral investment court, which it has advocated in front of UNCITRAL. Following the implementation of the CETA agreement, the Court of Justice of the European Union (ECJ) held that the ISDS terms were compatible with EU law.[608] This new model of agreement aims to demonstrate a greater desire to protect fundamental rights and values, which is a step forward

---

[603] Ibid.

[604] Note that the TTIP talks have been terminated since 2016, and the negotiation of this agreement is no longer moving forward. One of the principal points of debate when these negotiations were open was the inclusion of ISDS. This caused substantial public backlash in both the EU and the US. Many of the provisions that were to be incorporated into this agreement have since been incorporated in the Canada–EU investment agreement, discussed later in this chapter. See Mark Weaver, "The Proposed Transatlantic Trade and Investment Partnership (TTIP): ISDS Provisions, Reconciliation, and Future Trade Implications", (2014) 29 Emory Int'l L. Rev. 225.

[605] "CETA: EU and Canada agree on new approach on investment in trade agreement", European Commission, 29 February 2016, available at: https://ec.europa.eu/commission/presscorner/detail/sk/IP_16_399.

[606] Ibid.

[607] European Commission, "CETA Chapter by Chapter", available at https://ec.europa.eu/trade/policy/in-focus/ceta/ceta-chapter-by-chapter/.

[608] Opinion 1/17 of the Court of Justice of the European Union, 30 April 2019.

in protecting the rights of states over those of investors. UNCITRAL has formed a working group to discuss adopting this model of a multilateral court at the international level, and the EU and Canada have stated that, if such a court is established, then disputes under CETA will be brought to that court.[609] At the same time, the establishment of such a court would mark a major advancement on the global stage, in terms of ISDS reform.

3.3. THE *ACHMEA* CASE AND THE FUTURE OF ISDS IN EUROPE

On 6 March 2018, the ECJ dealt ISDS one of its greatest blows yet, in a landmark decision that is certain to have a major impact on ISDS in Europe, if not globally. In the case of *Slovakia v. Achmea* (the "*Achmea* case"), the ECJ ruled that the arbitration provision in a BIT between Slovakia and the Netherlands, which allowed for ISDS, was contrary to EU law, and that an arbitral tribunal is not the forum for arguing against matters of European law.[610] The Court's view was that there is no way to guarantee European law if it may be challenged at will in arbitral tribunals, rather than through the European courts. This case seemed to essentially render all of Europe's intra-European BITs void.

If the case itself did not finally end the use of intra-European BITs, a 2019 announcement by 28 EU Member States[611] made a political declaration that such agreements would, from then on, be terminated. On 15 January 2019, in a move largely consistent with movements on the continent since the enactment of the Lisbon Treaty, these Member States announced that they would be "terminat[ing] all bilateral investment treaties concluded between them by means of a plurilateral treaty, or, where it is mutually recognized as more expedient, bilaterally".[612] In addition, these states

---

[609] "Standing first instance and appeal investment court with full-time judges", United Nations Commission on International Trade Law, available at: https://uncitral.un.org/en/standing.

[610] "The Incompatibility of Intra-EU BITs with European-Union law," annotation following ECJ, *Slovak Republic v. Achmea BV*, Case 284/16, 6 March 2018.

[611] Signed by Austria, Belgium, Bulgaria, Cyprus, Croatia, Czechia, Denmark, France, Germany, Estonia, Greece, Ireland, Italy, Latvia, Lithuania, the Netherlands, Poland, Portugal, Romania, Slovakia, Slovenia, Spain and the United Kingdom.

[612] "Declaration of the Member States of 15 January 2019 on the legal consequences of the *Achmea* judgment and on investment protection", published 17 January 2019, available at: https://ec.europa.eu/info/publications/190117-bilateral-investment-treaties_en.

ordered investors not to bring any new cases against EU Member States, and asked that all ongoing cases be dropped.[613]

While the EU Member States have made the move towards declaring that in Europe, post-Lisbon, intra-European investment agreements will no longer be utilised or enforced, the *Achmea* case was not as clear about what will happen with extra-EU agreements. Some experts believe that the case means that the restrictions will be extended outside the continent, while others believe that it is a matter of hierarchy within the continent, pertaining to its own legal obligations.[614] There also remain certain open questions on what impact this case will have on multilateral investment treaties (MITs). The ICSID appears to remain firm on upholding the provisions of MITs, such as the Energy Charter Treaty, an international investment agreement, to which the EU is a party, that established a multilateral framework for cross-border cooperation in the energy industry, and which the ICSID has argued is of a different scope than BITs. As such, the ICSID has held that investors have the right to challenge that agreement in international arbitral tribunals; this was its decision in *Vattenfall v. Germany*,[615] and then again in *Landesbank Baden-Wurttemberg and others v. Kingdom of Spain*.[616]

To further complicate interpretation, investors have attempted to challenge the *Achmea* decision using the New York Convention. The EU Commission has had to attempt quickly to insert itself into these proceedings, most of which have been brought in the US, in New York courts. The Commission has argued that the public policy exception of the New York Convention applies to these cases. More particularly, it has argued that there are foreign policy implications of allowing enforcement of intra-EU awards.[617]

The implications of this debate for ISDS on the European continent are still in flux. One clear indication arising from *Achmea* and the events

---

[613] Ibid.

[614] Christopher Casey, "The End of Intra-EU Investor-State Dispute Settlement (ISDS): Implications for the United States", CRS Insight, 13 February 2019, available at: https://fas.org/sgp/crs/row/IN11041.pdf.

[615] *Vattenfall AB and others v. Federal Republic of Germany*, ICSID Case No. ARB/12/12.

[616] *Landesbank Baden-Wurttemberg (LBBW) et al. v. Kingdom of Spain*, ICSID Case No. ARB/15/45, award of 25 February 2019.

[617] Tania Singla, "*Achmea*: The Fate and Future of Intra-EU Investment Treaty Awards under the New York Convention", EJIL: Talk!, Blog of the European Journal of International Law, 8 May 2018, available at: https://www.ejiltalk.org/achmea-the-fate-and-future-of-intra-eu-investment-treaty-awards-under-the-new-york-convention/.

thereafter is that the EU is actively working towards the establishment of an investment court system. In short, the EU is arguing that such a court will create a more predictable, more transparent system, with greater oversight of arbitrators, and the ability to appeal decisions.[618] This is in line with the move towards terminating intra-European BITs, which have begun to be seen as including dated dispute settlement provisions. In the interim, the EU has been taking steps towards creating a hybrid system while an international court is being established, as demonstrated in the CETA.[619] The EU has also pursued similar set-ups in other agreements, with Vietnam and Indonesia, and has expressed that it will continue to pursue this hybrid model for as long as a multilateral tribunal has not been established. Whether the European model will be adopted on a larger international level remains to be seen. One can only imagine that the exit of the United Kingdom from the Union will only complicate moves forward. As Europe is one of the strongest economic blocs in the world, and remains a leader in shaping global policy, it is essential in looking at the future of ISDS to watch closely how the ripple effects of the *Achmea* case continue to evolve.

4. LATIN AMERICA AND THE CARIBBEAN

4.1. THE HISTORY OF ISDS IN LATIN AMERICA

Latin America, the birthplace of the Calvo Doctrine (see Chapter 6) has had a rocky relationship with ISDS since its inception. Bilateral treaties themselves have been the cornerstone of the region's international economic integration strategy for over three decades, and the region's countries have entered into more than 700 BITs since the 1990s.[620] This number includes agreements between Latin American countries;

---

[618] Tilbe Birengel, "European Union: A Shift from Arbitration to Multilateral Investment Court System at EU", Erdem & Erdem Law, 19 March 2019, available at: https://www.mondaq.com/turkey/arbitration-dispute-resolution/791418/a-shift-from-arbitration-to-multilateral-investment-court-system-at-eu.

[619] Ibid.

[620] "ISDS Reform in Latin America – Setting the stage: an Overview of ISDS in the Region", Center for the Advancement of the Rule of Law in the Americas, Georgetown University, available at: https://www.law.georgetown.edu/carola/wp-content/uploads/sites/29/2020/05/ISDS-Landscape-in-LA.pdf.

agreements between Latin American countries and developed countries such as the US and European countries; and a growing number of treaties between Latin American countries and developing countries, particularly in Asia.[621] Certain regional agreements that have also been formed during this same time, including the Andean Community,[622] Mercosur[623] and the Pacific Alliance.[624] Each of these BITs includes standard trade agreement provisions, such as reciprocal trade and elimination of tariffs. These agreements also cover a range of other issues, including foreign investment, government procurement, trade in services, and intellectual property.

While ISDS has made its way into many of these agreements, Latin America has consistently demonstrated hesitancy towards embracing this mechanism for dispute settlement. In 1964, the region famously gave what is referred to as the "Tokyo No", with Latin American countries unanimously voting against the ICSID Convention.[625] It was only under pressure from foreign companies that a majority of Latin American countries began adopting ISDS into their BITs. As the number of BITs that Latin American countries entered into increased exponentially in the 1990s, with the region turning its eyes towards greater international involvement, the use of ISDS in those agreements also increased. With the notable exception of Brazil, which will be discussed below, Latin American countries have gradually found ISDS included in their treaties with other countries, both in intercontinental agreements and in international agreements. However, for reasons that will be further discussed below, Latin American countries have, in the last decade, begun to demonstrate a desire to revert to their initial position against this mechanism.

---

[621] "Free Trade Agreements in South America. Trends, Prospects and Challenges", Banco de Desarrollo de América Latina, Public Policy and Productive Transformation Series, No. 7/2012, available at: https://scioteca.caf.com/bitstream/handle/123456789/365/caf_tomo_7_.pdf?sequence=1.

[622] Member States include Bolivia, Colombia, Ecuador and Peru. Chile, Argentina, Brazil, Paraguay and Uruguay are associate members, and Panama, Mexico and Spain are observers.

[623] Member States are Argentina, Brazil and Uruguay.

[624] Member States are Peru, Colombia and Chile.

[625] Nicolas Boeglin, "ICSID and Latin America: Criticism, withdrawal and the search for alternatives", Bretton Woods Project, 3 December 2013, available at: https://www.brettonwoodsproject.org/2013/12/icsid-latin-america/.

4.2. LATIN AMERICA'S STRUGGLE WITH ISDS

Since ISDS first made its way into Latin America BITs, the region has faced some of its fears about this dispute settlement mechanism head-on, with countries in the region having been challenged approximately 300 times by investors using ISDS. Since the 1990s, countries across the region have had internal processes and domestic policies challenged by foreign investors. This is particularly true of countries that have faced economic and political turmoil.

Latin America has faced the unique challenge of widely fluctuating economies in certain countries (for example, Argentina), which has made implementing domestic regulations essential in stabilising inflation and controlling the economy.[626] However, domestic policy that is set in response to a current crisis is more likely to run counter to investment agreements than decisions made during periods of growth, when the time can be taken to consider impacts on existing investments. The result, in Latin America, has been a significant portion of the total ICSID caseload coming from the region.[627] Argentina has been challenged 62 times, almost always as a result of the economic crises that the country has faced.[628] Venezuela, the most unstable country in the region, has also been brought into 51 cases.[629] Latin American countries have expressed their growing frustration with the ISDS system, which they view as often running contrary to their domestic needs. This is particularly true when countries such as Argentina believe that it is necessary to put in place certain domestic policies to prevent further economic decline, yet these policies are challenged by investors as contrary to their individual interests.

The box below provides an overview of the most notable cases in Latin America, which have led several Latin American countries to shift back to their initial view that ISDS should not be the mechanism of choice for dispute settlement.

---

[626]   Silvia Karina Fiezonni, "The Challenge of UNASUR Member Countries to Replace ICSID Arbitration", Beijing Law Review, 1 September 2011.
[627]   39% of cases at ICSID. See ibid.
[628]   See "ISDS Reform in Latin America – Setting the stage: an Overview of ISDS in the Region", Center for the Advancement of the Rule of Law in the Americas, Georgetown University, available at: https://www.law.georgetown.edu/carola/wp-content/uploads/sites/29/2020/05/ISDS-Landscape-in-LA.pdf.
[629]   Ibid.

Notable Cases in Latin America

Chevron v. Ecuador[630]

- *Chevron Corporation and Texaco Petroleum Company v. The Republic of Ecuador (I)*, PCA Case No. 2007-02/AA277
  - Case type: International Investment Agreement
  - Applicable arbitration rules: UNCITRAL Arbitration Rules (1976)
  - Investment treaty: Ecuador-United States BIT
  - Applicable legal instruments: Ecuador-United States BIT
  - Interim Award dated 1 December 2008
  - Partial Award on the Merits dated 30 March 2010
  - Final Award dated 31 August 2011

- *Chevron Corporation and Texaco Petroleum Corporation v. Ecuador (II)*, PCA Case No. 2009-23
  - Case type: International Investment Agreement
  - Applicable arbitration rules: UNCITRAL Arbitration Rules (1976)
  - Investment treaty: Ecuador-United States BIT
  - Applicable legal instruments: Ecuador-United States BIT
  - Case status: Pending

This case, ongoing for more than a decade, involved a major role reversal between Chevron and Ecuador. In the first case giving rise to this contentious relationship, a local court in Ecuador ruled against Chevron for its pollution of the Amazon between 1964 and 1992. In 2011, this court ordered Chevron to pay USD 9.5 billion. Later, Chevron brought a case against Ecuador at the Permanent Court of Arbitration in The Hague, under the UNCITRAL Arbitration Rules, and was successful, with the arbitration tribunal finding that Ecuador had violated the bilateral investment treaty and international law by delaying rulings on the commercial dispute. The tribunal awarded Chevron USD 96 million. This case remains an ongoing saga, with neither party willing to accept any decision as final.

---

[630] "Texaco/Chevron Lawsuits (re Ecuador)", available at: https://investmentpolicy. unctad.org/investment-dispute-settlement/cases/242/chevron-and-texpet-v-ecuador-i-.

Philip Morris v. Uruguay[631]

- Case type: International Investment Agreement
- Applicable arbitration rules: ICSID
- Investment treaty: Switzerland-Uruguay BIT
- Applicable legal instruments: Switzerland-Uruguay BIT
- Decision on Jurisdiction dated 2 July 2013
- Award dated 8 July 2016
- Concurring and Dissenting Opinion of Gary Born
- Decision on Rectification dated 26 September 2016

Philip Morris, a US company, challenged a Uruguayan regulation aimed at mitigating public health risks linked to tobacco consumption. The arbitral tribunal in this case ruled in favour of Uruguay, stating that the state does not need to prove a direct causal link between the regulation and any observed public health outcomes. It stated that it was sufficient that Uruguay was attempting to address a public health concern, when taken in good faith.

Pacific Rim v. El Salvador[632]

- Case type: International Investment Agreement, Foreign Investment Law
- Applicable arbitration rules: ICSID Convention – Arbitration Rules
- Investment treaty: The Central America Free Trade Agreement (CAFTA)
- Applicable legal instruments: CAFTA
- Decision on the Respondent's Preliminary Objections under CAFTA Articles 10.20.4 and 10.20.5 dated 2 August 2010
- Decision on the Respondent's Jurisdictional Objections dated 1 June 2012

Pacific Rim, a multinational mining corporation headquartered in Canada, brought a case against El Salvador for its denial of an

---

[631] *Philip Morris S.A. and Abal Hermanos S.A. v. Oriental Republic of Uruguay*, ICSID Case No. ARB/10/7, available at: https://investmentpolicy.unctad.org/investment-dispute-settlement/cases/368/philip-morris-v-uruguay.

[632] *Pac Rim Cayman LLC v. Republic of El Salvador*, ICSID Case No. ARB/09/12, available at: https://investmentpolicy.unctad.org/investment-dispute-settlement/cases/356/pac-rim-v-el-salvador.

underground mining concession. The arbitral tribunal, because it was to act on the basis of the local investment law, rejected the claim because of the company's lack of compliance with local mining law.

David Aven v. Costa Rica[633]

- Case type: International Investment Agreement
- Applicable arbitration rules: UNCITRAL (1976)
- Investment treaty: CAFTA-DR
- Applicable legal instruments: CAFTA-DR
- Final Award dated 18 September 2018

Claiming that Costa Rica had unfairly revoked tourist development permits, ICSID, again bound to rule on the basis of local law, dismissed the claim, finding that the investor was in breach of local law protecting wetlands and forests.

4.3. LATIN AMERICA'S RESPONSE TO ISDS CHALLENGES

The current trend in Latin America is a movement away from ISDS. Certain countries have never ratified the ICSID, including Brazil (which has never signed the Convention, as discussed below), Cuba, Mexico and the Dominican Republic.[634] Several Caribbean states have also not agreed to the jurisdiction of ICSID, including Barbuda, Belize, Dominica and Suriname.[635] Among those countries that did ratify the ICSID Convention, and include ISDS in their BITs, there are certain countries that have now withdrawn from the Convention. Bolivia withdrew from the Convention in 2007, followed by Ecuador in 2010, and Venezuela in 2012.[636] Nicaragua has also threatened to withdraw from the Convention.

---

[633] *David R. Aven, Samuel D. Aven, Giacomo A. Buscemi and others v. Republic of Costa Rica*, ICSID Case No. UNCT/15/3, available at: https://investmentpolicy.unctad.org/investment-dispute-settlement/cases/571/aven-and-others-v-costa-rica.

[634] Nicolas Boeglin, "ICSID and Latin America, Criticism: withdrawal and the search for alternatives", Bretton Woods Project, 3 December 2013, available at: https://www.brettonwoodsproject.org/2013/12/icsid-latin-america/.

[635] Ibid.

[636] Alejandro López Ortiz, José Joaquín Caicedo and William Ahern, "Two Solutions for One Problem: Latin America's Reactions to Concerns over Investor-State Arbitration", Transnational Dispute Management, TDM 2 (2016), available at: www.transnational-dispute-management.com.

Both Bolivia and Ecuador have also terminated the majority of their BITs, and certain countries have gone even further in expressing their disdain for ISDS. These countries have begun to enact more restrictive domestic policies. In Bolivia, for example, the New Bolivian Arbitration Act (2015) allows foreign investment only in certain public sectors, and orders that all investment arbitrations be seated in Bolivia.[637] There is some question as to whether these policies will hold, given the recent widespread public dissatisfactions in the region, including the movement in Bolivia which led to the resignation of Evo Morales, the country's president.

Other countries have been vocal in expressing concern over ISDS, particularly as the number of cases against Latin American countries has continued to rise. More specifically, countries in this region have argued, not unlike other developing countries, that international arbitration tribunals are biased and do not consider local context, or even necessity, when rendering decisions.[638] These complaints have led several countries, aside from those that have withdrawn from the ICSID Convention, to reconsider whether allowing ISDS is in their best interests. Many of these countries have adopted a "reform" approach to ISDS, whereby they seek to find a balance between state sovereignty and allowing ISDS.[639] These countries have explored the Asian model arising out of the CPTPP, whereby there is restricted ISDS, applied only to certain types of disputes, and, otherwise, state-to-state dispute settlement may be utilised, returning to the days of the Calvo Doctrine.

Latin America is somewhat different to other regions of the world, however. While some countries have gone to great lengths to distance themselves from ISDS and any agreements allowing such mechanism, others have seemingly embraced this method of dispute resolution. Mexico, for example, as previously mentioned, has accepted ISDS as part of the USMCA, and is also party to the CPTPP, which, as also previously mentioned, includes ISDS. Peru is also party to the CPTPP, and has not indicated that it has any major issues with the practice of ISDS. Some countries had not been involved in the negative aspects of ISDS until

---

[637]   Ibid.

[638]   Frédérique Youmbi Fasseu, "Current Debates on Investor-State Arbitration in Latin America", (2018) 12(45) Tla-melaua. Revista de Ciencias Sociales, pp. 190–207, available at: http://www.scielo.org.mx/pdf/tla/v12n45/2594-0716-tla-12-45-190.pdf.

[639]   Alejandro López Ortiz, José Joaquín Caicedo and William Ahern, "Two Solutions for One Problem: Latin America's Reactions to Concerns over Investor-State Arbitration", Transnational Dispute Management, TDM 2 (2016), available at: www.transnational-dispute-management.com.

recently: for example, Colombia, which has now been brought into three disputes by major multinational corporations, almost back-to-back.[640] Whether the positions of such countries, who have never, or had not until recently, been defendants in ISDS cases, will change remains to be seen, but is something worth watching as the global movement away from ISDS seems to take hold.

While no regional body has yet been established to provide another option for trans national dispute settlement in Latin America, during a Union of South American Nations (UNASUR) summit in 2010, Member States (including 12 South American countries) did agree to explore the creation of a Consultative Council of Justice and an International Centre for Conciliation, Mediation and Arbitration.[641] However, these tribunals have yet to be established. The trajectory of ISDS in South and Central America should continue to be watched as a possible indication of whether or not there will, in fact, be a major move away from ISDS in the developing world.

4.4. BRAZIL'S APPROACH TO ISDS

Given that Brazil has taken one of the sternest positions against ISDS, it is worth taking a moment to look more closely at the country's stance on ISDS. Brazil has made a point of arguing strongly that foreign investors in the country will be given no greater protection than its own citizens are afforded, and, as a result, has only recently ratified its first bilateral agreements.[642] The country did sign a total of 14 BITs between 1994 and 1999, but never ratified these agreements. As the rest of the world was diving into ISDS and BITs, Brazil purposefully opted out.

---

[640] Daniel Avila, "Balancing the Benefits of ISDS Provisions in Developing Economies: Colombia Faces its First Investor-State Disputes in ICSID and Demonstrates the Risks Associated with ISDS Clauses", (2018) 18 Houston Business and Tax Law Journal 317.

[641] Ibid.

[642] In the 1990s, Brazil signed, but never ratified 14 BITs, and had not sought any bilateral agreements since then. The country signed two BITs in 2015, one with Mozambique and the other with Angola; however, these agreements continue to be quite limited compared with other global agreements. See Joaquim de Paiva Muniz, "Brazil signs new bilateral investment treaties with Mozambique and Angola: new approach to BITs or 'toothless lions'?", Baker McKenzie Global Arbitration News, 7 April 2015, available at: https://globalarbitrationnews.com/20150407-brazil-signs-new-bilateral-investment-treaties/#.

Brazil has not, however, completely opted out of international agreements. The country has established its own form of bilateral treaty on investment, known as a Cooperation and Investment Facilitation Agreement (CFIA).[643] This is an international investment agreement model that does not incorporate investor-state dispute settlement in any way, and which creates a hybrid system of state-to-state arbitration and a sort of alternative, cooperative dispute settlement mechanism. CFIAs also put the focus on facilitation of investment, rather than on the protection/promotion of investment, as is found in BITs.[644] Moreover, the model brings public policy objectives into the mix, allowing for regulatory context to be given to investment guarantees, which provides greater protection of sovereignty.[645] The Brazilian model makes a clear shift from the traditional focuses of BITs, sending a clear message that the country will not put the interests of investors over its own state interests. This model is quite interesting, and as its use grows (as Brazil enters into more CFIAs), it is sure to garner greater interest in the international conversation on whether the existing BIT model, which encapsulates ISDS, should remain the world's dispute settlement mechanism of choice.

5. AFRICA

5.1. HISTORY OF ISDS IN AFRICA

African countries were some of the biggest proponents of ISDS when it was first introduced, and amongst the first signatories of the ICSID Convention.[646] This was in line with Africa's investment law regimes, which are aimed primarily at situating Africa in the global and regional international investment legal order, and expanding economic

---

[643] Geraldo Vidigal and Beatriz Stevens, "Brazil's New Model of Dispute Settlement for Investment: Return to the Past or Alternative for the Future?", (2018) 19(3) The Journal of World Investment & Trade, pp. 475–512, available at: https://brill.com/view/journals/jwit/19/3/article-p475_6.xml?language=en.

[644] Henrique Choer Moraes and Felipe Hees, "Breaking the BIT Mold: Brazil's Pioneering Approach to Investment Agreements", (2018) 112 AJIL Unbound, pp. 197–201, available at: https://doi.org/10.1017/aju.2018.59.

[645] Ibid.

[646] Makane Moïse Mbengue, "Africa's Voice in the Formation, Shaping and Redesign of International Investment Law", (2019) 34(2) ICSID Review – Foreign Investment Law Journal, pp. 455–481, available at: https://academic.oup.com/icsidreview/article-abstract/34/2/455/5680362.

partnerships beyond the continent.[647] ISDS was largely seen as a way of better attracting foreign investment, by providing investors certain dispute settlement rights that they would not otherwise have had under state-to-state dispute settlement. This was an attractive motive for supporting ISDS, given the need for African nations to increase development and improve their domestic economies.[648] Without African participation in the ICSID Convention, this agreement would likely have been unsuccessful.

The continent's countries have also been active signatories of BITs, having now collectively signed over 1,000 agreements with countries around the world.[649] Promoting BITs and ISDS has been a cornerstone of attracting FDI to the continent. This has largely been based on the premise that foreign investment is all good, and that it will automatically promote the growth and development of countries, which is often misguided.[650] Nevertheless, Africa followed the global model of increasing trade and investment through the use of BITs, which required embracing ISDS. Since signing and, in most cases, ratifying the ICSID Convention, however, African states' acceptance and appreciation of the ISDS system has slowly crumbled, as the continent has continuously faced more challenges with the system.

5.2. AFRICA'S STRUGGLE WITH ISDS

As time has passed, African governments have become some of the most vocal opponents of ISDS. Not unlike their Latin American counterparts, African nations have expressed concern over the exorbitant costs involved in carrying out international arbitration, as well as the crippling awards some

[647] Won Kidane, "Africa's International Investment Law Regimes", Oxford Bibliographies, 22 April 2020, available at: https://www.oxfordbibliographies.com/view/document/obo-9780199796953/obo-9780199796953-0209.xml.

[648] Antonio R. Parra, "The Participation of African States in the Making of the ICSID Convention", (2019) 34(2) ICSID Review – Foreign Investment Law Journal, pp. 270–277, available at: https://doi.org/10.1093/icsidreview/siz012.

[649] Makane Moïse Mbengue, "Africa's Voice in the Formation, Shaping and Redesign of International Investment Law", (2019) 34(2) ICSID Review – Foreign Investment Law Journal, pp. 455–481, available at: https://academic.oup.com/icsidreview/article-abstract/34/2/455/5680362.

[650] Xavier Carim, International Investment Agreements and Africa's Structural Transformation: A Perspective from South Africa, Geneva: South Centre, 2015, available at: https://www.southcentre.int/wp-content/uploads/2016/05/Bk_2015_Investment-Treaties_EN.pdf#page=142.

countries have had to pay as a result of international arbitral judgments.[651] Moreover, they have argued that there is an inherent lack of transparency in the ISDS process, which unfairly allows for foreign investors to challenge the legitimate public policies of their sovereign nations. There has been growing concern over the ability of large multinational corporations to shape the policies of developing African countries, seemingly without limit, hindering sustainable development.[652] This is a shift from the early days of ISDS, when, as previously discussed, African nations played a prominent role in the development of international systems that allowed for this mechanism.

Africa has a great reason for being increasingly frustrated with the ISDS system. The continent has been a steady target for disputes brought under the system, and states have, over and over again, seen their domestic policies questioned in front of international arbitrators. Approximately 11% of all arbitration disputes have involved African states.[653] Egypt has been the fifth most targeted country worldwide, with 34 registered ISDS cases against it, and Tanzania has been the most targeted country in sub-Saharan Africa, with six disputes, all of which were initiated by European investors.[654] Overall, investors have been successful in 64% of cases brought against African countries, with approximately one-third of the total cases still pending, meaning African states have been the most impacted by the frequent use of ISDS.[655] As mentioned, these claims have often led to exorbitant judgments. For example, in 2013, an arbitration court ordered Libya to pay USD 935 million in a dispute over a land-leasing contract for a tourism project, making it one of the largest known awards to date,

---

[651] Uché Ewelukwa Ofodile, "African States, Investor-State Arbitration and the ICSID Dispute Resolution System: Continuities, Changes and Challenges", (2019) 34(2) ICSID Review – Foreign Investment Law Journal, pp. 296–364, available at: doi:10.1093/icsidreview/siz031.

[652] Talkmore Chidede, "Investor-state dispute settlement in Africa and the AfCFTA Investment Protocol", tralacBlog, 11 December 2018, available at: https://www.tralac.org/blog/article/13787-investor-state-dispute-settlement-in-africa-and-the-afcfta-investment-protocol.html.

[653] "Impacts of investment arbitration against African states", Transnational Institute, 8 October 2019, available at: https://www.tni.org/en/isdsafrica.

[654] Talkmore Chidede, "Investor-state dispute settlement in Africa and the AfCFTA Investment Protocol", tralacBlog, 11 December 2018, available at: https://www.tralac.org/blog/article/13787-investor-state-dispute-settlement-in-africa-and-the-afcfta-investment-protocol.html.

[655] "Impacts of investment arbitration against African states", Transnational Institute, 8 October 2019, available at: https://www.tni.org/en/isdsafrica.

rendered against a country that was facing tremendous internal turmoil.[656] Total claims against African states since 1993 have totalled USD 55.5 billion, with investors having claimed over USD 1 billion in damages on ten separate occasions.[657] In one case, Egypt was ordered to pay USD 2 billion to Unión Fenosa as the result of what may be considered an exorbitant ruling.[658] Needless to say, these cases have greatly contributed to Africa's distrust of the ISDS system and desire to move away from this mechanism.

5.3. AFRICA'S RESPONSE TO ISDS CHALLENGES

The results of growing tensions between African nations and the ISDS system have been mixed. Certain countries have reviewed the BITs to which they are party, to determine whether the ISDS provisions should be modified. Other countries, including Tanzania and South Africa, have amended their domestic laws to refer investment disputes to national courts, moving even further away from the traditional ISDS model. Then, at the regional level, there has been an effort to establish regional mechanisms relating to investment, as will be discussed below. Moreover, there are certain indications that the continent as a whole may not be ready to fully reject ISDS.

As discussed at length in Chapter 3, Africa is home to a number of RECs, which hold substantial influence over investment policies on the continent. At the regional level, several African regional bodies have begun putting in place protections against unlimited ISDS.

For example, the SADC, through its Finance and Investment Protocol, has limited the use of ISDS, requiring that disputes be resolved in local courts and tribunals.[659] Further, the EAC Model Investment Treaty specifically includes a provision stipulating no ISDS.[660]

Similarly, in COMESA, the COMESA Common Investment Agreement provides for arbitration under ISDS to be brought to the COMESA Court of Justice. In this case, however, the law also leaves open the possibility

---

[656] Ibid.
[657] Ibid.
[658] *Unión Fenosa Gas, S.A. v. Arab Republic of Egypt*, ICSID Case No. ARB/14/4.
[659] "The arbitration game", The Economist, 11 October 2014, available at: https://www.economist.com/finance-and-economics/2014/10/11/the-arbitration-game.
[660] Uche Ewelukwa Ofodile, "African States, Investor-State Arbitration and the ICSID Dispute Resolution System: Continuities, Changes and Challenges", (2019) 34(2) ICSID Review, pp. 296–364, available at: doi:10.1093/icsidreview/siz031.

that claims between parties who are not party to COMESA can be brought to African arbitration tribunals, or to the international bodies (ICSID or UNCITRAL).[661] This leaves some doubt as to whether COMESA has, in fact, limited ISDS, given that countries belonging to different agreements may forum shop as needed.

In 2008, ECOWAS enacted the Supplementary Act adopting Community Rules on Investment and the Modalities for their Implementation with ECOWAS (ECOWAS SIA). This Act does not provide for ISDS, but, rather, includes a provision that investors use local remedies to resolve disputes. In 2018, it adopted the ECOWAS Common Investment Code (ECOWIC).[662] This Code provides for ISDS,[663] but states explicitly that: "[w]here recourse is made to arbitration, the arbitration may be conducted at any established public or private alternative dispute resolution centres or the arbitration division of the ECOWAS Court of Justice. Member States and investors are encouraged to utilise regional and national alternative dispute settlement institutions."[664] The Code has not yet entered into force.

A closer look at all these instruments shows that there is a new trend in African investment and investment-related instruments, advocating for an increased involvement of African dispute resolution centres and African judicial institutions in disputes involving African states.[665] This trend was initiated under the Pan African Investment Code (PAIC) of 2016.[666]

---

[661]   "COMESA: Dispute Settlement and Arbitration Developments", COMESA Court of Justice, 6–7 April 2017, available at: https://www.tralac.org/images/docs/11119/comesa-dispute-settlement-and-arbitration-developments-lady-justice-lombe-chibesakunda-tralac-annual-conference-april-2017.pdf.

[662]   Supplementary Act A/SA.1/12/18 adopting the ECOWAS Common Investment Code, available at: https://wacomp.projects.ecowas.int/wp-content/uploads/2020/03/SUPPLEMENTARY-ACT-ADOPTING-THE-ECOWAS-COMMON-INVESTMENT-CODE-EF.pdf.

[663]   Chapter 16, relating to dispute settlement mechanisms, provides for both state-to-state dispute settlement and ISDS.

[664]   Art. 54(2).

[665]   See Théobald Naud, Ben Sanderson and Maxime Desplats, "Investment Arbitration in Africa", Global Arbitration Review, 26 May 2021, available at: https://globalarbitrationreview.com/review/the-middle-eastern-and-african-arbitration-review/2021/article/investment-arbitration-in-africa.

[666]   The Pan African code, adopted in Nairobi in 2016, is the first continent-wide African model investment treaty ratified under the auspices of the African Union. But it is not yet officially adopted as a binding instrument See Art. 42: "Where recourse is made to arbitration … the arbitration may be conducted at any established African public or African private alternative dispute resolution center", available at: https://au.int/sites/default/files/documents/32844-doc-draft_pan-african_investment_code_december_2016_en.pdf.

One of the issues with reform under regional bodies, however, is the lack of uniformity between policies pertaining to the same country. States that are party to several agreements are given the ability to somewhat manipulate the process by forum shopping. Larger countries with greater resources are able to select from a larger pool of possible forums and procedures, based on what will favour them most during a particular case. This disadvantages smaller countries with fewer resources, and leads to overall confusion over what is, in fact, the governing principle, and in what circumstances ISDS will actually be applied. The SADC, for example, has not made clear in which cases its dispute settlement mechanisms are to be used over the ISDS mechanism existing under overlapping agreements, making the entire system less effective, and often leaving it ignored altogether, particularly given that investors often prefer the ISDS model permitted to them under certain international agreements.[667] As in other regions in Africa (for example, West Africa, where there are several regional bodies), several members of SADC are also members of COMESA. This adds to the confusion, and again diminishes the intention of moving away from ISDS, as investors have the option to search for more favourable forums (treaty shopping).

In addition to the reaction at the regional level, there are also mixed signs at the individual country level, largely demonstrating that Africa is not completely ready to let go of ISDS just yet. These include the fact that only South Africa has gone through the process of actually removing itself from BITs that include ISDS provisions, as will be further discussed below.[668] At the same time, countries continue to sign on to the ICSID, with Djibouti having ratified the agreement as recently as April 2019.[669] African nations also continue to enter into BITs that allow for ISDS.

---

[667] Tinyiko Ngobeni, "The Relevance of the Draft Pan African Investment Code (PAIC) in Light of the Formation of the African Continental Free Trade Area", Afronomics Law, 15 January 2019, available at: http://www.afronomicslaw.org/2019/01/11/the-relevance-of-the-draft-pan-african-investment-code-paic-in-light-of-the-formation-of-the-african-continental-free-trade-area/. See also Joost Pauwelyn, "Going Global, Regional, or Both – Dispute Settlement in the Southern African Development Community (SADC) and Overlaps with the WTO and Other Jurisdictions", (2004) Minnesota Journal of International Law, p. 215, available at: https://scholarship.law.duke.edu/cgi/viewcontent.cgi?article=1767&context=faculty_scholarship.

[668] Uche Ewelukwa Ofodile, "African States, Investor-State Arbitration and the ICSID Dispute Resolution System: Continuities, Changes and Challenges", (2019) 34(2) ICSID Review, pp. 296–364, available at: doi:10.1093/icsidreview/siz031.

[669] Ibid.

Some individual African countries have also begun revising their domestic laws to put more restrictions on the use of ISDS. Tanzania, for example, amended its Public Private Partnership Act in 2010 to eliminate international investment arbitration.[670] Thereafter, the same country began the process of terminating BITs that it does not feel are in its best interests.[671] Egypt has taken similar steps.[672]

In West Africa, several OHADA Member States, including Mali, Benin and Côte d'Ivoire, have amended their investment codes to extend ISDS to the CCJA.[673] Côte d'Ivoire went even further by narrowing their offer to arbitrate pursuant to the ICSID Convention.[674]

As will be discussed below, South Africa has gone one step further by terminating all of its BITs. The impact these domestic laws have on countries, and investors in the countries, may be quite small, however, particularly in countries where BITs or Regional Investment Treaties (RITs) also apply, and afford investors the right to bring claims as they deem necessary. In this vein, a growing number of BITs have begun incorporating provisions aimed at improving ISDS and/or adding new

---

[670] Amne Suedi, "The need for 'Africa-focused' arbitration and reform of Tanzania's Arbitration Act", bilaterals.org, 5 October 2020, available at: https://www.bilaterals.org/?the-need-for-africa-focused.

[671] Uche Ewelukwa Ofodile, "African States, Investor-State Arbitration and the ICSID Dispute Resolution System: Continuities, Changes and Challenges", (2019) 34(2) ICSID Review, pp. 296–364, available at: doi:10.1093/icsidreview/siz031.

[672] In 2017, Egypt enacted an Investment Law, providing a new dispute settlement mechanism including domestic litigation, amicable settlement and alternative dispute resolution (ADR), and administrative review by three specialised committees. In addition, the law allows for settlement through domestic or international ad hoc or institutional arbitration, subject to the agreement between the state and the investor. See: https://investmentpolicy.unctad.org/investment-laws/laws/167/egypt-investment-law-.

[673] See Mouhamed Kebe, "Nouveau Code des Investissements du Bénin: Focus sur les principales innovations", Afrimag, 12 November 2020, available at: https://afrimag.net/nouveau-code-investissements-benin-focus-sur-principales-innovations/.

[674] See Mouhamed Kebe, Mahamat Atteib and Mouhamoud Sangare, "Ivory Coast's New Investment Code: Focus on issues related to sustainable development and dispute settlement", Investment Treaty News, 19 September 2019, available at: https://cf.iisd.net/itn/en/2019/09/19/ivory-coasts-new-investment-code-focus-on-issues-related-to-sustainable-development-and-dispute-settlement-mouhamed-kebe-mahamat-atteib-mouhamoud-sangare/. On the same subject, see Arnaud Oulepo, "Cote-d'Ivoire Investment Code Amendments: Regaining Control over Investment Dispute Settlement", Kluwer Arbitration Blog, 20 May 2020, available at: http://arbitrationblog.kluwerarbitration.com/2020/05/20/cote-divoire-investment-code-amendments-regaining-control-over-investment-dispute-settlement/.

elements that otherwise change the mechanism.[675] Examples include the Brazil–Ethiopia BIT (2018), the Brazil–Malawi BIT (2015) and the Brazil–Mozambique BIT (2015).[676] There still remains, however, a question as to how these domestic laws and agreements will interplay with regional laws and processes.

5.4. SOUTH AFRICA AND ISDS

South Africa has gone further than any other country in moving away from ISDS and, therefore, warrants its own discussion here. As discussed in Chapter 6, South Africa enacted the Protection of Investment Act 22 of 2015, in which it limited ISDS to mediation or arbitration in domestic courts, tribunals or statutory bodies.[677] That same year, the country terminated all BITs that it had signed with European countries. This was done in an effort to better protect national interests, and to put the domestic needs of the country above those of investors.[678] At the same time, the country was focused on strengthening its own domestic courts, and improving their capacity to hear investment-related cases.

Similarly to other African nations' criticism of ISDS, South Africa's movement away from the mechanism was largely spurred by its own involvement in international arbitration, namely the *Piero Foresti, Laura de Carli v. Republic of South Africa* case (the "*Foresti* case").[679] This case was

---

[675] For instance, the new BIT model published by Morocco in December 2019 limits the range of disputes that can be subject to ISDS exclusively to those concerning a violation of the states' treaty obligations. In addition, the model requires the investor to exhaust local remedies before initiating international arbitration: see Hamed El-Kady and Yvan Rwananga, "Morocco's New Model BIT: Innovative features and policy considerations", Investment Treaty News, 20 June 2020, available at: https://www.iisd.org/itn/en/2020/06/20/moroccos-new-model-bit-innovative-features-and-policy-considerations-hamed-el-kady-yvan-rwananga/.

[676] Henrique Choer Moraes and Felipe Hees, "Breaking the BIT Mold: Brazil's Pioneering Approach to Investment Agreements", (2018) 112 AJIL Unbound, pp. 197–201, available at: https://doi.org/10.1017/aju.2018.59.

[677] South Africa Protection of Investment Act 22 of 2015.

[678] Mmiselo Freedom Qumba, "South Africa's move away from international investor-state dispute: a breakthrough or bad omen for Investment in the developing world?", (2019) 52(1) De Jure (Pretoria), available at: http://www.scielo.org.za/scielo.php?script=sci_arttext&pid=S2225-71602019000100021.

[679] *Piero Foresti, Laura de Carli and others v. Republic of South Africa*, ICSID Case No. ARB(AF)/07/1, available at: https://investmentpolicy.unctad.org/investment-dispute-settlement/cases/262/foresti-v-south-africa.

brought by Italian investors, who challenged the country's black economic empowerment legislation.[680] This followed an earlier case, known as the *Swiss Investor* case, wherein a Swiss citizen had challenged South Africa under the Swiss–RSA BIT, claiming that the country had failed to provide it with security under the agreement.[681] Ultimately, in that case, South Africa was found to have breached the agreement by not providing adequate protection of the claimant's property, which had been damaged by South African protestors.[682] In looking at the reasons why it had been challenged in these two cases, the country ultimately decided that its state interests outweighed the risks associated with leaving its BITs, which it found were not attracting FDI on their own. This major decision by the country has already had a ripple effect in the region, and on the continent, giving the SADC the confidence to limit the use of ISDS, as discussed above.

5.5. AFRICA'S FUTURE WITH ISDS

Regardless of the South African model that certain countries and regions have adopted, Africa largely remains tied to BITs and the ISDS provisions contained therein. Perhaps most notably, the draft Pan African Investment Code, a predecessor to the AfCFTA, drafted in 2015, did not completely reject ISDS.[683] This document seeks to promote sustainable development, and leaves it open to individual countries to decide whether or not to include ISDS in future agreements.[684] This, more than anything, indicates that, perhaps, the continent will not readily jump to the same decision to fully terminate all agreements involving ISDS that South Africa did. With the mix of approaches to addressing ISDS in mind, the best way for Africa to address its criticisms of the system, and to reduce the confusion existing under the current web of laws and regulations, is to include a

---

[680] South Africa Broad-based Black Economic Empowerment Act 53 of 2003, amended by Broad-based Black Economic Empowerment Act 46 of 2013, available at: https://www.gov.za/documents/broad-based-black-economic-empowerment-act.

[681] *Swiss Investor v. Republic of South Africa*, UNCITRAL, available at: https://jusmundi.com/en/document/decision/en-swiss-investor-v-republic-of-south-africa-final-award-tuesday-19th-october-2004#decision_5307.

[682] Ibid.

[683] Ibid.

[684] Ibid.

clear investment dispute resolution provision in the AfCFTA. As will be demonstrated in the next chapter, there is now an opportunity for African nations to make a decision as to whether, or to what extent, they will use the ISDS mechanism, and as to what type of unified front it will present to non-African investors.

.

CHAPTER 8

THE FUTURE OF AFRICAN
INVESTMENT DISPUTE SETTLEMENT

Africa as a continent is on the cusp of what could be a break in a decades-long cycle of poverty and economic shortcomings. Whether this cycle will be broken will depend on the ability of African nations to put in place policies that attract and protect foreign and intra-African investment. These policies must demonstrate to investors that the rule of law will be upheld; that equitable, local dispute settlement is possible; and that potential gains will be greater than the risks involved in investing in the continent. The enactment of the AfCFTA (or "the Agreement"), as previously discussed throughout this book, was a huge step in the right direction. This Agreement lays a solid foundation for increased intra-African trade in both goods and services, and looks to build on the collective strengths of African nations and citizens.

For AfCFTA to fulfil its potential, African nations must be focused on attracting greater FDI, both from within and outside the continent. As noted in a recent study by the World Bank, one of the most important aspects of the AfCFTA is the possibility that it will be able to substantially increase the flow of FDI into the continent.[685]

Increased FDI has the potential to create jobs and attract advanced technology and expertise. Foreign investment, if managed well, can build local capabilities and forge the connections that help countries integrate into regional and global value chains.[686] This, in turn, could have a substantial impact on Africa's dependence on extractive industries, and could build a more robust, sustainable economy across the continent.

---

[685] Roberto Echandi, Maryla Maliszewska, Victor Steenbergen, "Making the Most of the African Continental Free Trade Area: Leveraging Trade and Foreign Direct Investment to Boost Growth and Reduce Poverty" Washington, DC: World Bank 2022, available at: https://openknowledge.worldbank.org/handle/10986/37623.

[686] Ibid.

The importance of promoting resilient economies cannot be overstated, given the current ever-fluctuating global economy. Increasing investment on the continent, across industries, will be essential to Africa's efforts in becoming resilient. As the World Bank has noted, greater FDI through deep integration could raise Africa's exports as much as 32% by 2035, with intra-Africa exports growing by 109%, especially in the manufactured goods sectors.[687] Whether these huge gains will become a reality depends, in large part, on the ability of African nations to refine key components of the AfCFTA more clearly.

With all the potential of the Agreement in mind, and as AfCFTA comes into full force and effect, one of the most pressing issues is for African nations now to provide clear guidance as to what dispute settlement mechanisms are to be used under the Agreement. While Africa finds itself at the forefront of a bright economic future, State Parties to the AfCFTA must provide more comprehensive guidance as to how the Agreement will be implemented, in order for it to be truly effective. The dispute settlement mechanism detailed for the Agreement must strike the right balance between state and investor interests, ensuring that Africa is an attractive place for investment, including intra-African investment, while at the same time protecting the ability of African nations to promote sustainable development, using regulations that defend the public interest.

As noted in Chapter 5, AfCFTA's Dispute Resolution Protocol's Article 27 has substantially limited the other provisions of the Protocol by allowing for the possibility that all disputes under the Agreement be brought to arbitration, without adequately defining what the terms of such arbitration may be. At the same time, the AfCFTA as a whole is left open to further negotiation and definition of terms. If the AfCFTA is to be successful, African nations must come to the table and develop a clear, strong method for dispute resolution under the Agreement.

As previously discussed, the Agreement does include a Protocol on the Rules and Procedures on the Settlement of Disputes (the "Protocol"), which closely reflects the current dispute settlement mechanisms of the WTO.[688] This Protocol provides for the establishment of a DSB that will have the

---

[687]   Ibid.

[688]   Olabisi D. Akinkugbe, "Dispute Settlement under the African Continental Free Trade Area Agreement: A Preliminary Assessment", (2020) 28 Supp., African Journal of International and Comparative Law, p. 138, available at: https://digitalcommons. schulichlaw.dal.ca/cgi/viewcontent.cgi?article=1483&context=scholarly_works.

power to establish Dispute Settlement Panels and an Appellate Body.[689] At the same time, the Protocol provides that the parties may, by mutual agreement, refer disputes to arbitration, bypassing the DSB. However, the Protocol does not specify the details of either the DSB or the arbitration option, including where, and under what rules, disputes will be settled using either of these mechanisms. The African Union has made clear that the Protocol is to be further developed by Member States now that the Agreement has been enacted. This leaves open several questions, but also presents an opportunity for Africa to shape its own future in investment arbitration. To do so, however, the continent must move swiftly to consider what possibilities exist for dispute settlement under the AfCFTA.

Such consideration requires a deeper look at what currently exists, both inside and outside the continent, as well as what strengths should be built on, and what weaknesses must be improved on, under the new system. Chapter 2 highlighted how trade agreements and BITs have provided certain investor protections, such as investor-state dispute resolution mechanisms, that are designed to reduce regulatory risk.[690] This has proven attractive to investors, but has not addressed the perceived risks that are still prevalent on the continent. Factors such as a lack of government transparency, sudden changes in laws or regulations, breaches of contract, expropriation, or other regulatory risks can undermine investor confidence in a location and deter investment. This further raises the importance of creating a sound legal and regulatory environment under the AfCFTA, which is universal across the continent. As AfCFTA moves forward in defining its clauses, it is important to establish clear investor protections to reduce, or compensate for, the risks that exist on the continent, so as to provide investors with recourse, and to act as a policy commitment mechanism. This would build on the strengths of existing BITs, while also better considering the local context in which such agreements are made.

As was discussed in previous chapters, the intent of African nations in entering into BITs was, in many cases, to indicate to developed country

---

[689]   These bodies are to be comprised of experts in both law and international trade, who are independent from local governments.

[690]   Emma Aisbett, Matthias Busse and Peter Nunnenkamp, "Bilateral investment treaties as deterrents of host-country discretion: the impact of investor-state disputes on foreign direct investment in developing countries", (2018) 154(1) Review of World Economics (Weltwirtschaftliches Archiv), pp. 119–155, available at: https://ideas. repec.org/a/spr/weltar/v154y2018i1d10.1007_s10290-017-0285-1.html.

counterparties that their countries were open to foreign investment, and that they intended to protect investment domestically.[691] However, the relationships in developing country/developed country BITs can be seen as more one-sided than in those between two developed countries, given that there is an implied – albeit not typically expressed – understanding that the main purpose of the agreement is to increase investment into a developing nation, rather than to and from both nations. The implications of this perception have, arguably, hindered greater economic growth in Africa, by restricting African nations' ability to issue domestic laws that run contrary to BITs. African governments have expressed frustration about the limitations BITs impose on their sovereignty. African states that enter into BITs with developed nations limit their ability to freely regulate areas that may affect investment, and more often than not submit themselves to the will of international arbitral bodies (as discussed below).[692]

The use of BITs has laid bare certain weaknesses that must be addressed under AfCFTA. For example, investors under these agreements often overlook or ignore the internal responsibilities of governments, and misinterpret a reliance on foreign investment as a power to manipulate local law. This has a great deal to do with the dispute resolution mechanisms that have been included in these types of agreement. The existing dispute settlement mechanisms built into investment agreements almost always allow for ISDS. Using ISDS, investors have been quick to challenge proposed local laws or policy decisions that may run contrary to their investment expectations.[693] In most cases, little consideration is given to local need or objectives, which has led African leaders to express concern over a perceived infringement of their sovereign rights and obligations. At the same time, African governments have, historically, argued that international arbitration – investors' preferred method of dispute settlement – is extremely costly, and is perceived as biased towards investors, resulting in African nations having to pay large awards that

---

[691] United Nations Economic Commission for Africa, "Investment Policies and Bilateral Investment Treaties in Africa" (2016), available at: https://archive.uneca.org/publications/investment-policies-and-bilateral-investment-treaties-africa.

[692] Alec R. Johnson, "Rethinking Bilateral Investment Treaties in Sub-Saharan Africa", (2010) 59 Emory Law Journal, p. 919, available at: https://scholarlycommons.law.emory.edu/elj/vol59/iss4/3.

[693] Tsotang Tsietsi, "International Commercial Arbitration: Case Study of the Experiences of African States in the International Centre for Settlement of Investment Disputes", (2013) 47 International Lawyer, p. 249, available at: https://scholar.smu.edu/til/vol47/iss2/6.

further inhibit their economic growth.[694] There is clearly little confidence amongst African nations in the current dispute settlement mechanisms. This leaves room for new and substantial changes to be made under the AfCFTA. Africa now finds itself in a position to reshape dispute settlement on the continent in a way that can foster the growth of African nations long into the future.

The heart of any dispute settlement system is the type of court or tribunal in which disputes will be heard. Chapter 5 provided an in-depth look at the existing tribunals to which disputes involving African investment are currently referred. Where there is no specific law on the books dictating otherwise, local disputes are resolved in local courts. Everyday business in a country, for both locals and foreigners, is governed by local law. Every country on the continent has local, domestic courts that resolve business-related disputes in the same way that they resolve disputes between citizens. The size and capacity of these courts ranges dramatically from country to country. So, too, does the knowledge of local judges regarding business-related matters. In those countries where there is an authoritarian government, the independence of the judiciary is most certainly in question. In other, more established democracies, there are robust court systems which can have a strong influence over business practices within the country.

One of the key benefits of using domestic courts, from the perspective of African nations, is the tremendous understanding of local context that these courts inherently have. There is also an indisputable affordability and convenience to these courts, in the eyes of African nations and local investors. As business flourishes on the continent, it is presumed that local courts will also develop their understanding of business-related matters and their repository of business law precedents. That said, inept domestic courts have proven to frustrate even local investors. Foreign investors, particularly non-African investors, will, in most cases, outright reject local courts. More often than not, multinational corporations, when negotiating transactions on the African continent, will insist that disputes be brought outside the relevant country, and most typically out of the continent as a whole, to neutral international dispute settlement bodies.

The result of this frustration is that the most-used dispute settlement forum, particularly when non-African investors are party to an agreement,

---

[694]   Ibid.

is international investment arbitration.[695] Most bilateral investment agreements between African and non-African countries (as well as intra-African agreements) include international arbitration provisions that allow for investment disputes to be brought before an international arbitral tribunal. International arbitration allows a contracting party to bring a claim against the national of another contracting party, but does not allow domestic investors to bring a claim under this system.[696] The purpose of establishing this type of system is threefold, and includes: (i) attracting foreign investment, by allowing for a direct means of enforcement of international disputes on the part of international investors; (ii) depoliticising disputes; and (iii) allowing foreign investors an alternative to domestic courts.[697]

Finally, lying between international arbitration and domestic courts, there are regional arbitration tribunals and regional courts. By way of example, the OHADA, in addition to creating a set of uniform laws applicable to 17 Member States, has also established a CCJA. This court of 13 judges provides advice on proposed Uniform Acts and serves as a court of cassation. This court is seen as superior to national courts in matters pertaining to the Uniform Acts, and allows cases to be presented by either party, or by a national judge. Although this court is still building its reputation and legitimacy to a point where it can be trusted as much as more established centres like the ICC and ICSID, it is making strides in the right direction.[698] Other regional bodies include the KIAC, Mauritius' several arbitral institutions, and the still relatively new arbitration systems in Ghana and Kenya. These centres are attracting the attention of other

---

[695] The most commonly selected international tribunals include the ICC and the ICSID. The UNCITRAL Rules of Arbitration are commonly used to govern arbitrations not heard by these two tribunals, which both have their own rules and procedures. Other notable international arbitration tribunals include the LCIA, the ICDR, the HKIAC and the SIAC.

[696] Talkmore Chidede, "The Right to Regulate in Africa's International Investment Law Regime", (2019) 20(2) Oregon Review of International Law, pp. 437–468, available at: https://scholarsbank.uoregon.edu/xmlui/bitstream/handle/1794/24671/Chidede_ORIL20%282%29.pdf?sequence=1&isAllowed=y.

[697] Ibid.

[698] Babatunde Fagbayibo, "Towards the harmonisation of laws in Africa: is OHADA the way to go?" (2009) 42(3) Comparative and International Law Journal of Southern Africa, pp. 309–322, available at: https://www.jstor.org/stable/23253105?seq=1#page_scan_tab_contents.

African nations, who have, in some cases, begun to consider African dispute settlement bodies when choosing forums for resolving their conflicts. These tribunals, and the traction they have been gaining as of late, offer a strong insight into what could be successful at the continental level. The challenge of African parties to AfCFTA, therefore, is to build on the successes of these tribunals, while at the same time being careful not to repeat the setbacks some of them have had.

Taking collectively the strengths and weaknesses of each of the existing governing laws and dispute settlement forums in Africa, there is a strong argument that the African Union should establish a permanent tribunal for investment dispute resolution, located on the African continent. First and foremost, at this pivotal moment in the continent's history, Africa must demonstrate that it is able to create an amicable environment for investment that will, at the same time, push the continent forward in its development objectives. To do this, the Member States of AfCFTA, when further negotiating the Dispute Resolution Protocol, must create a forum that will allow for equitable dispute resolution that takes into consideration the needs of states as much as those of private investors.

A forum located on the African continent, with knowledge and experience of the local contexts within which disputes arise, will be crucial in gaining the support of African nations. Having the tribunal in Africa would also reduce costs and burdens for African governments. To foster accessibility, the African Union could have various satellite courts of the continental tribunal, allowing cases to be heard in a mutually agreed upon location convenient for the parties. At the same time, there should be one primary seat where the permanent staff and judges of the court should be located on a regular basis. On a continent as big as Africa, geography is crucial in ensuring the equitable treatment of parties. Moreover, it is essential that the tribunal be located in a stable, democratically strong country, where it is less likely to be impacted on by conflict or turmoil in the host country. Satellite offices will be essential in assuring equitability; however, it will also be necessary for the continent to carefully select where the principal seat of the tribunal will be located.

In developing this continental court, the African Union should also take care to make sure that the voices of all African nations are heard. Africa is a continent comprised of 54 different countries, all at varying levels of economic development, and each with its own needs. African Member States must consider this when drafting the rules of procedure for this court. Just as African nations do not want the desires of wealthy investors to overshadow their own needs, nor do smaller, less developed countries want their voices to be silenced by larger, stronger economies on the continent. If the continent is truly to develop collectively, then all countries must have an equal footing when it comes to dispute settlement. Equitable representation in the tribunal must be a top priority.

Cultural considerations must also play a central role in the shaping of this court. Globalisation and the increasing use of ISDS under international investment agreements have brought a greater need for arbitrators and advocates to develop critical cross-cultural competency skills. More and more parties to arbitrations hail from different legal systems, social traditions, faith-based customs and family backgrounds. These disparate perspectives permit disputants to look at the same set of facts and circumstances and interpret them differently. These disputants then bring those paradigms with them as they engage in the arbitration process, affording endless opportunities for cross-cultural misunderstandings, even among citizens of the same country. Thus, developing cultural sensitivity and cultivating awareness of subtle statements and actions in dispute settlement proceedings can lead to prompt recognition and identification of cultural issues, so that they can be addressed in the most useful manner.

Considering the cultural complexities, as well as African nations' legitimate concerns as to bias in international proceedings (among other justified complaints), a continental court under AfCFTA must be staffed by African judges and judicial staff. Judges at the proposed African continental court should not only be local to the continent, but they should also be from different countries throughout the continent. Both large and small countries should be represented. So, too, should countries with less developed and more developed legal systems, as well as both anglophone and francophone countries. Additionally, the judges selected should have the business knowledge that foreign investors would expect of a tribunal of such stature. This diversity of judges from varying countries would help reduce the bias and corruption concerns that exist in relation to local courts. It will also better ensure that smaller countries are treated equitably when in conflict with larger, wealthier countries. Moreover, foreign investors have, historically, expressed concerns that African courts are not familiar with business transactions, and this has turned them away from using local or regional courts. In developing a continental tribunal, it is important to recognise that there are plenty of African nationals, even from the smallest countries with small economies, with the capacity to consider complex investment disputes, who could serve on a continental court. Utilising local human capital from across the continent would achieve one of the key purposes of the AfCFTA, namely that local human resources are better utilised to meet local needs.

Perhaps the greatest benefit of having a continental tribunal will be the contextual awareness that is added by having local judges who are familiar with the most pressing issues on the African continent. African-bred judges will have greater concern for the impact that investments in the continent are having. African judges will be more likely to consider the social, environmental and labour consequences of investments. This will give them a unique perspective on the reasoning behind why states may take certain policy decisions, and allow them to weigh that reasoning with investors' interests. This will, in turn, serve the purpose of balancing Africa's sustainable development goals with investment decisions. With this in mind, judges should be carefully selected from each of the Member States of the AfCFTA. As is provided in the Articles of the current Dispute Settlement Protocol for the DSB process, judges hearing a given case should not be from either of the countries that are party to the dispute.

As has also been suggested under the Dispute Settlement Protocol, the continental tribunal should have an appeals process, allowing parties to challenge decisions based on law or evident misinterpretation of facts. States have long complained of the finality of arbitration decisions rendered by party-selected arbitrators, without any higher-level reconsideration. An appeals process utilising tenured judges would diminish this concern and, once again, build consistency. Again, this appellate tribunal should have clearly defined procedures and directives, defined during the negotiation process of the AfCFTA.

The new AfCFTA dispute settlement system should primarily be focused on the needs of African countries, rather than being built around the desires of foreign investors. The African Union must do better to protect the interests of its Member States – all of its Member States – and must do so through creating a stronger, more equitable dispute settlement mechanism. As Africa moves forward with the implementation of the AfCFTA, it is essential that dispute settlement be at the forefront of discussions. Investors will be looking at how well their rights are protected under the new agreement when deciding how extensively to move into the continent, and, at the same time, governments will be more likely to buy into the agreement if it allows for greater protection of their rights than the existing mechanisms.

While it will be difficult to come to a final continental consensus, and change may be slow, African State Parties to the AfCFTA must decide to what extent ISDS will be utilised to resolve investment disputes on the continent. As currently written, the Dispute Settlement Protocol appears to point towards state-to-state dispute settlement, with all the language used referring to State Parties, without mention of investors or non-state actors. In considering the current world landscape as it pertains to ISDS, as discussed in Chapter 7, rather than moving completely towards state-to-state dispute settlement, Africa should consider the possibility of a limited, regulated ISDS. The limited approach utilised under the new USMCA and the CPTPP (the successor to the TPP Agreement, which is poised to be ratified by the remaining Member States) agreements would offer a strong solution to many of the grievances expressed by African states, while at the same time allowing investors to bring legitimate claims for breaches of the Agreement. One limitation that could, for example, be included, as is currently alluded to under the Dispute Settlement Protocol, is a limitation on compensation as a remedy for an aggrieved party. This would alleviate the concerns over overly burdensome judgments, which, as discussed, have been one of the major sticking points in African opposition to ISDS.

The EU model that appears to be taking shape after the *Achmea* case, wherein the laws of the EU are taking precedence over the needs of investors, should be used as a guide in the African negotiation of the AfCFTA. The final terms of the AfCFTA should specify the supremacy of African continental law, and should place clear limits on the cases in which private investors will be able to challenge domestic law. There should be express provisions built into the Agreement that protect individual countries' rights to regulate for the public good. For example, there should be limitations on challenges to environmental and public health laws. This has been done under the CPTPP and USMCA, and appears also to be the direction that Europe is heading in. Africans should take note of the progression of the debate on ISDS as it is continuously evolving around the world.

That said, the AfCFTA dispute settlement provisions should not completely exclude state-to-state dispute settlement, but should, rather, adapt an either-or approach to ISDS and state-to-state dispute settlement. When considering state-to-state dispute settlement in the context of the African continent, there are several key specificities that are important to pause and consider. As has been reiterated throughout this book, the sustainable development objectives of African nations, more than anywhere else in the world, are essential in ensuring a prosperous future for the continent. States are balancing an array of different needs; everything from strengthening the rule of law to food security, and from providing health services to creating jobs, must be considered if countries hope to reduce the current level of poverty and, quite frankly, if they wish to better attract foreign investment. Without improved infrastructure, for example, foreign investors will be wary of entering many markets. They will also be hesitant to enter a market that cannot guarantee protection of contracts. The long-term objectives of African states, therefore, must be built into current policies and laws.

While foreign investment will play a key role in creating strong economies that can lift countries from developing to developed status, there must also be advances made in local development, in order to ensure the same trajectory. By way of example, in the extractive sectors, there is often a reliance on foreign investors to provide the technical assistance necessary to extract natural resources. At the same time, however, the country where the natural resource is located must ensure that the environment is protected, so as to not cause issues with food security or raise health concerns among local populations. There must also exist a strong rule of law, so as to protect against illegal extraction, and to ensure that the foreign investor is protected against third-party intervention into their projects. To improve the local economy, states must also ensure that the extraction project involves local workers, and creates better job opportunities for surrounding communities. Every project has a long list of different considerations for the state, while often the sole consideration of investors is profit.

State-to-state dispute settlement, the mechanism built into AfCFTA under the Dispute Settlement Protocol, for claims brought to the DSB, allows states to better consider their internal needs, without direct challenges from investors who may view legitimate development objectives as contrary to their potential profit. Allowing states to have a voice in arguing their public policy reasoning for certain decisions will protect against infringement on sovereignty, and will allow local governments to maintain adequate control over domestic policy. Moreover, state-to-state dispute resolution carried out on the continent will allow holistic consideration of the needs, not only of individual countries, but of the continent as a whole. This mechanism could contribute to Africa's intention of becoming more self-reliant.

At the same time, there are certain considerations that must be weighed in relation to state-to-state dispute settlement. For example, the willingness of states to bring claims on behalf of their nationals may hinge on the same problem of costliness that exists under international arbitration, and not on the legitimate needs of an investor, or on the black-and-white terms of a contractual agreement. Additionally, the capacities of African nations vary tremendously from one state to another.

Larger countries with more resources[699] have greater capacity to bring claims, and to then be successful in the pursuit of those claims, than smaller countries with fewer resources.[700] Moreover, there are varying levels of relationships between different governments on the continent, and there is a risk that political interests may boil over into investment dispute settlement. For these reasons, a compromise position, where ISDS is limited, but state-to-state dispute settlement may also be used for cases that may have a more widespread impact – as opposed a complete move to state-to-state dispute settlement – is likely the best option for the continent. This would allow investors the opportunity to defend themselves when facing breaches of contract, but would, at the same time, allow governments to maintain their own sovereignty. Of course, the procedural rules built into the AfCFTA must ensure that states will maintain certain rights, even when faced with an ISDS claim.

Taking all of this into consideration, it is also important that Africa, as previously mentioned, develops a dispute resolution mechanism that does not create the same issues that exist under the current ISDS-dominated system. What that means is that the system developed under AfCFTA should not place small-economy countries with fewer resources in a more vulnerable position than their more affluent counterparts. This also means that the system should focus inwards, rather than outwards. The AfCFTA dispute settlement system should be focused on the needs of African countries, rather than the desires of foreign investors. The African Union must do better to protect the interests of its Member States – all of its Member States – and must do so by creating a stronger, more equitable dispute settlement mechanism.

---

[699]   Examples would include South Africa, Kenya or Nigeria (should the country decide to join), among others.

[700]   Examples would include the Gambia, Gabon or Democratic Republic of Congo, among others.

BIBLIOGRAPHY

"2014–2015 West Africa Ebola Crisis: Impact Update", The World Bank, available at: https://www.worldbank.org/en/topic/macroeconomics/publication/2014-2015-west-africa-ebola-crisis-impact-update.

"2019: Natural disasters claim more than 1200 lives across East and Southern Africa", ReliefWeb, available at: https://reliefweb.int/report/world/2019-natural-disasters-claim-more-1200-lives-across-east-and-southern-africa.

Segnonna Horace Abjolohoun, "The Njemanze ECOWAS Court Ruling and 'Universal' Jurisdiction: Implications for the 'Grand African Human Rights System'", I.CONnect, available at: http://www.iconnectblog.com/2017/11/the-njemanze-ecowas-court-ruling-and-universal-jurisdiction-implications-for-the-grand-african-human-rights-system/.

"About ICSID", International Centre for Settlement of Investment Disputes, available at: https://icsid.worldbank.org/en/Pages/about/default.aspx.

"About the Sustainable Development Goals", United Nations, available at: https://www.un.org/sustainabledevelopment/sustainable-development-goals/.

"A Business Guide to the African Continental Free Trade Area Agreement", International Trade Centre, available at: https://cpccaf.org/XCMD.RE9fU2hPQko 8MjU+MDAwMDAtMC0wMjgtMDAwMDAwMDAzODA2Mw==.html.

Pia Accounci, "Most Favoured Nation Treatment", in Peter Muchlinski, Frederico Ortino and Christopher Schreur (eds.), The Oxford Handbook of International Investment Law, Oxford: OUP, 2008, pp. 363–401.

"Action Plan for Boosting Intra-African Trade and Fast-Tracking the Establishment of a Pan-American Free Trade Area", available at: https://au.int/sites/default/files/newsevents/workingdocuments/27214-wd-cfta_action_plan_ti6174_e_original.pdf.

"Africa and the Rule of Law", International Development Law Organization, 18 May 2016, available at: https://www.idlo.int/news/policy-statements/africa-and-rule-law.

"Africa Continental Free Trade Area – Questions and Answers", United Nations Economic Commission for Africa, available at: https://repository.uneca.org/handle/10855/43253.

"Africa Report", The World Bank, available at: https://www.worldbank.org/en/region/afr/overview.

African Development Bank, "African Economic Outlook 2018", available at: https://www.afdb.org/fileadmin/uploads/afdb/Documents/Publications/African_Economic_Outlook_2018_-_EN.pdf.

"African Economic Outlook 2018", African Development Bank Group, ch. 3, available at: https://www.afdb.org/fileadmin/uploads/afdb/Documents/Publications/2018AEO/African_Economic_Outlook_2018_-_EN_Chapter3.pdf.

Emma Aisbett, Matthias Busse and Peter Nunnenkamp, "Bilateral investment treaties as deterrents of host-country discretion: the impact of investor-state disputes on foreign direct investment in developing countries", (2018) 154(1) Review of World Economics (Weltwirtschaftliches Archiv), pp. 119–155, available at: https://ideas.repec.org/a/spr/weltar/v154y2018i1d10.1007_s10290-017-0285-1.html.

Oludara Akanmidu, "How Nigeria got hit with a $9.6 billion gas deal judgment debt in a UK court", available at: https://qz.com/africa/1710707/how-nigeria-got-hit-with-a-9-6-billion-judgment-debt-in-the-uk/.

Olabisi D Akinkugbe, "Dispute Settlement Under the African Continental Free Trade Area Agreement: A Preliminary Assessment", (2020) 28 Supp., African Journal of International and Comparative Law, p. 138, available at: SSRN: https://ssrn.com/abstract=3403745 or http://dx.doi.org/10.2139/ssrn.3403745.

——, "Reverse Contributors? African State Parties, ICSID and the Development of International Investment Law", (2019) 34(2) ICSID Review, pp. 434–454, available at: doi:10.1093/icsidreview/siz010.

Adeoye O. Akinola, "The Politics and Challenges of ECOWAS' Common Currency", VDM Verlag Dr. Müller, 2 September 2011.

Karen Alter and Laurence Helfer, "A New Human Rights Court for West Africa: The ECOWAS Community Court of Justice," SSRN Electronic Journal, October 2013, available at: https://www.researchgate.net/publication/256026224_A_New_Human_Rights_Court_for_West_Africa_The_ECOWAS_Community_Court_of_Justice.

Carrie Anderer, "Bilateral Investment Treaties and the EU Legal Order: Implications of the Lisbon Treaty," (2010) 35(3) Brooklyn Journal of International Law, available at: https://brooklynworks.brooklaw.edu/cgi/viewcontent.cgi?article=1152&context=bjil.

Soamiely Andriamananjara, "Understanding the Importance of the Tripartite Free Trade Area", Brookings Institution, 17 June 2015, available at: https://www.brookings.edu/blog/africa-in-focus/2015/06/17/understanding-the-importance-of-the-tripartite-free-trade-area/.

Sylvain Andzongo, "Visa confusion hinders trade, travel in central Africa" available at: https://www.reuters.com/article/uk-africa-central-trade-idUKKBN0OS0FX20150612.

"An Impact Assessment of OHADA Reforms", International Finance Corporation's OHAD Investment Climate Program, 2018, available at: http://www.ohada.com/content/newsletters/4643/rapport-ohada-ifc.pdf.

"An overview of judicial review in parts of Africa", Hogan Lovells, available at: https://www.hoganlovells.com/en/publications/an-overview-of-judicial-review-in-parts-of-africa.

ArentFox Schiff, "Wait Is Over: USMCA Border Enforcement Begins" 5 January 2021, available at: https://www.afslaw.com/perspectives/alerts/wait-over-usmca-border-enforcement-begins.

Brian J. Arnold, "An introduction to tax treaties," available at: https://www.un.org/esa/ffd/wp-content/uploads/2015/10/TT_Introduction_Eng.pdf.

Ernest Aryeetey, "Is there a tension between democracy and economic development in Africa?", Brookings Institution, 11 March 2019, available at: https://www.brookings.edu/blog/africa-in-focus/2019/03/11/is-there-a-tension-between-democracy-and-economic-development-in-africa/.

"Assessing Regional Integration in Africa", United Nations Economic Commission in Africa, May 2010, available at: https://www.unece.org/fileadmin/DAM/trade/TF_JointUNRCsApproach/ECA_IntraAfricanTrade.pdf.

Amindeh Blaise Atabong, "Cameroon Town's Residents Say Chinese-Run Quarry Damaging their Homes", Epoch Times, 9 June 2019, available at: https://www.theepochtimes.com/cameroon-town-residents-say-chinese-run-quarry-damaging-their-homes_2943839.html.

Raziah Athman, "Africa-China Trade Grows by 19%", available at: http://www.africanews.com/2017/08/04/africa-china-trade-grows-by-19-percent-in-2017//.

Robert Basedow, "A Legal History of the EU's International Investment Policy", (2016) 17(5) Journal of World Investment and Trade, pp. 743–772, available at: http://eprints.lse.ac.uk/86423/1/Basedow_Legal%20history_2018.pdf.

"Basic Information", Economic Community of West African States (ECOWAS), available at: https://ecoslate.github.io/about-ecowas/basic-information/index.htm.

"Basic Purpose and Concepts – 1.3 Definition of Services Trade and Modes of Supply", World Trade Organization, available at: https://www.wto.org/english/tratop_e/serv_e/cbt_course_e/c1s3p1_e.htm.

Joe Bavier, "Guinea not Flexible on Simandou Infrastructure – Minister," available at: https://www.reuters.com/article/africa-mining-guinea/guinea-not-flexible-on-simandou-infrastructure-minister-idUSL5N2016E3.

Renaud Beauchard and Mahutodji Jimmy Vital Kodo, "Can OHADA Increase Legal Certainty in Africa?" (2011), available at: http://documents.worldbank.org/curated/en/266761467990085419/pdf/659890WP00PUBL010Can0OHADA0Increase.pdf.

Nathalie Bernasconi-Osterwalder, "State–State Dispute Settlement in Investment Treaties", International Institute for Sustainable Development, October 2014, available at: https://www.iisd.org/system/files/publications/best-practices-state-state-dispute-settlement-investment-treaties.pdf.

Tilbe Birengel, "European Union: A Shift from Arbitration to Multilateral Investment Court System at EU", Erdem & Erdem Law, March 2019, available at: https://www.mondaq.com/turkey/arbitration-dispute-resolution/791418/a-shift-from-arbitration-to-multilateral-investment-court-system-at-eu.

Bruce A. Blonigen and Ronald B. Davies, "Do Bilateral Tax Treaties Promote Foreign Direct Investment?", in Karl P. Sauvant and Lisa E. Sachs (eds.), The Effect of Treaties on Foreign Direct Investment: Bilateral Investment Treaties, Double Taxation Treaties, and Investment Flows, New York: Oxford Academic, 2009, pp. 461–484, available at: https://doi.org/10.1093/acprof:oso/9780195388534.003.0017.

Markus Bockenforde, Babacar Kante, Yuhniwo Ngenge and H. Kwasi Prempeh, "Judicial Review Systems in West Africa A Comparative Analysis", International Institute for Democracy and Electoral Assistance, available at: https://www.idea.int/sites/default/files/publications/judicial-review-systems-in-west-africa.pdf.

Nicolas Boeglin, "ICSID and Latin America, Criticism, Withdrawal and the Search for Alternatives", Bretton Woods Project, 3 December 2013, available at: https://www.brettonwoodsproject.org/2013/12/icsid-latin-america/.

Peter Van den Bossche and Werner Zdouc, The Law and Policy of the World Trade Organisation, Cambridge: CUP, pp. 30–340, 2017, available at: https://doi.org/10.1017/9781316662496.005.

"Breaking the BIT Mold: Brazil's Pioneering Approach to Investment Agreements", available at: https://doi.org/10.1017/aju.2018.59.

"Bridging Africa's Infrastructure Gap", World Finance, available at: https://www.worldfinance.com/infrastructure-investment/project-finance/bridging-africas-infrastructure-gap.

William W. Burke-White, "The Argentine Financial Crisis: State Liability Under BITs and the Legitimacy of the ICSID System", 24 January 2008, University of Pennsylvania Carey Law School, available at: https://scholarship.law.upenn.edu/cgi/viewcontent.cgi?article=1192&context=faculty_scholarship.

Xavier Carim, "International Investment Agreements and Africa's Structural Transformation: A Perspective from South Africa", available at: https://www.southcentre.int/wp-content/uploads/2016/05/Bk_2015_Investment-Treaties_EN.pdf#page=142.

"Case Studies: Investor-State Attacks on Public Interest Policies", PublicCitizen, available at: https://www.citizen.org/wp-content/uploads/egregious-investor-state-attacks-case-studies_4-1.pdf.

Christopher Casey, "The End of Intra-EU Investor-State Dispute Settlement (ISDS): Implications for the United States", CRS Insight, 13 February 2019, available at: https://fas.org/sgp/crs/row/IN11041.pdf.

"CEN-SAD – The Community of Sahel-Saharan States", United Nations Economic Commission for Africa, available at: https://archive.uneca.org/oria/pages/cen-sad-community-sahel-saharan-states.

"Central Africa Regional Integration Strategy Paper 2019-2025", African Development Bank Group, available at: https://www.afdb.org/sites/default/files/documents/strategy-documents/central_africa_risp_2019-_english_version_020619_final_version.pdf.

"Central African Economic and Monetary Community", International Democracy Watch, available at: http://www.internationaldemocracywatch.org/index.php/central-african-economic-and-monetary-community.

Centre for Democracy and Development, "West Africa Insight: ECOWAS at 40," available at: https://www.osiwa.org/wp-content/uploads/2016/09/ECOWAS-at-40-Full-Report.pdf.

"CETA: EU and Canada agree on new approach on investment in trade agreement," European Commission, 2016, available at: https://ec.europa.eu/commission/presscorner/detail/sk/IP_16_399.

Wilson Chapman, "Africa to Lead World in Population Growth", US News, 10 July 2019, available at: https://www.usnews.com/news/best-countries/articles/2019-07-10/africa-to-lead-world-in-population-growth.

Andrew Chatzky, James McBride and Mohammed Aly Sergie, "NAFTA and the USMCA: Weighing the Impact of North American Trade", Council on Foreign Relations, 1 July 2020, available at: https://www.cfr.org/backgrounder/naftas-economic-impact.

Talkmore Chidede, "The Right to Regulate in Africa's International Investment Law Regime", (2019) 20(2) Oregon Review of International Law, pp. 437–468, available at: https://scholarsbank.uoregon.edu/xmlui/bitstream/handle/1794/24671/Chidede_ORIL20%282%29.pdf?sequence=1&isAllowed=y.

Henrique Choer Moraes and Felipe Hees, "Breaking the BIT Mold: Brazil's Pioneering Approach to Investment Agreements", (2018) 112 AJIL Unbound, pp. 197–201, available at: https://doi.org/10.1017/aju.2018.59.

Allison D. Christians, "Tax Treaties for Investment and Aid to Sub-Saharan Africa: A Case Study", (2006) 71(2) Brooklyn Law Review, pp. 639–713, available at: https://brooklynworks.brooklaw.edu/cgi/viewcontent.cgi?referer=&httpsredir=1&article=1385&context=blr.

Chris Cleverly, "Future of Currency in W. Africa: CFA Franc Collapse and Eco Inadequacy", available at: https://cointelegraph.com/news/future-of-currency-in-w-africa-cfa-franc-collapse-and-eco-inadequacy.

"Climate Risk Profile: Guinea", United States Agency for International Development, available at: https://www.climatelinks.org/resources/guinea-climate-risk-profile.

"Climate Risk Profile: West Africa", ReliefWeb, available at: https://reliefweb.int/report/world/climate-risk-profile-west-africa.

"COMESA at Twenty: of the Successes, Challenges and Promises", Addis Standard, 7 April 2015, available at: http://addisstandard.com/comesa-at-twenty-of-the-successes-challenges-and-promises/.

"COMESA: Dispute Settlement and Arbitration Developments", COMESA Court of Justice, 6–7 April 2017, available at: https://www.tralac.org/images/docs/11119/comesa-dispute-settlement-and-arbitration-developments-lady-justice-lombe-chibesakunda-tralac-annual-conference-april-2017.pdf.

"Common Market for Eastern and Southern Africa", Office of the United States Trade Representative, available at: https://ustr.gov/countries-regions/africa/regional-economic-communities-rec/common-market-eastern-and-southern-africa-comesa.

Cornell Law School, "Bilateral Investment Treaty," available at: https://www.law.cornell.edu/wex/bilateral_investment_treaty.

"Corruption in Guinea", WorldData, available at: https://www.worlddata.info/africa/guinea/corruption.php.

Dr Johanne M. Cox, Expropriation in Investment Treaty Arbitration, Oxford: OUP, 2019.

"CPTPP: Investor-State Dispute Settlement", Australian Government Department of Foreign Affairs and Trade, available at: https://www.dfat.gov.au/trade/agreements/in-force/cptpp/official-documents/Pages/official-documents.

"Declaration of the Member States of 15 January 2019 on the Legal Consequences of the *Achmea* Judgment and on Investment Protection", 17 January 2019, available at: https://ec.europa.eu/info/publications/190117-bilateral-investment-treaties_en.

Kim Yi Dionne, "Why West African Governments are Struggling in Response to Ebola," available at: https://www.washingtonpost.com/news/monkey-cage/wp/2014/07/15/why-west-african-governments-are-struggling-in-response-to-ebola/.

"Doing Business in Africa: Risks, Trends, and Opportunities Roundtable", Brookings Institution, October 2016, available at: https://www.brookings.edu/events/doing-business-in-africa-a-risks-trends-and-opportunities-roundtable-2/.

De Rudolf Dolzer and Margrete Stevens, "Bilateral Investment Treaties", The Hague/Boston: Martinus Nijhoff Publishers, 1995.

"Domestic and International Arbitration: Perspectives from African Arbitration Practitioners", SOAS Arbitration in Africa Survey, 2020, available at: https://eprints.soas.ac.uk/33162/1/2020%20Arbitration%20in%20Africa%20Survey%20Report%2030.06.2020.pdf.

Gaston Kenfack Douajni, "Recent Developments in OHADA Arbitration," Global Arbitration Review, 11 April 2019, available at: https://globalarbitrationreview.com/chapter/1190118/recent-developments-in-ohada-arbitration.

Pascaline Dupas and Jonathan Robinson, "The (hidden) costs of political instability: Evidence from Kenya's 2007 election crisis," (2012) 99 Journal of Development Economics, pp. 314–329, available at: https://web.stanford.edu/~pdupas/Coping_DupasRobinson.pdf.

"EAC – East African Community", United Nations Commission for Africa, available at: https://www.eac.int/.

"ECCAS – Economic Community of Central African States", United Nations Economic Commission for Africa, available at: https://www.uneca.org/oria/pages/eccas-economic-community-central-african-state.

Roberto Echandi, Maryla Maliszewska and Victor Steenbergen, "Making the Most of the African Continental Free Trade Area: Leveraging Trade and Foreign Direct Investment to Boost Growth and Reduce Poverty" Washington, DC: World Bank 2022, available at: https://openknowledge.worldbank.org/handle/10986/37623.

"Economic Community of Central African States", International Democracy Watch, available at: http://www.internationaldemocracywatch.org/index.php/economic-community-of-central-african-states-.

"Economic Development in Africa – Report 2019", United Nations Conference on Trade and Development, available at: https://unctad.org/webflyer/economic-development-africa-report-2019.

"ECOWAS – Economic Community of West African States", United Nations Economic Commission for Africa, available at: https://www.uneca.org/oria/pages/ecowas-economic-community-west-african-states.

Egypt and Community of Sahel-Saharan States, available at: https://www.sis.gov.eg/section/2614/101?lang=en-us.

"Entry into Force of the United States–Mexico–Canada Agreement", Press Statement of Michael R. Pompeo, Secretary of State of the United States, 1 July 2020, available at: https://ee.usembassy.gov/2020-07-02-5/.

Andre-Michel Essoungou, "Africa's Least Developed: Lands of Opportunity", Africa Renewal, August 2011, available at: https://www.un.org/africarenewal/magazine/august-2011/africas-least-developed-lands-opportunity.

"Executive Summary of the Environmental and Social Assessment – Rift Valley Railways Project," African Development Bank Group, available at: https://www.afdb.org/fileadmin/uploads/afdb/Documents/Environmental-and-Social-Assessments/RVR%20ESIA%20Exec%20Summary_English%20final.pdf.

"Extractive Industries," The World Bank, available at: https://www.worldbank.org/en/topic/extractiveindustries/overview.

"EY Attractiveness Reports (2019)", Ernst and Young, available at: https://www.ey.com/en_us/attractiveness.

Babatunde Fagbayibo, "Towards the harmonisation of laws in Africa, is OHADA the way to Go?", (2009) 42(3) The Comparative and International Law Journal of Southern Africa, pp. 309–322, available at: https://www.jstor.org/stable/23253105?seq=1#page_scan_tab_contents.

Frédérique Youmbi Fasseu, "Current Debates on Investor-State Arbitration in Latin America", (2018) 12(45) Tla-melaua. Revista de Ciencias Sociales, pp. 190–207, available at: http://www.scielo.org.mx/pdf/tla/v12n45/2594-0716-tla-12-45-190.pdf.

Silvia Karina Fiezonni, "The Challenge of UNASUR Member Countries to Replace ICSID Arbitration," Beijing Law Review, 1 September 2011.

Will Fitzgibbon, "What's a Tax Treaty and Why Should I care?" 2019, available at: https://www.icij.org/investigations/mauritius-leaks/whats-a-tax-treaty-and-why-should-i-care/.

"Foreign Direct Investment in Africa: Performance and Potential," United Nations Conference on Trade and Development, available at: https://unctad.org/en/Docs/poiteiitm15.pdf.

"Free Trade Agreements in South America. Trends, Prospects and Challenges", Banco de Desarrollo de América Latina, available at: https://scioteca.caf.com/bitstream/handle/123456789/365/caf_tomo_7_.pdf?sequence=1.

"From Regional Economic Communities to a Continental Free Trade Area", United Nations Conference on Trade and Development, available at: https://unctad.org/en/PublicationsLibrary/webditc2017d1_en.pdf.

Lixiao Fu, "Legal review on investor-state dispute settlement under TPP" (2017) 2 Research on Modern Higher Education, pp. 155–161, 10.24104/rmhe/2017.02.02003, available at: https://www.researchgate.net/publication/314219390_Legal_review_on_investor-state_dispute_settlement_under_TPP.

Noemi Gal-Or, "The Concept of Appeal in International Dispute Settlement" (2008) 19(1) EJIL, pp. 43–65 doi: 10.1093/ejil/chm054, available at: http://ejil.org/pdfs/19/1/177.pdf.

David A. Gantz, "Addressing Dispute Resolution Institutions in a NAFTA Renegotiation", Rice University's Baker Institute for Public Policy, April 2018, available at: https://www.bakerinstitute.org/media/files/files/fa4d9adf/mex-pub-nafta-040218-1.pdf.

Christiane Gerstetter and Nils Meyer-Ohlendorf, "Investor-State Dispute Settlement Under TTIP – A Risk for Environmental Regulation?" (31 December 2013), Heinrich Böll Stiftung TTIP Series, available at SSRN: https://ssrn.com/abstract=2416450.

Umar Ghori, "Investment Court System or 'Regional' Dispute Settlement?: The Uncertain Future of Investor-State Dispute Settlement," (2018) 30(1) Bond Law Review, pp. 83–17, available at: http://www.austlii.edu.au/au/journals/BondLawRw/2018/7.pdf.

Ahmad Ali Ghouri, "The Evolution of Bilateral Investment Treaties, Investment Treaty Arbitration and International Investment Law", (2011) 14(6) International Arbitration Law Review, pp. 189–204, available at: https://ssrn.com/abstract=1970561.

Jola Gjuzi, "Stabilization Clauses in International Investment Law: A Sustainable Development Approach", ch. 2, Cham: Springer International Publishing, 2018, available at: https://www.springerprofessional.de/en/meaning-evolution-rationale-sources-and-typology-of-stabilizatio/16314714.

Lemessa Bayissa Gobena, "Power, Justice and Trust: a Moderated Mediation Analysis of Tax Compliance among Ethiopian Business Owners", (2016) 52 Journal of Economic Psychology, pp. 24–37, available at: sciencedirect.com/science/article/abs/pii/S0167487015001397.

Christina Golubski, "Africa in the News: AfCFTA enters into force", Brookings Institution, 1 June 2019, available at: https://www.brookings.edu/blog/africa-in-focus/2019/06/01/africa-in-the-news-afcfta-enters-into-force-south-africa-and-senegal-tackle-climate-change-and-presidents-inaugurated-in-nigeria-and-malawi/.

"Guinea and UNDP launch new adaptation project to prepare for climate change impacts", PreventionWeb, available at: https://www.preventionweb.net/news/view/67155.

"Guinea Country Profile", BBC News, available at: https://www.bbc.com/news/world-africa-13442051.

"Guinea Economy Profile 2019", Index Mundi, available at: https://www.indexmundi.com/guinea/economy_profile.html.

"Guinea Events of 2018", Human Rights Watch, available at: https://www.hrw.org/world-report/2019/country-chapters/guinea.

"Guinea Overview", The World Bank in Guinea, available at: https://www.worldbank.org/en/country/guinea/overview.

Kwabena Gyimah-Brempong, "Corruption, economic growth and income inequality in Africa", (2002) 3 Economics of Governance, pp. 183–209, available at: https://www.usf.edu/arts-sciences/departments/economics/documents/corruption.growth.inequality.africa.econgov.02.pdf.

Harry Hanauer and Lyle J. Morris, "China in Africa Implications of a Deepening Relationship", Rand Corporation, available at: https://www.rand.org/pubs/research_briefs/RB9760.html.

Stephanie Hanson, "Corruption in Sub-Saharan Africa", Council on Foreign Relations, 6 August 2009, available at: https://www.cfr.org/backgrounder/corruption-sub-saharan-africa.

Matthew Happold, "Investor-State Dispute Settlement using the ECOWAS Court of Justice: An Analysis and Some Proposals," (2019) 34(2) ICSID Review, pp. 496–518, available at: doi:10.1093/icsidreview/siz028.

Ernest Harsch, "Making African Integration a Reality", Africa Renewal, September 2002, available at: https://www.un.org/africarenewal/magazine/september-2002/making-african-integration-reality.

Martin Hearson, "Tax Treaties in Sub-Saharan Africa: A Critical Review", London School of Economics, 2015, available at: http://eprints.lse.ac.uk/67903/1/Hearson_Tax_treaties_in_sub-Saharan_Africa.pdf.

——, "When do Developing Countries Negotiate Away their Corporate Tax Base?" (2018) 30 Journal of International Development, pp. 233–255, available at: https://onlinelibrary.wiley.com/doi/pdf/10.1002/jid.3351.

Charlotte Heyl, "The Judiciary and the Rule of Law in Africa", Oxford Research Encyclopedias, available at: https://oxfordre.com/politics/view/10.1093/acrefore/9780190228637.001.0001/acrefore-9780190228637-e-1352.

Edith Honan, "Chinese-built Railway to Cut Through National Park in Kenya's Capital", Reuters, 31 July 2015, available at: https://www.reuters.com/article/kenya-railway-wildlife/chinese-built-railway-to-cut-through-national-park-in-kenyas-capital-idUSL1N10B0OQ20150731.

ICC, "ICC Arbitration figures reveal new record for awards in 2018," 11 June 2019, available at: https://iccwbo.org/media-wall/news-speeches/icc-arbitration-figures-reveal-new-record-cases-awards-2018/.

——, "ICC Court to Launch Africa Commission", Paris, 19 July 2018, available at: https://iccwbo.org/media-wall/news-speeches/icc-court-launch-africa-commission/.

——, "ICC Court Releases Full Statistical Report for 2017", available at: https://iccwbo.org/media-wall/news-speeches/icc-court-releases-full-statistical-report-for-2017/.

"IGAD – Intergovernmental Authority on Development", United Nations Economic Commission for Africa, available at: https://archive.uneca.org/oria/pages/igad-intergovernmental-authority-development.

"IISD Best Practices Series: State-to-State Dispute Settlement in Investment Treaties", IISD, October 2014, available at: https://www.iisd.org/sites/default/files/publications/best-practices-state-state-dispute-settlement-investment-treaties.pdf.

"Impact of Corruption on Nigeria's economy", PricewaterhouseCoopers, available at: https://www.pwc.com/ng/en/press-room/impact-of-corruption-on-nigeria-s-economy.html.

"Impacts of Investment Arbitration Against African States", Transnational Institute, October 2019, available at: https://www.tni.org/en/isdsafrica.

"Inter-Governmental Authority on Development", United States Agency for International Development, available at: https://www.usaid.gov/documents/1860/inter-governmental-authority-development.

International Institute for Sustainable Development, "Assessing the Impacts of Investment Treaties: Overview of the Evidence" (2017), available at: https://www.iisd.org/sites/default/files/publications/assessing-impacts-investment-treaties.pdf.

"International Investment Agreements: Key Issues Volume I", United Nations Conference on Trade and Development, available at: https://unctad.org/en/Docs/iteiit200410_en.pdf.

"Investment and ISDS", New Zealand Foreign Affairs and Trade, available at: https://www.mfat.govt.nz/en/trade/free-trade-agreements/free-trade-agreements-in-force/cptpp/understanding-cptpp/investment-and-isds/.

"ISDS: Important Questions and Answers", Office of the United States Trade Representative, available at: https://ustr.gov/about-us/policy-offices/press-office/blog/2015/march/isds-important-questions-and-answers.

"ISDS Reform in Latin America – Setting the State an Overview of ISDS in the Region", Center for the Advancement of the Rule of Law in the Americas, Georgetown University, available at: https://www.law.georgetown.edu/carola/wp-content/uploads/sites/29/2020/05/ISDS-Landscape-in-LA.pdf.

Mike Ives, "China's Belt and Road Initiative Threatens to Pave the Planet", 16 December 2019, available at: https://www.sierraclub.org/sierra/2020-1-january-february/feature/chinas-belt-and-road-initiative-threatens-pave-planet.

Prince Jaiblai, "International Journal of Financial Studies, Determinants of FDI in Sub-Saharan Economies: A study of DATA from 1990-2017," available at: https://ideas.repec.org/a/gam/jijfss/v7y2019i3p43-d256918.html.

Alec R. Johnson, "Rethinking Bilateral Investment Treaties in Sub-Saharan Africa," (2010) 59 Emory Law Journal, p. 919, available at: http://law.emory.edu/elj/content/volume-59/issue-4/comments/bilateral-investment-treaties-sub-saharan-aftica.html.

Lise Johnson, Lisa Sachs, Brooke Güven and Jesse Coleman, "Costs and Benefits of Investment Treaties", Columbia Centre on Sustainable Investment, March 2018, available at: http://ccsi.columbia.edu/files/2018/04/07-Columbia-IIA-investor-policy-briefing-ENG-mr.pdf.

Patrick Juillard, "Calvo doctrine/Calvo clause", in Rüdiger Wolfrum (ed.), Max Planck Encyclopedia of Public International Law, Oxford: Oxford Public International Law, 2012, vol. i.

Gabrielle Kaufmann-Kohler Michele Potestà, "Investor-State Dispute Settlement and National Courts. Current Framework and Reform Options", *European Yearbook of International Economic Law*, Cham: Springer, 2020.

Yomi Kazeem, "West Africa's 'Eco' single currency ambition has a slim chance of success", Quartz Africa, July 2019, available at: https://qz.com/africa/1657000/will-west-africas-eco-currency-succeed/.

Mouhamed Kebe, "Dispute Settlement under China's Belt and Road Initiative – African Perspective", December 2019.

——, "How Can OHADA Boost Integration and Investment in Africa?", Geni & Kebe SCP, available at: https://www.hg.org/legal-articles/how-can-ohada-boost-integration-and-investment-in-africa-19603.

——, "The Attractiveness of the New OHADA Arbitration Act", Geni & Kebe SCP, 13 December 2018, available at: https://www.lexology.com/library/detail.aspx?g=680f77e3-1b8c-4327-87c1-183a7abc45f4.

Mouhamed Kebe, Mahamat Atteib and Mouhamoud Sangare, "Ivory Coast's New Investment Code: Focus on issues related to sustainable development and dispute settlement", Investment Treaty News, 19 September 2019, available at: https://www.iisd.org/itn/en/2019/09/19/ivory-coasts-new-investment-code-focus-on-issues-related-to-sustainable-development-and-dispute-settlement-mouhamed-kebe-mahamat-atteib-mouhamoud-sangare/.

Thomas Kendra, Thibaud Roujou de Boubee and Ledea Sawadogo-Lewis, "The Paris Court upholds the supranational nature of OHADA law in dismissing annulment application", 14 February 2019, available at: https://www.hlarbitrationlaw.com/2019/02/the-paris-court-upholds-the-supranational-nature-of-ohada-law-in-dismissing-annulment-application-ca-paris-16-25484-20-december-2018/.

"Kenya Halts Lamu Coal Power Project at World Heritage Site", BBC News, 26 June 2019, available at: https://www.bbc.com/news/world-africa-48771519.

Parag Khanna, "At First Glance, the Story of Accenture Reads", Foreign Policy, available at: https://foreignpolicy.com/2016/03/15/these-25-companies-are-more-powerful-than-many-countries-multinational-corporate-wealth-power/.

Won Kidane, "The Culture of Investment: An African Perspective," (2019) 34(2) ICSID Review, pp. 411–433, available at: doi:10.1093/icsidreview/siz027.

Sung Teak Kim, "Adjudicating Violations of International Law: Defining the Scope of Jurisdiction under the Alien Tort Statute – Trajano v. Marcos", (1994) 27(2) Cornell International Law Journal.

Mek Kinnear and Paul Jean Le Cannu, "Concluding Remarks: ICSID and African States Leading International Investment Law Reform", (2019) 34(2) ICSID Review, pp. 542–551, available at: doi:10.1093/icsidreview/siz026.

Mark Klaver and Michael Trebilcock, "Chinese Investment in Africa: Strengthening the balance sheet", available at: http://www.glawcal.org.uk/glawcal-comments/pros-and-cons-of-chinese-investments-in-africa.

Ezra Klein, "What the most controversial part of Obama's trade deal really does", 10 November 2015, available at: https://www.vox.com/2015/11/10/9698698/tpp-investor-state-dispute-settlement.

Apollinaire Kouton, "Droits-BENIN : Des juges condamnés pour corruption à la prison ferme, une leçon pour tout le pays", Inter-Press Service News Agency, available at: http://ipsnews.net/francais/2004/06/08/droits-benin-des-juges-condamnes-pour-corruption-a-la-prison-ferme-unelecon-pour-tout-le-pays/.

Rebecca Kysar, "Unraveling the Tax Treaty," New York University School of Law, Spring 2019, available at: http://www.law.nyu.edu/sites/default/files/upload_documents/Unraveling%20the%20Tax%20Treaty%20-%20Kysar_0.pdf.

Dasmani Laary, "22 Ghanaian judges suspended over corruption scandal", The Africa Report, 10 September 2015, available at: https://www.theafricareport.com/2596/22-ghanaian-judges-suspended-over-corruption-scandal/.

Jerry L. Lai, "A Tale of Two Treaties: A Study of NAFTA and the USMCA's Investor-State Dispute Settlement Mechanisms", (2021) 35 Emory Int'l L. Rev. 259, available at: https://scholarlycommons.law.emory.edu/eilr/vol35/iss2/3.

Pierre Lalive, "The First 'World Bank' Arbitration (*Holiday Inns v. Morocco*) – Some Legal Problems", (1980) 51(1) British Yearbook of International Law, pp. 123–162, available at: https://doi.org/10.1093/bybil/51.1.123.

Benoit Lebars, "The Evolution of Investment Arbitration in Africa", Global Arbitration Review, May 2018, available at: https://globalarbitrationreview.com/review/the-middle-eastern-and-african-arbitration-review/2018/article/the-evolution-of-investment-arbitration-in-africa.

Alejandro López Ortiz, José Joaquín Caicedo and William Ahern, "Two Solutions for One Problem: Latin America's Reactions to Concerns over Investor-State Arbitration", TDM 2 (2016), available at: www.transnational-dispute-management.com.

Amanda Lucey, "How ECOWAS has got peacebuilding right", ReliefWeb, 1 December 2016, available at: https://reliefweb.int/report/world/how-ecowas-has-got-peacebuilding-right.

Payce Madden, "Africa in the News: WAEMU's eco implementation, Sahel security update, and Foresight Africa Launch", Brookings Institution, 18 January 2020, available at: https://www.brookings.edu/blog/africa-in-focus/2020/01/18/africa-in-the-news-waemus-eco-implementation-sahel-security-update-and-foresight-africa-launch/.

Lungelo Magubane, "Investment Protection Legislation in South Africa", Return to Africa Connected: Issue 1, DLA Piper, November 2018, available at: https://www.dlapiper.com/en/southafrica/insights/publications/2018/11/africa-connected-doing-business-in-africa/investment-projection-legislation-in-south-africa/.

Abdullah H. Makame, "The East African Integration: Achievements and Challenges", GREAT Insights, Volume 1, Issue 6, August 2012, available at: https://ecdpm.org/great-insights/trade-and-development-making-the-link/east-african-integration-achievements-challenges/.

Mahnaz Malik, "The Full Protection and Security Standard Comes of Age: Yet another challenge for states in investment treaty arbitration?", International Institute for Sustainable Development, November 2011, available at: https://www.iisd.org/pdf/2011/full_protection.pdf.

"Mamamah airport: Sierra Leone cancels China-Funded Project", BBC News, 10 October 2018, available at: https://www.bbc.com/news/world-africa-45809810.

Jephias Mapuva and Loveness Muyengwa-Mapuva, "The SADC regional bloc: what challenges and prospects for regional integration?", (2014) 18 Law, Democracy and Development, pp. 22–36, available at: http://www.scielo.org.za/scielo.php?script= sci_arttext&pid=S2077-49072014000100002.

Julie Martin, "Kenya and Mauritius sign new tax treaty following court nullification of earlier agreement", MNE Tax, 15 April 2019, available at: https://mnetax.com/ kenya-and-mauritius-sign-new-tax-treaty-following-court-nullification-of-earlier-agreement-33414.

Frederic Maury and Joel Te-Lessia Assoko, "Senegal: le gisement de Faleme adeau ou fardeau", 23 September 2013, available at: https://www.jeuneafrique.com/16514/ economie/s-n-gal-le-gisement-de-fal-m-cadeau-ou-fardeau/.

Makane Moïse Mbengue, "Africa's Voice in the Formation, Shaping and Redesign of International Investment Law", (2019) 34(2) ICSID Review – Foreign Investment Law Journal, pp. 455–481, available at: https://academic.oup.com/icsidreview/ article-abstract/34/2/455/5680362.

James McBride, Andrew Chatzky and Anshu Siripurapu, "What is the Trans-Pacific Partnership (TPP)?", Council on Foreign Relations, available at: https://www.cfr. org/backgrounder/what-trans-pacific-partnership-tpp.

Jaime de Melo, "A Fresh Look at Africa's Integration in Regional Economic Communities", ICTSD, 13 October 2017, available at: https://www.ictsd.org/bridges-news/bridges-africa/news/a-fresh-look-at-africa%E2%80%99s-integration-in-regional-economic.

Jaime de Melo and Yvonne Tsikata, "Regional Integration in Africa : Challenges and Prospects", Foundation pour Les Etudes et Recherches sur le Développement International, available at: https://ferdi.fr/dl/df-6Lm5LieRw5yaW5shkAeNSSBj/ ferdi-p93-regional-integration-in-africa-challenges-and-prospects.pdf.

"Member States", Southern African Development Community, available at: https:// www.sadc.int/member-states.

Memorandum by Charles H. Sullivan headed "Entry of Foreign Investors into the United States under Treaties of Friendship, Commerce and Navigation", dated 23 November 1949, NARA, Record Group 59, Department of State File No. 611.004/5-350.

Max Mendez-Parra, Sherillyn Raga and Lily Sommer, "Africa and the United Kingdom", 2020, available at: https://cdn.odi.org/media/documents/africa_uk_ investment.pdf.

Muhabie Mekonnen Mengistu, "Multiplicity of African Regional Economic Communities and Overlapping Memberships: A Challenge for African Integration", January 2015, available at: https://www.researchgate.net/publication/293009606_ Multiplicity_of_African_Regional_Economic_Communities_and_Overlapping_ Memberships_A_Challenge_for_African_Integration.

"Ministry of East African Community and Regional Development", Republic of Kenya, available at: https://meac.go.ke/eac-achievements/.

Bill Mitchell, "Modern Monetary Theory – Introduction – The Last Colonial Currency: A History of the CFA Franc – Party 3", 8 January 2020, available at: http://bilbo.economicoutlook.net/blog/?p=44038.

Andrew Mizner, "The future is now for African Arbitration", Commercial Dispute Resolution, 23 May 2019, available at: https://www.cdr-news.com/categories/arbitration-and-adr/9573-the-future-is-now-for-african-arbitration.

Zachary Mollengarden, "One-Stop Dispute Resolution on the Belt and Road: Toward an International Commercial Court with Chinese Characteristics", (2019) 36(1) Pacific Basin Law Journal, pp. 65–111, available at: https://escholarship.org/content/qt43q7s46n/qt43q7s46n.pdf?t=pm8ts1.

Alhousseini Mouloul, "Understanding the Organization for the Harmonization of Business Laws in Africa", 2nd ed., June 2009, available at: http://www.ohada.com/content/newsletters/1403/Comprendre-l-Ohada-en.pdf.

"Most Corrupt Countries 2020", World Population Review, available at: http://worldpopulationreview.com/countries/most-corrupt-countries/.

Torque Mude, "Challenges and Prospects for the Transformation of the Common Market for Eastern and Southern Africa by 2025", Midlands State University, available at: http://www.jpanafrican.org/docs/vol12no6/12.6-9-Mude.pdf.

Andrew Muhammad, Anna E. D'Souza and William Amponsah, "Violence, Political Instability, and International Trade: Evidence from Kenya's Cut Flower Sector", 1 October 2011, available at: https://ssrn.com/abstract=1961207.

Ombeni N. Mwasha, "The Benefits of Regional Economic Integration for Developing Countries in Africa: A Case of East African Community", (2008) Korea Review of International Studies, pp. 69–92, available at: https://www.semanticscholar.org/paper/The-Benefits-of-Regional-Economic-Integration-for-%3A-Mwasha/18beea4e9968371264a4a0b3a577d657073bde88.

Patricia Mukiri Mwithiga, "The Challenges of Regional Integration in the East African Community", available at: https://link.springer.com/chapter/10.1057/9781137462084_5.

Paul Nantulya, "Implications for Africa from China's One Belt One Road Strategy", March 2019, available at: https://africacenter.org/spotlight/implications-for-africa-china-one-belt-one-road-strategy/.

Theobald Naud, Ben Sanderson and Andrea Lapunzina Veronelli, "Recent Trends in Investment Arbitration in Africa", DLA Piper, 11 April 2019, available at: https://globalarbitrationreview.com/insight/the-middle-eastern-and-african-arbitration-review-2019/1190119/recent-trends-in-investment-arbitration-in-africa.

Andrew Newcombe and Lluis Paradell, "Law and Practice of Investment Treaties: Standard of Treatment Chapter 1, Historical Development of Investment Treaty Law," Kluwer Law International, Chapter 1, 2009, available at: https://papers.ssrn.com/sol3/papers.cfm?abstract_id=1375600.

Tinyiko Ngobeni, "The Relevance of the Draft Pan African Investment Code (PAIC) in Light of the formation of the African Continental Free Trade Area", 15 January 2019, available at: http://www.afronomicslaw.org/2019/01/11/the-relevance-of-the-draft-pan-african-investment-code-paic-in-light-of-the-formation-of-the-african-continental-free-trade-area/.

Dominic Nsikan, "Top 6 Achievements of the ECOWAS", West African Countries, 2 October 2017, available at: https://www.westafricancountries.com/top-6-achievements-of-the-ecowas/.

Peter Nunnenkamp and Manoj Pant, "Why the case for a multilateral agreement on investment is weak", 2003, available at: https://www.econstor.eu/bitstream/10419/2931/1/kd400.pdf.

Ayodele Odusola, "Addressing the Foreign Direct Investment Paradox in Africa", available at: https://www.un.org/africarenewal/web-features/addressing-foreign-direct-investment-paradox-africa.

Uche Ewelukwa Ofodile, "African States, Investor-State Arbitration and the ICSID Dispute Resolution System: Continuities, Changes and Challenges" (2019) 34(2) ICSID Review, pp. 296–364, available at: doi:10.1093/icsidreview/siz031.

Emilia Onyema, "2020 Arbitration in Africa Survey Report", 30 June 2020, available at: https://eprints.soas.ac.uk/33162/1/2020%20Arbitration%20in%20Africa%20Survey%20Report%2030.06.2020.pdf.

Aloysius Uche Ordu, "An Evaluation of the single currency agenda in the ECOWAS region", Brookings Institution, September 2019, available at: https://www.brookings.edu/blog/africa-in-focus/2019/09/24/an-evaluation-of-the-single-currency-agenda-in-the-ecowas-region/.

Organization for the Harmonization of Business Law in Africa, "Organization", available at: https://www.ohada.org/index.php/en/ohada-in-a-nutshell/history.

Overview of COMESA, available at: https://www.comesa.int/overview-of-comesa/.

William L. Owen, "Investment Arbitration under NAFTA Chapter 11: A Threat to Sovereignty of Member States?", (2015) 39 Canada–United States Law Journal, pp. 55–67, available at: https://scholarlycommons.law.case.edu/cgi/viewcontent.cgi?article=2488&context=cuslj.

Joost Pauwelyn, "Going Global, Regional, or Both – Dispute Settlement in the Southern African Development Community (SADC) and Overlaps with the WTO and Other Jurisdictions", (2004) Minnesota Journal of International Law, p. 215, available at: https://scholarship.law.duke.edu/cgi/viewcontent.cgi?article=1767&context=faculty_scholarship.

Facundo Perez-Aznar, "The Recent Argentina-Qatar BIT and the Challenges of Investment Negotiations", 12 June 2017, available at: https://www.iisd.org/itn/2017/06/12/recent-argentina-qatar-bit-challenges-investment-negotiations-facundo-perez-aznar/.

Manuel Perez-Rocha, "When Corporations Sue Governments", New York Times, 3 December 2014, available at: https://www.nytimes.com/2014/12/04/opinion/when-corporations-sue-governments.html.

Michele Potesta, "Investor-State Dispute Settlement and National Courts", SpringerOpen, 2020, available at: https://doi.org/10.1007/978-3-030-44164-7.

——, *Republic of Italy v. Republic of Cuba*", (2012) 106(2) American Journal of International Law, available at: https://www.cambridge.org/core/journals/american-journal-of-international-law/article/republic-of-italy-v-republic-of-cub a/15DAB44D01A94E1ABBD4E17E1F2358DF.

Andre Pottas, "Addressing Africa's Infrastructure Challenges," Deloitte, available at: https://www2.deloitte.com/t/dam/Deloitte/global/Documents/Energy-and-Resources/dttl-er-africasinfrastructure-08082013.pdf.

John A. Powell, Elsadig Elsheikh and Hossein Ayazi, "The Trans-Pacific Partnership: Corporations before People and Democracy", Haas Institute, University of California Berkeley, May 2016, available at: https://escholarship.org/content/qt3b62p6v0/qt3b62p6v0_noSplash_5ebb097cb314dfeff25a61915c831820.pdf?t= qc4v1u.

H. Kwasi Prempeh, "Africa's 'constitutionalism revival': false start or new dawn?" (2007) 5(3) International Journal of Constitutional Law, pp. 495–506, available at: https://academic.oup.com/icon/article/5/3/469/647353.

"Principles of the trading system", World Trade Organization, available at: https://www.wto.org/english/thewto_e/whatis_e/tif_e/fact2_e.htm.

Evert-jan Quak and Hannah Timmis, "Double Taxation Agreements and Developing Countries", 1 June 2018, available at: https://assets.publishing.service.gov.uk/media/5b3b610040f0b645fd592202/Double-Taxation-Treaties_and_Developing_Countries.pdf.

"Quick Review – The Arab Maghreb Union (AMU): The Forgotten Dream", NATO Strategic Direction – South, 12 May 2018, available at: https://thesouthernhub.org/resources/site1/General/NSD-S%20Hub%20Publications/The_Arab_Maghreb_Union.pdf.

Mmiselo Freedom Qumba, "South Africa's Move Away from International Investor-State Dispute: a Breakthrough or Bad Omen for Investment in the Developing World?", (2019) 52(1) De Jure (Pretoria), available at: http://www.scielo.org.za/scielo.php?script=sci_arttext&pid=S2225-71602019000100021.

Fiza Qureshi, "Revisiting the nexus among foreign direct investment, corruption and growth in developing and developed markets", available at: https://www.sciencedirect.com/science/article/pii/S2214845020300405.

Rafiq Raji, "Moody's dim outlook on African Banks", African Business, 2 March 2020, available at: https://africanbusinessmagazine.com/african-banker/moodys-dim-outlook-on-african-banks/.

Lucy Reed, Jan Paulsson and Nigel Blackaby, "Guide to ICSID Arbitration", Wolters Kluwer Law and Business, December 2010.

"Regional Economic Communities", United Nations Economic Commission for Africa, available at: https://au.int/en/organs/recs.

Pearl Risberg, "The Give-and-Take of BRI in Africa" in New Perspectives in Foreign Policy, Issue 17, 8 April 2019, available at: https://www.csis.org/give-and-take-bri-africa.

James Roberts, Ted Bromund and Riddhi Dasgupta, "Straight Talk on the ISDS Provisions in the Trans-Pacific Partnership", The Heritage Foundation Issue Brief, No. 4564, 17 May 2016, available at: http://report.heritage.org/ib4564.

Diana Rosert, "The Stakes are High: A review of the financial costs of investment treaty arbitration", International Institute for Sustainable Development, July 2014, available at: https://www.iisd.org/sites/default/files/publications/stakes-are-high-review-financial-costs-investment-treaty-arbitration.pdf.

"SADC Major Achievements and Challenges", available at: https://www.sadc.int/files/7713/5826/4978/Achievements_booklet.pdf.

"SADC – Southern African Development Community. History and Treaty", United Nations Economic Commission for Africa, available at: https://www.sadc.int/pages/history-and-treaty.

Tahmina Sahibli, "The Relationship of EU Law and Bilateral Investment Treaties", 2015, available at: https://www.diva-portal.org/smash/get/diva2:903370/fulltext01.pdf.

Saliou Samb, "Rio Tinto fails to clinch sale of Guinea iron ore project", Reuters, available at: https://www.reuters.com/article/us-rio-tinto-deals-chinalco-simandou/rio-tinto-fails-to-clinch-sale-of-guinea-iron-ore-project-idUSKCN1N3010.

Tim R. Samples, "Winning and Losing in Investor–State Dispute Settlement", (2019) 56(1) Am Bus Law J, pp. 115–175, doi:10.1111/ablj.12136, available at: https://onlinelibrary.wiley.com/doi/10.1111/ablj.12136.

Kwadwo Sarkodie and Joseph Otoo, "The Rise and Rise of Arbitration in Africa", African Law and Business, 5 April 2018, available at: https://www.africanlawbusiness.com/news/8105-the-rise-and-rise-of-arbitration-in-africa.

Christoph Schreuer "The relevance of Public International Law in International Commercial Arbitration: Investment Disputes", 2006, available at www.univie.ac.at/intlaw/pdf/csunpublpaper_1.pdf.

Stuart P. Seidel, "International Trade Compliance Update", Baker McKenzie, May 2019, available at: https://www.lexology.com/library/detail.aspx?g=fd2a8cf3-03a6-426f-89c1-7ab8dbf24ac5.

Samson L. Sempasa, "Obstacles to International Commercial Arbitration in African Countries," (1992) 41(2) The International and Comparative Law Quarterly, pp. 387–413.

Landry Signe, "How Africa is Bucking the Isolationist Trend", Foreign Affairs, 23 May 2018, available at: https://www.foreignaffairs.com/articles/africa/2018-05-23/how-africa-bucking-isolationist-trend.

"Simandou Iron Ore Project", Mining Technology, available at: https://www.mining-technology.com/projects/simandou-iron-ore-project-guinea/.

Reuben Simukoko, "Achievements and Failures of the East African Community" Best of Africa, available at: https://thebestofafrica.org/content/successes-and-failures-of-the-east-african-community.

Tania Singla, "*Achmea*: The Fate and Future of Intra-EU Investment Treaty Awards under the New York Convention," Blog of the European Journal of International Law, 8 May 2018, available at: https://www.ejiltalk.org/achmea-the-fate-and-future-of-intra-eu-investment-treaty-awards-under-the-new-york-convention/.

Elliot Smith, "The US–China trade rivalry is underway in Africa, and Washington is playing catch-up", CNBC, October 2019, available at: https://www.cnbc.com/2019/10/09/the-us-china-trade-rivalry-is-underway-in-africa.html.

Noah Smith, "The Dark Side of Globalization: Why Seattle's 1999 Protesters were Right", The Atlantic, 6 January 2014, available at: https://www.theatlantic.com/business/archive/2014/01/the-dark-side-of-globalization-why-seattles-1999-protesters-were-right/282831/.

Anita Sobjak, "2018 OECD Global Anti-Corruption & Integrity Forum – Corruption Risks in Infrastructure Investments in Sub-Saharan Africa", February 2018, available at: https://www.oecd.org/corruption/integrity-forum/academic-papers/Sobjak.pdf.

Mireya Solísm, "Trump withdrawing from the Trans-Pacific Partnership", 24 March 2017, available at: https://www.brookings.edu/blog/unpacked/2017/03/24/trump-withdrawing-from-the-trans-pacific-partnership/.

Vera Songwe, "Intra-African Trade: A path to economic diversification and inclusion", Brookings Institution, 11 January 2019, available at: https://www.brookings.edu/research/intra-african-trade-a-path-to-economic-diversification-and-inclusion/.

M. Sornarajah, "Compensation for nationalisation of foreign investments", in M. Sornarajah (ed.), The International Law on Foreign Investment, Cambridge: CUP, 2010, pp. 412–452, doi:10.1017/CBO9780511841439.014.

"Southern Africa Development Community", International Democracy Watch, available at: http://www.internationaldemocracywatch.org/index.php/southern-africa-development-community.

Southern African Development Community, "Towards a Common Future", available at: https://www.sadc.int/themes/social-human-development/.

Mariama Sow, "Figures of the Week: Africa's intra-and extra-regional trade", available at: https://www.brookings.edu/blog/africa-in-focus/2018/03/29/figures-of-the-week-africas-intra-and-extra-regional-trade/.

Standard Bank, "Africa's Oil and Gas Potential," available at https://corporateandinvestment.standardbank.com/cib/global/sector/capabilities/oil-and-gas/Africa%27s-Oil-and-Gas-potential.

"Standing first instance and appeal investment court with full-time judges", United Nations Commission on International Trade Law, available at: https://uncitral.un.org/en/standing.

Amne Suedi, "The need for 'Africa-focused' arbitration and reform of Tanzania's Arbitration Act", available at: https://www.bilaterals.org/?the-need-for-africa-focused.

"Summary of the Trans-Pacific Partnership Agreement", available at: http://www.sice.oas.org/TPD/TPP/Negotiations/Summary_TPP_October_2015_e.pdf.

Ana Swanson and Jim Tankersley, "Trump Just Signed the U.S.M.C.A. Here's What's in the New NAFTA", The New York Times, 1 July 2020, available at: https://www.nytimes.com/2020/01/29/business/economy/usmca-deal.html.

Amadou Sy and Mariama Sow, "Four Questions on the State of the West African Economic and Monetary Union and Implications", Brookings Institution, 15 March 2016, available at https://www.brookings.edu/blog/africa-in-focus/2016/03/15/four-questions-on-the-state-of-the-west-african-economic-and-monetary-union-and-implications-for-other-regional-economic-communities/.

"Rodrigo Tavares and Vanessa Tang, "Regional economic integration in Africa: impediments progress?", (2011) 18(2), South African Journal of International Affairs, pp. 217–233, available at: https://www.tandfonline.com/doi/abs/10.1080/10220461.2011.588826.

"Tax Treaties", Tax Justice Network, available at: https://www.taxjustice.net/topics/corporate-tax/tax-treaties/.

"Tax Treaty between Mauritius and Senegal Terminated", Orbitax, 2019, available at: https://www.orbitax.com/news/archive.php/Tax-Treaty-between-Mauritius-a-40865.

"Taxation, Senegal Denounces Double Taxation Agreement with Mauritius and Threatens to Abandon the Deal", AfricaNews, 2019, available at: https://www.africanews.com/2019/07/11/senegal-mauritius-tax-row/.

"Texaco/Chevron Lawsuits (re Ecuador)", Business and Human Rights Resource Centre, available at: https://www.business-humanrights.org/en/texacochevron-lawsuits-re-ecuador.

"The Africa Investment Report 2016", FDI Intelligence, available at: https://www.camara.es/sites/default/files/publicaciones/the-africa-investment-report-2016.pdf.

"The Arbitration Game", The Economist, 11 October 2014, available at: https://www.economist.com/finance-and-economics/2014/10/11/the-arbitration-game.

"The Case for Investing in Africa", McKinsey and Company, available at: https://www.mckinsey.com/featured-insights/middle-east-and-africa/the-case-for-investing-in-africa.

"The Current State and Future of International Arbitration: Regional Perspectives", International Bar Association, August 2015, available at: https://cvdvn.files.wordpress.com/2018/10/int-arbitration-report-2015.pdf.

"The Economic Consequences of Conflicts", IMF, available at: https://www.elibrary.imf.org/view/book/9781484396865/ch002.xml.

"The European Union: What it is and What it Does", European Commission, available at: https://op.europa.eu/webpub/com/eu-what-it-is/en/.

"The Facts on Investor-State Dispute Settlement", Office of the United States Trade Representative, available at: https://ustr.gov/about-us/policy-offices/press-office/blog/2014/March/Facts-Investor-State%20Dispute-Settlement-Safeguarding-Public-Interest-Protecting-Investors.

"The ICSID Caseload – Statistics", International Centre for Settlement of Investment Disputes, available at: https://icsid.worldbank.org/en/Documents/resources/ICSID%20Web%20Stats%202018-1(English).pdf.

"The Incompatibility of Intra-EU BITs with European-Union law", annotation following *ECJ, 6 March 2018, Case 284/16, Slovak Republic v. Achmea BV.*

"The Investor-State Dispute Settlement Mechanism: An Examination of Benefits and Costs", CATO Institute, 20 May 2014, available at: https://www.cato.org/events/investor-state-dispute-settlement-mechanism-examination-benefits-costs.

"The Regional Economic Communities (RECs) of the African Union", Office of the Special Adviser on Africa, available at: https://www.un.org/en/africa/osaa/peace/recs.shtml.

"The Rocky History of NAFTA", Reuters, 1 September 2017, available at: https://www.reuters.com/article/us-trade-nafta-timeline/the-rocky-history-of-nafta-idUSKCN1BC5IL.

The World Bank, "Doing Business Region Profile Sub-Saharan Africa", 2020, available at: https://www.doingbusiness.org/content/dam/doingBusiness/media/Profiles/Regional/DB2020/SSA.pdf.

Stephen Thomsen, "Foreign Direct Investment in Africa: the Private-Sector Response to Improved Governance", Chatham House, available at: https://www.chathamhouse.org/sites/default/files/public/Research/International%20Economics/bpafrica-fdi.pdf.

Andrew Thompson, "Who is Free Trade Really for in Latin America?", World Politics Review, 23 September 2019, available at: https://www.worldpoliticsreview.com/articles/28209/who-is-free-trade-really-for-in-latin-america#:~:text=By%20size%20and%20economic%20importance,and%20the%20Pacific%20Alliance%2C%20a.

Alexander Edberg Thorén and Fredrik Azelius, "ECOWAS and WAEMU as Tools for Promoting Export Diversification", available at: http://lup.lub.lu.se/luur/download?func=downloadFile&recordOId=8877024&fileOId=8877029.

Catherine Titi, "International Investment Law and the European Union: Towards a New Generation of International Investment Agreements," (2015) 26(3) The European Journal of International Law, pp. 639–661, available at: http://www.ejil.org/pdfs/26/3/2598.pdf.

"Trade Policy Review: Members of the West African Economic and Monetary Union (WAEMU)", Tralac, 26 October 2017, available at: https://www.tralac.org/news/article/12324-trade-policy-review-members-of-the-west-african-economic-and-monetary-union-waemu.html.

"Trans-Pacific Partnership Investment and ISDS", New Zealand Government, available at: https://tpp.mfat.govt.nz/assets/docs/TPP_factsheet_Investment.pdf.

"Treaties of Friendship, Commerce and Trade", Oxford Public International Law, available at: https://opil.ouplaw.com/view/10.1093/law:epil/9780199231690/law-9780199231690-e1482.

Alexander Trepelkov, Harry Tonino and Dominika Halka, "United Nations Handbook on Selected Issues in Administration of Double Tax Treaties for Developing Countries", 2013, available at: https://www.un.org/esa/ffd/wp-content/uploads/2014/08/UN_Handbook_DTT_Admin.pdf.

Tsotang Tsietsi, "International Commercial Arbitration: Case Study of the Experiences of African States in the International Centre for Settlement of Investment Disputes", available at: https://scholar.smu.edu/cgi/viewcontent.cgi?article=1582&context=til.

Ko-Yung Tung, "Investor-State Dispute Settlement under the Trans-Pacific Partnership", (2015) 23(1) The California International Law Journal, available at: https://media2.mofo.com/documents/150800investorstatedisputesettlement.pdf.

UNCTAD, "Handbook of Statistics 2019", available at: https://unctad.org/system/files/official-document/tdstat44_en.pdf.

——, "International Investment Agreements Navigator", available at: https://investmentpolicy.unctad.org/international-investment-agreements.

United Nations, "International Investment Agreements: Key Issues" (2004), available at: https://unctad.org/en/Docs/iteiit200410_en.pdf.

United Nations Economic Commission for Africa, "Investment Policies and Bilateral Investment Treaties in Africa", available at: https://archive.uneca.org/publications/investment-policies-and-bilateral-investment-treaties-africa.

"USMCA Curbs How Much Investors Can Sue Countries – Sort Of," International Institute for Sustainable Development, available at: https://www.iisd.org/library/usmca-investors.

Martin Valasek, Alison Fitzgerald and Jenna Anen de Jong, "Major changes for investor-state dispute settlement in new United States–Mexico–Canada Agreement", October 2018, available at https://www.nortonrosefulbright.com/en/knowledge/publications/91d41adf/major-changes-for-investor-state-dispute-settlement-in-new-united-states-mexico-canada-agreement.

Kenneth J. Vandevelde, Bilateral Investment Treaties: History, Policy and Interpretation, Oxford/New York: OUP, 2010.

——, "The First Bilateral Investment Treaties: U.S. Postwar Friendship, Commerce, and Navigation Treaties", Oxford: OUP, 2017.

Geraldo Vidigal and Beatriz Stevens, "Brazil's New Model of Dispute Settlement for Investment: Return to the Past or Alternative for the Future?", (2018) 19(3) The Journal of World Investment & Trade, pp. 475–512, available at: https://brill.com/view/journals/jwit/19/3/article-p475_6.xml?language=en.

M. Angeles Villareal and Ian F. Fergusson, "The North American Free Trade Agreement (NAFTA)", CRS Report R42965, Washington DC, Congressional Research Service, available at: http://digitalcommons.ilr.cornell.edu/key_workplace/1411/.

Tania Voon and Elizabeth Sheargold, "The Trans-Pacific Partnership", (2016) 5(2), British Journal of American Legal Studies, pp. 341–370, doi: https://doi.org/10.1515/bjals-2016-0012.

Mohamed S. Abdel Wahab, "ICSID's Relevance for Africa: A Symbiotic Bond Beyond Time", (2019) 34(2) ICSID Review, pp. 519–541, available at: doi:10.1093/icsidreview/siz022.

Luke Warford, "Africa is Moving Toward a Massive and Important Free Trade Agreement", The Washington Post, 14 July 2016, available at: https://www.washingtonpost.com/news/monkey-cage/wp/2016/07/14/the-7-things-you-need-to-know-about-africas-continental-free-trade-area/?utm_term=.c8c2a586d85d.

Jereon Warner, "The Fantasy of the Grand Inga Hydroelectric Project on the River Congo", MDPI, 26 February 2019, available at: https://www.mdpi.com/2073-4441/11/3/407.

Mark Weaver, "The Proposed Transatlantic Trade and Investment Partnership (TTIP): ISDS Provisions, Reconciliation, and Future Trade Implications", (2014) 29 Emory Int'l L. Rev. 225.

Adam Wernick, "Congo pushes for a mega-dam project, with no environmental impact studies", 3 July 2016, available at: https://www.pri.org/stories/2016-07-03/congo-pushes-mega-dam-project-no-environmental-impact-studies.

"West Africa – Trade Policy", European Commission, available at: http://ec.europa.eu/trade/policy/countries-and-regions/regions/west-africa/.

"Why Justice in Africa is Slow and Unfair", The Economist, 1 June 2017, available at: https://www.economist.com/middle-east-and-africa/2017/07/01/why-justice-in-africa-is-slow-and-unfair.

Paul D. Williams, "A New African Model of Coercion? Assessing the ECOWAS Mission in The Gambia", Global Observatory, 16 March 2017, available at: https://theglobalobservatory.org/2017/03/ecowas-gambia-barrow-jammeh-african-union/.

"WIR-Foreign direct investment to Africa fell by 21% in 2017, says United Nations report," UNCTAD, available at: https://unctad.org/en/pages/PressRelease.aspx?OriginalVersionID=461.

Stephen Woolcock, "EU Trade and Investment Policymaking after the Lisbon Treaty", (2010) 45(1) Intereconomics, pp. 22–25, available at: https://www.intereconomics.eu/contents/year/2010/number/1/article/eu-trade-and-investment-policymaking-after-the-lisbon-treaty.html.

"World Investment Report 2018", United Nations Conference on Trade and Development, available at: https://unctad.org/en/PublicationsLibrary/wir2018_en.pdf.

Eleanor Wragg, "USMCA enters into force, sort of", Global Trade Review, 1 July 2020, available at: https://www.gtreview.com/news/americas/usmca-enters-into-force-sort-of/.

Jason Yackee, "New Trade Agreements Don't Need ISDS", CATO Institute, 19 May 2015, available at: https://www.cato-unbound.org/2015/05/19/jason-yackee/new-trade-agreements-dont-need-isds.

Sophia Yan, "China's Ambition Dealt Blow Ahead of G20 as Tanzania and Kenya Projects Grind to Halt", The Telegraph, 27 June 2019, available at: https://www.telegraph.co.uk/news/2019/06/27/tanzania-suspends-10-billion-port-project-new-blow-chinas-belt/.

Feleke Habtamu Zeleke, "African Continental Free Trade Area (AfCFTA): A Corner Stone for Pan-Africanism and Dispute Settlement Mechanisms," Addis Ababa University, School of Law, Ethiopia, available at: https://www.academia.edu/84632188/African_Continental_Free_Trade_Area_AfCFTA_A_Corner_Stone_for_Pan_Africanism_and_Dispute_Settlement_Mechanisms.

INDEX

ABOUT THE AUTHOR

Mouhamed Kebe is an attorney and the Managing Partner of GENI & KEBE, a full services law firm member of DLA Piper Africa, based in Senegal and Ivory Coast, with affiliate offices across several jurisdictions mainly in the Organization for the Harmonisation of Business Law in Africa (OHADA) region (Benin, Burkina Faso, Cameroon, Chad, Gabon, Guinea, Mali, Mauritania, Niger, Togo). He is a member of the Senegalese Bar and the Ivorian Bar and is top-ranked in Chambers Global, the International Finance Law Review and Who's Who Legal Mining. He is also a member of the Court of Arbitration of the ICC, a member of the panel of arbitrators of the Common Court of Justice and Arbitration of the OHADA, and a member of the panel of arbitrators of the China International Economic and Trade Arbitration Commission (CIETAC).